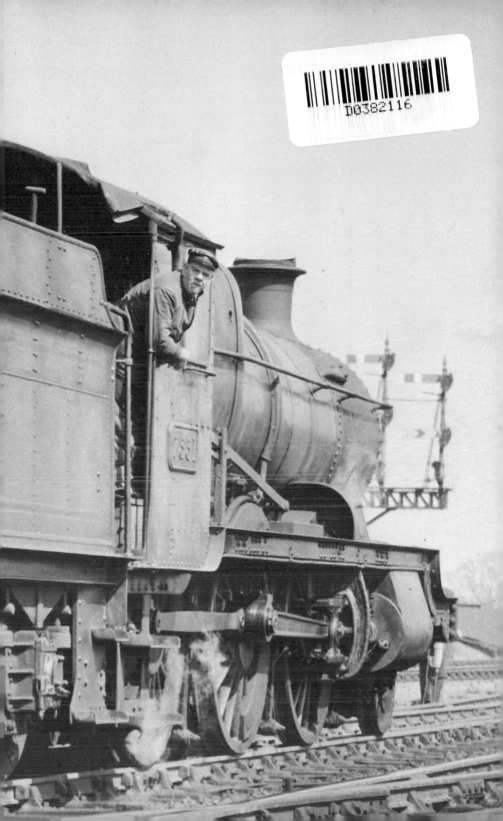

CASTLES TO WARSHIPS

Castles to Warships

ON THE GREAT WESTERN FOOTPLATE

JACK GARDNER

John Murray

© Jack Gardner 1986

First published 1986
by John Murray (Publishers) Ltd
50 Albemarle Street, London WIX 4BD

Typeset by Inforum Ltd, Portsmouth
Printed and bound in Great Britain
by The Bath Press, Avon

British Library CIP data
Gardner, J.
Castles to warships: on the Great
Western footplate,
1. British Rail. *Western Region*
——History
I. Title
385′.092′4   HE 3018
ISBN 0–7195–4265–0

CONTENTS

ILLUSTRATIONS

Between pages 102 *and* 103

FRONT ENDPAPER: See Plate 28; REAR ENDPAPER: See Plate 23

Sources of Illustrations

1, 16, 21: Mike Esau; 2, 3, 11, 14, 15, 24, 27: the Author; 4: Brian L. Davis; 5: BR/OPC; 6, 7: BBC Hulton Picture Library; 8: Popperfoto; 9, 12, 13: Kenneth Leech; 10: Lens; 17: E. Wilmshurst; 18, 28: C. J. Blay, from collection of Brian L. Davis; 19, 22, 23: H. G. Forsythe; 20: John Ashman, FRPS; 25, 29: David Withey; 26: R. J. Blenkinsop; Author's collection.

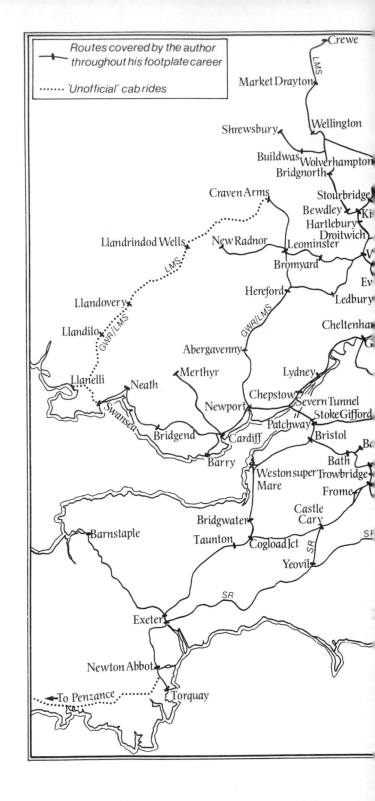

Routes covered by the author throughout his footplate career

'Unofficial' cab rides

Crewe
Market Drayton
LMS
Shrewsbury
Wellington
Buildwas Wolverhampton
Bridgnorth
Craven Arms
Stourbridge
Bewdley Ki
Hartlebury Droitwich
Llandrindod Wells New Radnor Leominster
Bromyard Ev
Hereford Ledbury
Llandovery
Cheltenha
Llandilo GWR/LMS
GWR/LMS
Abergavenny
Llanelli Neath Merthyr Lydney
Chepstow
Swansea Newport Severn Tunnel
Stoke Gifford
Patchway
Bridgend Cardiff Bristol
Barry Bath
Weston super Trowbridge
Mare Frome
Barnstaple Bridgwater Castle Cary
Taunton Cogload Jct SR
Yeovil
SR
Exeter
Newton Abbot
To Penzance Torquay

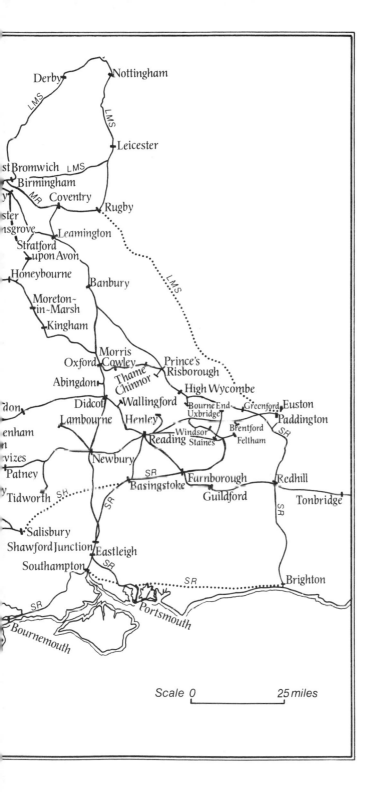

Scale 0   25 miles

GREAT WESTERN RAILWAY.

TERMS OF ENGAGEMENT OF WAGES STAFF.

1. An employee must devote himself exclusively to the service of the Company, must reside at or near the place of his employment, attend for duty during such hours as may be required, be loyal and obedient and conform to all Rules and Regulations of the Company.

2. He must abstain from any act that may injuriously affect the interests of the Company, and, except in the proper performance of his duties, must not make public or communicate to any person information concerning the business of the Company.

3. Wages will be calculated as from the day upon which duties are commenced, and will be paid weekly in the course of each following week at such times as may be convenient to the Company, subject to statutory deductions under (for example) the National Health Pensions and Unemployment Insurance Acts, and to deductions of payments due under the Rules of any benefit society established or authorised by the Company. (Particulars of the existing Societies may be obtained on application).

4. Seven days' previous notice in writing of termination of service shall be given on either side, provided that in case of drunkenness, disobedience of orders, negligence, or misconduct or absence from duty without leave, the Company reserve the right to dismiss an employee without notice.

5. No wages will be payable in respect of periods of absence from duty.

6. These terms of engagement will continue to apply throughout the period of employee's service with the Company, subject to any agreed variations.

To be completed by accepted applicants :—

I, the undersigned, having made myself acquainted with the above terms and conditions, agree to abide by the same and to conform to all the rules and regulations of the Company.

Signature *W J Gardner*

Date *3-8-1936*

Witness :—

Signature *Parke*

Grade *Clerk*

PADDINGTON STATION,

LONDON, W.

A Copy of the terms of engagement is to be handed to the Signatory.

ONE

Time for decision

MY FIRST THOUGHTS of working on the Great Western Railway came one evening in June 1936. I had just finished my meal after working overtime at a factory in my home town of Worcester. My father sat reading his newspaper, slowly he lowered it as if afraid to face me and, in a matter-of-fact way, asked 'How would you like to work on the footplate, John?'

'Work on the footplate. What's that?' I asked.

He looked a bit bewildered for a moment, then said, 'You know, on the engines.'

'Oh that,' I murmured.

There was a pause before he continued by expounding all the virtues of the job he could possibly think of including the better pay offered. Free passes and uniform were made to seem something special, the importance of the job was not even considered. To give him his due he did point out the disadvantages such as the hard work, the dirt and the unusual hours of duty, saying quite emphatically, 'You'll always be at work when others are off. Holiday times are when you notice it most. Mind you it could be several years before you're made a fireman, and even then you may be only twenty.'

I was allowed several minutes to absorb the pros and cons before he added a further comment, 'A fireman's wage of £2 17s is a good living wage, you can get married on that.'

Being expected to consider marriage as well set me back, not knowing quite what to say. We talked around it for some time before Dad said, 'Give it some thought, sleep on it.'

I needed to. How could I, at the age of sixteen, be expected to have thoughts of marriage? Several days passed with my mind in turmoil. I had what I considered to be a good job as an apprentice in Archdale's machine tool factory, at the time I seemed happy with my lot. Two years had passed since leaving school and this was my third job. Would it be wise for me to change again? Although Dad had been a lifelong railwayman he had never spoken much of his work, let alone try to push me on to the railway.

I remember well the placards on the station hoarding bemoaning the railway's lot: 'Give the railways a fair deal.' They also pleaded with the general public by advertising: 'Travel at a penny a mile.'

I doubted the wisdom of changing to a job with an uncertain future. The thought of hard work didn't bother me, I was already suffering from that. Whether I would be interested was the thought that kept welling up in my mind. Until now the railways had held little fascination for me. Only a few months before, while working in the factory which lay alongside the line from Worcester to the North the call was heard, 'Come and see this new train.'

The enthusiasm with which the call was made fetched men from all over the factory floor myself included.

There, travelling along the embankment was something quite new, a diesel rail-car – its front and rear ends beautifully rounded off and raked back to form a streamlining of the latest style. It glided along effortlessly, its engines muffled by the factory noises, no smoke or steam to suggest it even belonged to the railway. Quite unimpressed I returned to my bench, one of the first to do so.

Within seconds Mr Jones, the works manager, was on the scene taking names of all he could catch for the purpose of deducting pay. My lack of interest had kept my pay packet intact. The one thing I remembered about the rail-car was the number 4 painted on its side.

The only interest I had ever shown was, I suppose, when Mum and Dad took me with the rest of the family on seaside excursions to places such as Barry Island or Porthcawl and Weston-super-Mare, all within easy reach of Worcester. I was more interested in the seaside than the means of getting there. With all this lack of interest it is a wonder that I ever took up an eventual lifetime of railways.

After several days my mind was made up. When my father came home one evening I told him, 'Dad, I'm going to have a try.'

'I'll see what I can do but don't be disappointed if you're unlucky.'

This was quite a surprise after all that had passed and being left to consider for so long. I asked, 'Why should I be disappointed?'

'Well, it's like this. Footplate jobs are not easy to get, there's always plenty after them. I'll ask the Superintendent, see what he has to say.'

The next day as Mr Armstrong walked the platform on the way to his office my father buttonholed him and got the go-ahead for me to apply. Even then this was only the beginning, there was a long way yet.

My father carefully guided me through my application and it was duly posted. Ages seemed to pass before I had a reply requesting me to report to the railway works for an interview. I arrived with doubt still in my mind and was directed to the messroom. It was a bare, spartan place, rows of long wooden benches ranged along each side of tables, all of them bleached white with years of scrubbing. I was surprised to find a large number of lads already waiting, wondering what to do, when in came a very tall man smartly dressed in a suit. He surveyed the gathering and immediately raised his voice. Looking at several who had sat down he said briskly 'Who told you to sit? Stand up until I tell you.'

This first taste of railway discipline came from Mr Ross, the Superintendent's chief clerk, who then proceeded to give us a lecture in no uncertain terms. Having dealt with the first offenders, he then addressed us all. 'There are only three vacancies and I can count twenty-one of you here. Those of you that can't take discipline can leave now.' He looked over his glasses and paused, silence reigned. After completing the register the object of the interview got under way. First the most important eyesight test, the usual card followed by small bundles of wood in various colours.

'Pick out the reds,' was the simple order. 'Now the green. Now sit down over there and keep quiet.'

Sitting there quietly whispering to each other we were aware of Mr Ross's eyes menacing us. Presently one of the cheeky ones was heard to say 'What do I do with this wool? Knit something?'

Mr Ross replied instantly: 'No, leave that here, I'll give you some more to take home. Catch your next train home, there's no need to wait any longer.'

A simple maths and dictation test followed and we all sat around again while each in turn faced Mr Ross for a personal interview. I was a little dismayed at his rather sharp remarks about my effort, saying 'You couldn't have done much worse, could you?'

I remembered my father's guiding influence: it doesn't cost anything to be polite.

'No sir,' I replied.

'Don't let this worry you, we'll let you know.'

I didn't think so at the time but I later realised that he was probably sounding me out for respect.

Once again while waiting one lad called out 'Are we going to be long? I've got a train to catch.'

'Is there anyone else in the same hurry?' asked Mr Ross.

Another voice said 'Yes, I am.'

'Then both of you catch your train. Sorry you've wasted your day. Goodbye.'

Those few unruly ones together with some who had failed the eyesight test reduced the odds of failing but at the same time proved the point on discipline.

After a further polite lecture explaining that the successful ones would be required to undergo a full medical exam at Swindon he finished with 'Wait until you hear from us.'

In due course I received a letter directing me to travel to Swindon; it also contained a free pass and detailed instructions on which trains to travel on and the route to follow at Swindon. We met several hopefuls at the station and more at Swindon.

We passed through the ticket barrier, each one of us studying his directions. The ticket collector, having seen it all before, offered his assistance and pointed the way. Turning right from the station we made our way along a high wall built with stone blocks which one of the more knowledgeable informed us had been taken from the excavations of Box tunnel. At intervals large doors broke the monotony, all except one being closed. Through this we could see a vast expanse of factories, the home of the Great Western Railway.

A uniformed watchman allowed us only a fleeting glimpse, in any case our destination was further along the road. As we wandered along we speculated on the various buildings ranged opposite the wall; many of them had a sombre exterior. Did they belong to the railway or was it just part of the design of the era?

The end of the road turned sharp left at the park. Another check of the instructions confirmed that the large Victorian building about 300 yards on the left would be our goal. A brass plate on the wall proclaimed its name: Park House. We were here.

We paused before entering, inside the hall was bleak. Not daring to sit down we stood around waiting and taking in the surroundings. There were several doors, one small window and at the end a large staircase rose to the right, turning back to disappear from view.

Very soon a man came down the stairs, he was rather small with a round red face, balding from the forehead. Perched half-way down his nose was a pair of small round spectacles. He referred to the papers he carried and with a slight tilt of his head forward looked over his specs. 'So you're the lot from Worcester, I suppose.' After checking our names against the list he said, 'Sit down over there,' nodding towards the seat. 'Come upstairs when your name is called.'

After several lads had gone my name was called from the top of the stairs. As I climbed up, a fellow sufferer trotted across the landing naked; glancing back, he said, 'In that door, mate. Good luck.'

Inside, a very strict-looking doctor said 'While you're standing read that chart, go down as far as you can.' Then the wool test again followed by a tricky test with coloured beads. He gave me a box with three holes in the lid, each leading into separate compartments.

'Sort out the reds, greens and yellows into separate holes. Use the tweezers.'

This was as much a test of nerves as eyesight.

Then came the usual strip, cough, and then height measurement. 'Yes, only just good enough,' he remarked. 'Here, take this bottle and give me a sample,' he said, handing me the bottle. 'Go along to the toilet at the end.'

Now I knew where the naked fellow had been going.

I returned and the doctor disappeared behind a screen saying, as he went, 'You can get dressed now.'

I was still dressing when he returned to his desk and started writing on a slip of paper. Craning my neck I just made out my name then he turned to me.

'Do you know that footplate work is very hard, can you work hard?'

'Yes, sir, I'm used to it,' I replied.

'How do you know about it?'

'My father's a railwayman, sir, he works on the station.'

'Did he suggest you apply for this job?'

'Yes, sir, he told me all he could about it.'

'In that case I think you'll do,' he concluded.

With a final addition to the paper with the word Passed and his best wishes he said, 'Take this paper downstairs to the clerk.'

It seemed that my interview had been completed by the doctor himself.

My feet hardly touched the stairs on the way down. The clerk suddenly became very important to me; his order to sit down at a table was quickly carried out. The paper he placed in front of me was headed CONTRACT OF SERVICE. 'Read this,' he said. After a while he returned, 'Do you fully understand it?' he asked.

'Yes,' I replied, not bothering too much. I thought that can sort itself out later.

In the corner sat one lad looking pleased with himself. I cocked a thumb at him. The clerk promptly rebuked me. 'Never mind him, give me five shillings.'

'What's that for?' I asked.

'To join the MAS.' Then noting my look of concern he carried on to explain, 'It's a scheme called the Mutual Assurance Society, run by the GWR to provide sick-pay and a pension when you retire at sixty.'

I replied, 'I don't need a pension, I'm only sixteen.'

'You'll need one when you're sixty, besides, if you don't join you can't start on the footplate, it's compulsory.'

Reluctantly I handed over my five shillings; this hurt, it was almost a week's wages.

Having signed on the dotted line I was then told that I had a job for life, providing I never acquired a criminal record.

'Wait with that lad in the corner.'

Two of us now sat there looking pleased with ourselves; he happened to be the only one of the bunch whom I had befriended. We sat for a while before he introduced himself as Doug Bennet, I recriprocated before he observed 'There's only three jobs. I wonder who the other will be?' In colloquial Worcester he added 'We're in, kid, it don't really matter.'

We speculated on which of the two we knew was left. Our deliberations ceased when one came down the stairs, placed a slip of paper on the desk and quickly left. Soon the other one came, he went through the same ritual as us, then we were called to join him at the table.

'I kept you two waiting, better to travel home together.'

He completed the day's procedures by issuing each of us a rule-book and general appendix and then entering our names in the register with an individual number for each. Mine was

24747, the number that was to follow me all my career.

The clerk looked up a service to get us home. 'Catch the 4.26 p.m. to Didcot, change there and again at Oxford.'

Five hours had passed since we first arrived, I was glad to get away. Armed with our books the three of us retraced our way along the boundary wall, not having much to say except consider why it should be us who finally got through. Doug was certain that his success could be attributed only to having several relations already employed, while Fred, the other chap, was equally satisfied that he owed his good fortune to his father being a driver at Kidderminster. For myself, I was beginning to appreciate that my own father's approach to the Superintendent had an influence on my success. Whatever the reasons, it was not far from nepotism. The principle of preferring railwaymen's sons existed.

At the station the signals came to life, the coloured pictures in the general appendix together with details of the various types more than captured our imaginations, so many different types in one place overwhelmed us. Somewhat bemused we retired to the refreshment rooms for a much-needed cup of tea. The normal price was twopence but by showing our passes we paid only a penny, quite a saving in those days.

The day was getting long. We had started with the 7.15 from Worcester, changing at Ledbury to ride on a very scenic branch line through the Wye valley to Gloucester and up the Stroud valley to Swindon. The return route started facing away from home as far as Didcot then turning back to complete a round trip. I remember very little of the return, being much too tired to bother. Waiting at Oxford I recall looking at a row of terrace houses behind the bay line but I missed the fast run from Oxford to Worcester. I was asleep most of the way unaware that I was riding the renowned 4.45 p.m. from Paddington.

It was nearly eight when I reached home. As I entered the back alley of our terrace I glanced over the wall to see my father looking out anxiously. Unmoved, he allowed me to enter then said, 'Well, you've passed then, John.'

'How do you know that?' I asked.

'I can see, you've got your books. Besides, I knew before I left work, Mr Ross found out for me.'

My father had actually known before me.

'When do you start?' he asked, anxious to get me installed.

'Don't know yet,' was my reply. 'They're going to send me a letter.'

'I'm interested to know because I've taken out a free pass for a trip to Weymouth on August Sunday. If you start before then you won't be able to use it.'

Food was on the table so I was spared any further questions.

In due course a letter arrived directing me to report to Worcester shed on August Bank Holiday Monday. In a way I was quite disappointed at losing my holiday but I couldn't say that I wasn't warned. 'You'll always be at work when others are off' came sooner than expected. However, the trip to Weymouth was on.

August Sunday came. We were up early to walk the two miles to the station to catch the excursion. It was still dark, the train filling the long platform. We boarded it well to the rear, the loco appearing to be a long way off. Nothing much to do but sit.

At 4.30 we were off with a long journey ahead. The train rumbled on, hardly a sound from the loco. At Evesham our coach was off the platform but there was life of some sort up the front. Off we moved again in the faint light of dawn until my father stirred me while we were ascending Honeybourne bank. 'Look out of the window, John, we've got two engines on.'

Looking out I could see the two locos working hard on the heavy gradient, the firelight glowing red on the steam from the chimney and the dawn creeping over the top of the hill we were climbing, giving just enough light to pick out the train as it weaved its way through the trees to the summit. As the locos entered the tunnel a little reminder came. 'Better close the window now, you'll get smuts in your eyes.'

I pulled the window up by its strap and latched it in its slot, once again settling down.

Very little else remained in my memory of the journey there and back except that my father insisted on taking me to see the

loco before the return. I went along grudgingly to listen to him
telling the crew of my pending start. The loco number was 4007
Swallowfield Park which my father pointed out and became
indelibly fixed in my mind.

It was turned twelve when we arrived back at Worcester and
after the long walk home I crept into bed at 2 a.m.

My new alarm clock was set for five o'clock with a promise
from my father that he would make certain that I got up. As it
happened I was up without help, walking in a trance. My light
breakfast eaten I picked up the sandwiches my mother had
stayed up to pack and I was away on my bike. The morning was
crisp and fresh, out in the air I came to life, the world was my
oyster, at least the town was. No one else stirred, I found myself
alone. I decided to take a longer route knowing that I could get a
good view of the shed from a high vantage point along the
railway walk.

The walk runs along the top of the embankment skirting the
loop line from Wales to the North, joining the main line from
London at the tunnel junction a little to my left. Looking east
towards London the station could be seen; from here a loop line
ran across to join the South Wales line forming a triangle in
which nestled the loco sheds. Most of the area to the left and in
front was occupied by railway workshops, sidings, and goods
shed. In the yard I could see a signal box which controlled the
large number of freight movements in the yard.

Down below the panorama I had come this particular way to
see stretched out before me. The layout of the shed was very
unusual inasmuch as it had two separate sheds with a shunting
yard in between. Nearest the loop line below me lay the goods
shed with four roads; built along its side the offices and cabins
were ranged. Over the other side beyond the small shunting
yard lay the passenger shed next to the main line. Scattered
about the shed fronts and spilling over into the yard locos were
everywhere with men tending them or walking to and fro.

For a short time I took in the scene, watching the lazy smoke
curling up from some of the chimneys while others blasted
theirs skywards under the control of the firemen preparing for

the road. Suddenly I became aware of the time, it was getting close to six o'clock. Realising that I now belonged down there I freewheeled slowly down the walk and across the little bridge over the loop line. The fence on my left, made from second-hand sleepers and tarred to preserve them for ever, had an opening through which I could see the office only a few feet away, a point from which the time clerk kept a watchful eye.

I had arrived. It was 6 a.m., 3 August 1936.

To the left of the window stood the door – a heavy wooden barrier made to last and painted in the inevitable chocolate and cream of the Great Western. Inside, the stone floor of the lobby gave cold comfort, fanlights in the roof took the place of windows. Several doors led off to offices and on the right the partition was made up from the floor with brick; a counter protruded both inside and out with the partition continuing as glazed wooden framework to the ceiling. Two small sash windows were built in to communicate with the clerk.

As I stood wondering a voice called out from round the corner, 'Knock that window there, this one's for drivers and firemen.'

It was Doug, who had arrived early and was waiting on the seat round the corner, deciding to make his début with the other two new boys.

The window slid up, a friendly clerk asked, 'Are you one of the new boys?'

'Yes,' I replied.

He looked through some papers. 'Your name must be Gardner then.'

'Yes, W.J.'

From a small wooden tray partitioned into slots he took out a round brass disc with the number 22 stamped on it. Round the edge the words GWR LOCO CARRIAGE AND WAGON DPT indicated its ownership. With a wry smile he said 'Don't lose this, you can't get any pay without it.' Then added, 'Don't confuse it with the number given to you at Swindon.'

Doug then asked, 'Wonder where Fred's got to?'

We knew he had to come from Kidderminster and thought

he may not have made it. Within moments, though, he turned up with one of the senior cleaners. He was a big fellow by our standards and after booking on duty offered to escort us to the cabin, the name given to the mess room.

The three of us trailed behind, turning right in the lobby to the door leading into the shed. Our guide pushed the door open and, turning, said, 'Mind the steps, they're sometimes slippery.'

The door opened to reveal a dingy, smoky shed. Directly in front stood a black, grimy and very dirty loco.

Doug asked, 'Have we got to clean that?'

The big fellow said, 'Yes, they're all like that, there's over a hundred of them.'

A look of dismay passed around us, noted by our senior. 'Don't worry, there'll be plenty of us in the winter months to square them up.'

He led us along the shed. Through the open end doors I had a completely different view of the shed and sidings which I had seen only a few minutes ago from the walk. A window with a counter was let into the wall on the left, behind which stood the storesman, a polite nod and a smile greeted us, he was another relation of Doug's. The next door was slightly ajar. 'This is it,' said our escort, passing in, leaving us to follow.

Inside, I looked around tentatively; there were about twenty cleaners with eyes fixed on us mainly with a disdainful look. The cabin seemed full although it was quite large, some 30 ft by 15 ft. Long bench-type seats were fixed all round the walls painted with the inevitable chocolate. The walls above were washed in cream, the standard colour scheme. Two long tables with metal tops stood one each side. At the end a huge fireplace occupied nearly the whole of the wall, a large fire burned even though it was summer with a two-gallon kettle standing on the side in readiness for the mealbreak. On the outside wall two metal-framed windows looked out on to the loop line, the light being supplemented by fanlights in the roof. Heavy rafters supported the roof which was a continuation of the shed roof; hanging by its own pipe from above was a solitary gaslight.

The three of us sat down at the end, no one else spoke to us. Within a few minutes the door flew open and a call came in with a strong nasal accent: 'Blow up.'

It was the chargeman cleaner calling us to work. They all seemed reluctant to get up. The call was soon repeated, this time from inside the door. The whole gang were soon outside followed by three little lambs.

The chargeman stood at his cupboard in the corner dispensing wrath with each issue of cleaning materials. He was a short grey-haired man with a squashed face, a bit like Popeye. His words were difficult to understand because of his nasal accent, it did nothing to help him when he raised his voice in anger.

Dick Gammon was his name, normally called Dick but when he annoyed the lads it was reduced to Gam, not very complimentary.

The cleaning oil, or 'blue billy', as it was called, was doled out with the cotton waste in a miserly manner to the last ounce; why the meanness with the waste I don't know, it was only the sweepings from the mill floors. Looking round his charges he sent them in gangs of two or four with their instructions as if to settle old scores. Eventually he came to us. The big chap that had led us along to the cabin had already been told to stand by. Dick turned to him, 'You can take these for the day, take them on the 9.5 Paddington. Take these scrapers and get some of the muck off the wheels.'

We were with the only one to have spoken to us so far.

'Follow me, we'll go across the sidings. We're not allowed this way when shunting is being carried out.'

Before we left Dick said 'Hang on a minute,' and waddled off up the shed, returning in a few minutes with some old overalls for me to borrow.

'Don't you have any at home?' he asked.

'No, at my last job I hired them by the week.'

'Use these until you get an issue, let me have them back.'

Doug remarked 'He's not so bad after all.'

Our new leader turned and introduced himself as Bill Obrey, then in turn asked our names. Mine, I told him, was William

John. He replied, 'Right, you'll be Jack.' There was no argument, I was named for life. 'Right, step over the rails, never
tread on them.'

I asked 'Why?'

'Your shoes will get slippery with oil and it's easy to slip on
the shiny rails.'

We followed him to the passenger shed, passing the coaling
stage on our left with an old-fashioned steam crane lifting
10-cwt tubs of coal on to a tender. Volumes of dust flew as it
poured down prompting the remark from Bill 'That's what
makes the locos so dirty, that and fire-dropping.'

Arriving at the passenger shed Bill led us to a loco standing in
the middle road. The road nearest to us was empty, giving an
uninterrupted view of the loco we were to clean. 'This is it,' said
Bill.

To my astonishment it was none other than 4007 *Swallowfield Park*, the loco that had hauled my excursion trip the day
before and brought me back only a few hours earlier.

Standing on the platform at Weymouth it hadn't made much
impression on me but from ground-level its size seemed enormous, my 5 ft 6 in. was dwarfed by its 6 ft 8½ in. wheels,
which disappeared up into the splashers out of sight. Looking
further up, the boiler reached almost to the smoke shutes, in
fact the chimney was partly hidden in the shute. I had no
difficulty in standing under the main frame.

'Dick wants the wheels cleaned,' said Bill. 'Take a scraper
each and get on with them.'

We were allocated a wheel each. I was the unlucky one, I had
the leading driver hidden behind the outside motion bars,
connecting and coupling rods.

'Scrape all the grease off, I'm going to wipe the boiler off.'

Armed with my scraper I set to work not knowing where to
start, I couldn't get my hand in properly to manipulate the
scraper. Bill gave me a parting shot, 'You'll have to roll your
sleeves up.'

It wasn't long before my hands and arms were as mucky as
the wheels. Long soggy lumps of grease fell to the floor

gradually revealing the shape of the rim and later the colour, black.

Very little conversation passed between us, we were too engrossed in our new-found occupation. Bill had not given us any waste and it now seemed a hopeless task, the muck clung to everything. He eventually came down from his dizzy heights on top of the boiler to inspect our efforts.

'Is this the best you can do? Dick won't be very pleased with this.'

My wheel looked the worst and I was the first to make excuses but they fell on deaf ears. 'I suppose you had better have some waste,' said Bill.

As if giving away something special he produced the second-hand waste he had wiped the boiler with. 'Can't give you clean waste for that. Better get a move on, don't forget there are three more big wheels on the other side.'

About this time the crew came to carry out their preparation in readiness for the road. It was 7.30, we had been over an hour cleaning a wheel each.

The driver, an elderly man nearing retirement I thought, came along and gave us our first taste of misery. 'What are you lot doing here? I don't want you in my way when I'm oiling.'

'It's all right, they won't get in your way,' said Bill, defending us. 'Come on, let's go round the other side for a while out of his way.' Round the other side Bill said, 'Get on as quickly as you can, the loco goes off shed in an hour, we have to be finished before then.' To be sure of doing so Bill gave us a hand.

Presently the grumpy driver called out, 'Get your gang out of the way, I want to move it.'

The driver needed to move the loco to make some of the moving parts more accessible, in doing so he turned the wheels round to reveal the dirty side which had been hidden in the splashers. It was disheartening; it seemed I had worked all this time for nothing. To make matters worse the chargeman turned up to see our progress. 'What have you been up to all morning, Bill? This is no good.'

Bill jumped in with his explanation that the loco had only just been moved. 'Don't worry, Dick, we'll soon have that licked off.'

'Don't be long then, it's off shed soon.'

Most of the offending dirt was cleaned off and the loco moved outside for water. While this was being done someone turned up with a camera and took my picture on the front of the loco. A memento of my first day at work.

Throughout this time 5042 *Winchester Castle* had been standing in front, a gang of four had been working on it. It was now moved forward and our 4007 moved to couple to it. At 8.30 the leading driver blew his whistle with the code for leaving the shed to indicate to the signalman that they were ready. We watched as these two majestic locos left the shed in a cloud of steam from their open cylinder cocks to travel the few hundred yards to the station, the front one for the 8.55 express to Paddington and the rear one to work the 9.5 stopper to Oxford then fast to Paddington.

Already a certain amount of pride within me was beginning to manifest itself. As the locos left the shed we turned to Bill who was talking to Dick.

Dick gave us a short sharp lecture in pride in the job before leading us via the correct walking route back to the goods shed. Here we collected more rations of cleaning materials. Dick asked Bill 'Can you take them on that one over there?' pointing to a small loco in a yard siding.

'Yes,' said Bill. 'That'll be all right.'

'Keep a good watch on them when the shunters are about, don't want anybody getting hurt on their first day.'

Bill had willingly accepted this loco knowing that it would be an easy job to take us up to mealbreak. The loco in question was a small 'Dean' 0–6–0 tender used mainly for goods and occasional light passenger work. It was quite a small loco, built about the turn of the century. The straight boiler stood high above the frame allowing plenty of room to see right through. The rather short smokebox carried a tall slender chimney and in the centre of the boiler stood a dome rather large by proportion. On the top of the firebox the safety valve cover emulated the chimney and two brass whistles completed the fittings. The cab design was peculiar to the Great Western, providing little cover for the crew. At the front were two round windows known as spectacles, above which the cab roof extended back barely 3 ft, the sides dropped a few inches before curving forward then dropping and sweeping in a long curve towards the tender. The driver and fireman had their seats attached to the side of the cab well outside the cover of the roof, in fact they did most of their work standing in the open. Outside the loco was completely uncluttered, all the motions were neatly tucked away inside between the frames under the boiler.

The old thing was equally as dirty as the other one we did but because of its size it looked less formidable. Instead of scraping the wheels Bill directed Fred and me to climb into the motion. Before doing so he gave us instructions on how to protect ourselves by putting a NOT TO BE MOVED board on each end of the loco and never to get in unless someone else was there to keep watch.

'Before you get in and get yourself plastered wipe round as far as you can reach, it'll save you getting a lot of dirt on your overalls. Wipe the bottom of the boiler as well.' Bill was trying to show us the best way to approach the job. There wasn't really room for two of us in there but Dick had said 'Get them in the motions.'

Bill gave us a little clean waste each which I found difficult to use, bits fell off diminishing the pad to almost nothing.

'Bill, can I have some more waste?' I asked.

'No, you'll have to do with what you've got.' He then added 'You'll need some to clean your hands with soon. Don't be too long, the driver will be here soon, I don't want him moaning as well,' he said, as he wiped away at the side rods.

We finished just in time. The driver came along and, as expected, greeted us with grumbles.

'Are they all like this?' I asked Bill.

'You'll have a job to please many of them. It's the same when you go out firing, have to watch your step.'

Bill explained that this particular man was on this goods turn regularly because he had suffered injury from falling off a loco and was given light duties. This was a feature of the job, a guaranteed job even if ill health or accident befell anyone.

To me he was an old groaner, in fact all the men I had seen until now looked old – probably an illusion of youth. I was already wondering how long it would be before I could expect to become a fireman. I turned to Bill, 'How long have you been a cleaner?'

'About three years,' he replied. 'I expect to be made a fireman early next year.'

'That's a long time to wait, isn't it?'

'Not really, some have waited twelve years or more in the past. You see, about three years. It's worth waiting for, the time will go quickly.'

The hour or so we were on this loco passed by and towards ten o'clock Bill gave us some waste each which he had saved to clean our hands. With a crafty eye on the chargeman we made our way to the cabin for our mealbreak.

In the cabin a bucket of hot water waited. The unwritten rule was for the first in to collect it and then have first wash, the rest followed with the seniors and the pushers elbowing out the juniors. The three newcomers sat back, no soap or towel.

Bill took pity on us. 'Borrow mine for today, bring your own tomorrow.'

Before we ate we all dashed to the office to put our time checks in to book off duty for half an hour, they were too mean to pay us for eating. On return there was another setback: none of us had the means of making tea. Bill came to our rescue again with a much-needed cup of fresh tea. The break passed quickly, we three sat at the end of the cabin, partly because we sensed it was our place and also realising that a hierarchy existed. As we became more senior we would move along.

Bill had left us to sit with his mates but we knew they were talking about us and wondered whether an initiation ceremony was being contemplated. If this was so we never knew, for, spot on at ten-thirty, Dick flung open the door with his raucous cry 'Blow up' and this time everyone left without fuss, a much better response. The reason was soon obvious, it was time to dash back to the office to take out our checks again and book back on duty, a bit late and a quarter of an hour's pay was lost. Dick believed in hitting the pocket to get obedience.

Outside at the cupboard Dick held us back while he doled out more meager rations to the rest and then turned to Bill. 'Take them over to the Super's office.'

We trailed behind Bill, retracing our steps along the official path to the passenger shed then on past the signal box to a wide footboard crossing over the main lines at the end of the platform and then on into the goods yard. On the left I noticed the messroom where I had made my first visit. Facing us as we walked there stood a large office block, its red exterior grimy with age and many layers of soot deposited by passing locos over the years.

Bill had remained silent all the way over except for watching our safety on the crossing. Surveying the building he said, 'This is it. Now how do we find the way in? Haven't been here for a long time. This visit is quite usual, Mr Ross only wants to complete some formalities and give you a pep talk.'

We were called in one at a time, the senior one first. As we all started on the same day seniority was determined by age. I was second, already I had a junior.

Mr Ross greeted me with a friendly 'Good morning, sit down please.' He placed in front of me a CONTRACT OF SERVICE form asking as he did so 'Do you remember reading this at Swindon and do you understand it?'

Because I had skipped it the first time I asked if I could read it again.

'Certainly, pleased to know you're interested.' After allowing me time he said, 'If you're happy will you please sign and date it.' He followed by witnessing my signature and handing me a copy explaining that what I had signed for was my side of the bargain in return for life-long employment with the Company.

Back at the shed Dick waited for our return to give us his own lectures. 'I'm easy to get along with if you do your work and don't try to play me up. Don't listen to those others, they're not a very good example. Bill will tell you how to go on.' Doug reinforced his earlier assessment of Dick, 'I told you he wasn't so bad.'

Dick then handed out more waste and oil saying 'Clean that one for the Blowers.' The order we found out later meant the loco was working a goods train to Blowers Green, a small place beyond Stourbridge.

Another type of loco waited our attention, this time a 49xx, a 'Hall' class, a mixed-traffic loco which would complete its day by returning and continuing through to London with an express goods. It didn't vary in its appearance as regards dirt; once again piles of greasy muck faced us.

Dick realised the state it was in and had said to Bill, 'Do the best you can with it, only do the tops.' Perhaps he was taking pity on us and letting us off the terrible job of cleaning the wheels, or was it his intention to introduce us to climbing about on the boiler. Whatever the reason it was a pleasant change trying to get some sort of shine on the green paintwork. In my mind I had conjured up thoughts of several years wallowing in muck. I couldn't imagine these locos being any different.

The rest of the day passed slowly although some of the time had been taken up with the office visit. Perhaps it was because my late night and early morning was now catching up with me.

The boiler and tender sides eventually looked a bit more reasonable with the bold Great Western lettering getting more than its share of attention, a mark of my developing interest.

A little before 2.30 Dick came round to have another word. 'There's a lot more to it than you thought, you haven't started cleaning yet. You can have a go at the brass tomorrow.' He finished with a little encouragement by saying 'You've done well for your first day, go and get cleaned up.'

Those few words of added encouragement was all I needed to convince me that I had made the right decision. I put my check in at 2.30 feeling confident.

TWO

Cleaning engines

AT HOME, my father was just ready to leave when I came puffing in. I had hurried in the hope of catching him before he left for work.

'How did it go then, John?' he asked.

'Not too bad, a lot dirtier than I thought. I'm told it gets easier as it goes.' Then I went on to tell him 'We cleaned 4007, the one on our train yesterday, at least we did the wheels, it was much too dirty to do it all in the time.'

'What train did it work?'

'The 9.5 to Paddington.'

'I'll look out for it when it comes back.'

'Don't bother, it didn't look very good.'

'I've got to go now, get a good night's sleep, you'll feel better tomorrow.'

That advice was heeded but not needed.

At that particular time my reflections were that I had worked a bank holiday and wasn't able to justify it. In those days they didn't give a day in lieu for a day worked.

While I scrubbed away at my hands in the kitchen sink wondering whether the natural colour would ever come back my mother asked, 'Where did you get those overalls from?'

'The chargeman lent them to me, I've got to give them back when I get an issue.'

'Have I got to get them cleaned?' she asked. 'I'll never get all that grease off. Whatever will they be like at the end of the week.'

I evaded the issue by asking, 'Can you find me an old towel

and a bit of soap to take, they all had some except us.' Then I thought, ask for tea, sugar and milk.

I was in bed quite early and got up next morning very refreshed. Taking the normal route to the shed I booked on duty with an air of belonging to the job. Having taken my time check I made my way to the cabin to find my two new colleagues and only a few others there. The large gang of the day before were dispersed to various spare firing duties, upgraded to firemen on a day-to-day basis. This was the reason for the heavy layers of grime on the locos, there was no one to clean them. Bill, our mentor of the day before, was among them, so were all those forbidding senior fellows, leaving only those who were too junior to carry out firing duties. With so much space we moved along the seats to feel less cut off, not so much out of things.

Washing at mealbreak and making tea was much more civilised and before they all came back at the end of the summer service I was well settled in.

In the meantime Dick treated us casual, he kept us three together giving out waste and oil and instructions on what to do. He also kept to his word and insisted on us polishing the brass on all the 'Castle' class locos. The medium used to scour the brass was brick dust ground from old fire bricks after they had done a stint in the fire box, nothing wasted.

Dick left us alone to go along quietly, keeping an eye on us, from time to time scrutinising our efforts and passing caustic remarks such as, 'You're not cleaning it, only smudging it over. Let's see you get some of the dirt off.'

At the end of the summer service the senior cleaners returned, their services not required now the extra trains and holiday leave were ended. Some of them were arrogant towards Dick, rude and unco-operative. No wonder he treated them severely.

We were soon organised into gangs, Dick sorting out as best he could the miscreants to keep them together and at the same time giving the younger ones the chance to settle in without too much bad influence. At least that was the reason he gave us.

We three were kept together and put with a chap of about a year's seniority.

Dick said, 'You take these three, Den, you're the captain of the nobby.'

'What's that, Dick, am I in charge?'

'Yes, that's right, you're responsible, any trouble and you answer for it.' That was another way of getting someone else to maintain discipline.

Den Insole was our new mate's name. He explained that he had been out firing for a short time. 'Lucky, really, at my age,' he added.

He decided that we should split into two pairs, each to clean one side on a regular basis. We tossed, Fred and I did the driver's side, sharing the privilege of cleaning the motions underneath.

Under Den's guidance we worked with a will, starting each loco by polishing the brass to make it look as if we were really doing something, followed by the boiler and tender then the wheels and motions, using up the second-hand waste as taught by Bill.

Dick thought our work was good enough to keep us regularly on the two Londons. This arrangement was good for us, too; having regular locos made life easier, we could reap the rewards of our labours and what's more take more pride in the job.

The locos got much better, so much so that the two pairs of us became competitive, each trying to outshine the other. The brass safety valve and the copper top of the chimney had a definite demarcation line right down the centre, quite often with a better shine one side than the other. The division down the front of the smokebox was too much for Dick, who soon ordered us to stop our nonsense and show the rest how well we could do it.

Den's enthusiasm went a long way towards improving our efforts, he was always in the best of spirits, cheerfully urging us on. His entry into the ranks of cleaners was less of a shock than mine; his father was a fireman at Kingham, a small depot operating mainly on the branch line between Gloucester and

Banbury. On school holidays and often on other days he was taken on the footplate for whole days at a time. Many times he held us spellbound as he related yarns of the various happenings and the casual way the branch was worked, how his father taught him the arts of firing and all the little things that go towards making an efficient fireman.

Fred had left our gang to return to his home depot and was replaced by a new entrant Ted Wigley. He and I worked together smoothly, ensuring no interruption with the efficiency of the work.

It was not without problems that I got to this stage. I was experiencing some difficulty in getting up at 5.30 a.m. each day, and several warnings were issued to me from Dick. In general I arrived fifteen to thirty minutes late at least twice a week. I just couldn't wake up. Threats of dismissal made no difference, my late arrivals continued. My father was also getting worried, often reminding me that I would lose my job and if I did it would be difficult to get another.

The showdown came one morning. The previous day I had had a severe telling-off from Dick saying 'If you come late again this week you'll have to see the gaffer.' When I eventually got out of bed and saw the time my heart sank: it was 6.30.

I scrambled into my clothes and away without a cup of tea – I don't know why because I felt this was the end anyhow. It was with a heavy heart that I entered the time office that morning. The time clerk refused to book me on duty saying 'I've had instructions from the chargeman not to book you on duty if you're more than a few minutes late.' He continued with, 'You'll have to see Mr Elms when he comes. You can wait there if you like or sit in the cabin.'

'What time will he see me?' I asked.

'He gets here just before eight, he'll probably see you then.'

I knew I had got a bad name for being late and didn't want to sit in full view of everyone to let them know I was waiting to see the foreman on a disciplinary case. I made my way to the cabin and spent a long miserable hour. Dick looked in just before eight. 'Better go along and wait for Mr Elms to come, it'll look better if you're waiting for him.'

I sat outside his office and didn't wait long before he arrived. I stood up as he walked towards me. He was a tall man with a slight stoop and as he approached he bent a little lower as he asked 'Have you come late again, young man?'

'Yes, sir.'

'What time did you arrive?'

'Seven o'clock, sir.'

'Come into the office, we'll have to talk about this.' He sat down and continued his questioning. 'Do you want to stay on the job?'

'Yes, sir.'

'Then why don't you make more effort to get here? You're no good as a fireman if you get late in the mornings, trains would be making late starts.'

'I do try, sir, but I don't hear the clock go off.'

'I suppose you have the clock by the side of the bed.'

'Yes, sir, it's a new one.'

'When you wind it up at night do you have to reset it?'

'Yes, sir, I always make sure I've set it.'

'I think I know what you're doing. You must be hearing it and turning it off without realising it.'

After a little pause he went on to suggest 'How about if you put the clock over the other side of the room?'

'Yes, sir, I've got somewhere to put it but I wouldn't hear it go off.'

'Has it got a loud bell?'

'Yes, sir, quite loud.'

'I'll tell you what I'll do. If you put it over the other side tonight and promise me faithfully to tell me the truth in the morning if you don't hear it, I'll let you off. It's either that or a week's notice if you come late again.'

That night I did his bidding, the clock seemed so far away I was certain that I could never hear it. The morning came with me in a bemused state, there was a distant ringing. Suddenly I realised it was my clock, I shot out of bed delighted that I would be in time for work.

Having stopped the clock and being out of bed I was now aware of Mr Elms' scheme. There was no reason why I should turn over and go to sleep again.

Just before six the time clerk was surprised to see me so bright and cheerful. 'Made it this morning,' he said. When the chargeman met me he looked amazed but said 'I'm glad to see you here on time, don't want to see you late again. Carry on with your mates.'

Den then had a go at me. 'You had a near squeak then, mate, Dick told us you were getting the sack. I've been telling you it would happen but you took no notice.'

'I have taken notice, but I just didn't wake up.'

'Well what happened to get you here this morning? Did he put the fear of Christ up you?'

'He did that all right,' I replied and related the episode in the foreman's office.

Round about 8.15 just before the loco went off Mr Elms arrived on the scene, something he had never done before. I was on the top framing cleaning the brass when I looked down to see him beckoning me to get down. Face to face again he said, 'You look pleased with yourself. I understand you were right time this morning.'

'Yes, sir, no trouble at all.'

'Did you put the clock over the other side and did you hear it?'

'Yes, sir, I heard it all right and had to get out to stop it,' I said, with a knowing smile.

'You needn't look so pleased with yourself. Now we both know it works just don't come late again or it's certain sack for you.'

He left me a little shaken. What if I came late for some other reason, I thought? During the next forty-five years on the railways I made damned sure that I did arrive for work on time.

My first winter was a hard one, there was plenty of frost and inclement weather to suffer. Normally the 'Castle' class we cleaned for the first London stood outside the shed with its tender half inside. The east wind blew on to the boiler and very little heat escaped to warm us up but this was considerably better than doing the tender. We were not supplied with trestles or ladders. The only way to clean the expanse of the sides was to hang on with one hand to the top of the tender while making the best of a 2 in. toe-hold on the ledge along the bottom and polishing away with the other hand. Coal stacked on the tender made it difficult at the best of times, in winter ice along the rim made matters even worse. Dick still expected immaculate cleaning. Our own efforts had grown on him, he now expected a higher standard than ever before. The shed doorway had a very limited opening, so small in fact that a loco had to be driven through at the slowest possible speed to prevent any rocking that might occur from scraping the tender on the wall. The clearance of little more than an inch made it impossible to clean right through and even when we had worked from both sides there was still a stripe down the centre to be cleaned when the loco was moved.

In bad weather we naturally hoped to get on the footplate for warmth, even to help the fireman if we could, although this was strictly against the rules. The foreman, Dick and everyone else were adamant that we should not get on the footplate. Why this should be I never knew – it was the best place to learn our future job. Perhaps it was a matter of insurance or, more likely, discipline.

Quite often we defied him and offered to help the fireman who in turn agreed to look out for Dick. Sometimes the drivers kept a look-out as well because when we helped the fireman he was free to help the driver. At times our own mates would fail to let us know when he was about, just for the fun of seeing us get a telling off. Dick would stand only so much of this and every so often without hesitation he had us booked off duty from the time he caught us, which was often as early as eight in the morning; not much fun getting up at five for only two hours' pay.

A habit that started in the winter to help us warm up was to sneak in and make a cup of tea. All too often Dick caught us at it with the inevitable loss of time. One particular occasion that comes to mind was when it was my turn to make it. I made my way over to the cabin keeping a sharp look-out all the way, dodging round locos to avoid detection. I made it to the cabin safely, made the tea and quietly opened the door. The first sight I saw was Dick sitting on a loco near the door. How was I to get out without being seen? I was certain he knew I was in there, my first thoughts were of going out through the window but when I looked out I noticed the foreman in his office looking my way. I doubt if he was looking for me but he effectively blocked off that exit. There was no other way but to run the gauntlet. Another look out and Dick was looking the other way. I eased the door open as little as I could and slithered out quite confident I had escaped. Back at the loco I told them, 'Dick was sitting on a footplate near the cabin door, I had a job to get out.'

'Did he see you?' asked Den.

'I don't think so, he was looking the other way when I came out. I thought of getting out through the window but Mr Elms was looking my way.'

'We shall have to keep a look-out for him, that's all.'

As we sat snugly on the footplate pouring out the tea Dick was seen to walk across to the coal stage.

'Keep an eye on him,' said Den. 'It looks as if you've got away with it.'

Our enjoyment was suddenly shattered by a horrible voice shouting up at us 'What the hell are you up to?'

Dick had once again outwitted us by coming round the back of the shed.

We all tried to get off the other side but he bawled, 'Come on down this side, I want to talk to you lot.'

We faced him hoping to wriggle our way out of it.

He looked at us and asked, 'Well, who made it?'

We stood there with no intention of telling him.

He waited for a moment, then looking straight at me said, 'It was you, wasn't it? I saw you trying to get out of the door without opening it. Book off the lot of you. Go home, put your checks in.'

'Now look what you've done,' said Den.

'It wasn't my fault. How was I to know he was waiting for me?'

As we washed hands we forgot our recriminations and decided that Dick wasn't going to win again.

'I know what we'll do,' said Den. 'We'll take a tea can out with us and make it over there. He'll have a job to catch us then.'

From then on we proudly sneaked the can and ingredients out under his nose and succeeded in making tea by boiling the water in the firebox of any suitable loco. It often came out smoky but who cared, we kept out of trouble.

Some of the senior lads had very little respect for Dick and his authority. They seldom got caught as they regularly played him up. He did, in fact, come round to saying we were a good bunch by comparison. They used every ploy they knew to dodge work, their efforts at cleaning were poor, none of Dick's bad language made any impression. They even made tea and drank it in front of him while they attempted to clean with the other hand. One of their tricks was to get in a firebox of a dead loco to play cards, particularly on a Saturday morning when Dick tended to allow a little more laxity. The usual thing was to take a can of tea and a couple of flare lamps for light. The lamps were styled the same as Aladdin's lamp with a long spout holding a wick which trailed down into the vessel of paraffin. When it burned it gave off pungent smoke and fumes. Two of these in a firebox was enough to choke anyone but they considered it worth it.

The day came when Dick caught up with them. It was generally believed that someone had told him where they were. Whatever his source of information they found the fire-hole doors slowly closing. Panic reigned, there was no way of opening the doors from the inside. Then to make matters worse the ashpan dampers were closed, cutting off all air. By the time a fitter heard their calls for help and let them out there was no sign of the chargeman, he left them to find out for themselves who had done it. On the next pay day, alas, they found a reduction in their pay packets.

It wasn't long before the lads settled the score. One day Dick was spotted asleep in his little hut, a corrugated iron structure about 8 × 6 ft. Inside was a small stove, its chimney pipe protruding through the curved roof. They made certain that he was asleep then one of them climbed up and dropped three fog detonators down the chimney pipe, completing the mischief by placing some waste inside the pipe. Quietly the iron door was closed and the outside bolt put over. Several of us cleaning locos nearby watched with interest and when these lads disappeared we thought it wise to do the same. From a vantage point further away we waited; it seemed ages before the detonators went off and then only with a *phutt*. Presently all hell was let loose. Dick panicked and hit the inside of the hut making a terrible din. He must have been choking to death in there. None of us dared go near for fear of getting the blame but we all felt we should; there was always the possibility of the culprits taking their revenge on us. As we peeped from our hiding place half decided to let him out; a fitter passing by heard his ravings and let him out. When the door opened Dick emerged in a cloud of smoke and dust, eyes streaming, partly with rage but most certainly from the conditions he had suffered. Without hesitation he charged off towards the shed, no doubt to tell Mr Elms. He was forestalled, someone had already told him and he was on his way. In the meantime we had returned to cleaning our loco and from a vantage point on the boiler watched and heard the meeting. Dick spluttered his story out but was answered with a curt reply, 'You should leave them alone, you cause more trouble than they do, I've told you about it before. Serves you right.'

Smugly we thought that's put him right but we soon had to change our attitude.

Mr Elms was down below. 'Come on down and tell me all you know about this trouble.'

We protested our innocence without much conviction. Turning to Den he asked, 'How was it that being so near you didn't see anything?'

Quick as a flash Den replied 'We were working on the other side, sir.'

I could read disbelief in his face but he didn't relent. Not realising that we had heard his remarks to Dick he concluded by assuring us that 'If I hear of anything like this again you'll all get the sack.'

Mr Elms then made a round-up of all the lads, giving them all the same threat but for some uncanny reason he sorted out the real culprits and gave them a day's leave without pay.

The pranks were brought to an end in general but there was an occasion when we all got into trouble. One morning after break Dick came to the door with his usual 'Blow up'. A voice from the cabin was heard to murmur a rude remark. The door opened and Dick stood there red in the face, 'Right, who said it?' he asked.

We were all amazed to think that he had even been able to hear it and looked round one another rather amused. This infuriated him even more and he stamped off up the shed to once again report to Mr Elms. He also instructed the time clerk not to book us on duty again until it was sorted out.

After a few minutes he returned with the boss.

'Well,' said Mr Elms, 'if the person who was rude to the chargeman will own up the matter will be settled.'

The guilty one kept quiet, we had all agreed to cover him, it was such a trivial matter. Mr Elms didn't like the silence, after looking round and waiting some time he repeated his request adding 'If you don't say now you'll all go home. Is there anyone else who knows who it was?'

That was a forlorn hope; we may have fought among ourselves but never would we do a thing like that. The continued silence brought the expected reply.

'All right then, all of you go home, come back to work when you're sent for.'

We were left to talk it over and before leaving came to a firm understanding that no one had said anything. As we walked along the shed we passed Dick who was heard to remark, in undertones, 'Got you this time.' This was Wednesday morning and we had no idea when we would be back.

I found it difficult to explain to my father why I was losing pay to cover another lad but it was such an issue where mates stuck together.

On Friday a note came saying that I should report at ten o'clock on Saturday morning. On arrival the orders were to wait in the cabin until we were called. We all agreed to stick to our story of not hearing anything but had doubts about one lad, who was a possible tell-tale. Very soon Dick appeared at the door and called out six names. I was not among them. 'The rest of you wait here for your names to be called,' said Dick.

More speculation followed, from the selection made it was obvious that these were the chargeman's best boys. What was he up to? The picture unfolded a while later when the door opened again and my name was called out. 'Jack Gardner, you come alone.'

Dick turned to leave, the lads gave their best wishes and a reminder not to let the side down.

Following Dick along the shed he turned to me. 'I don't know how you've got involved in this. You've turned out to be all right. If you know who said it you should tell.'

I could suppose only that he was trying to coerce me into turning traitor. I never thought that he had held me in such high regard.

A very subservient young man entered Mr Elms' office; I had been there before. Sitting with Mr Elms was Mr Armstrong, the superintendent. He studied the list of reports in front of him and turned to Dick. 'Shouldn't this one have been with the others we've seen?'

Dick looked a bit silly, going pink in the face as he replied, 'I suppose so but I thought he might be able to help us and tell us something.'

'Well, can you?' asked the super.

'No, sir, I didn't hear anything said.'

'Can you tell us who might have said it then?'

'Said what, sir?' I asked.

'It's no good you saying you don't know but if you won't tell I can't make you.'

Mr Elms then stepped in. 'We had some trouble with him at

the start but he's been good since, never gives any bother now, one of the better lads.'

Mr Armstrong then continued. 'The six I saw together were regarded as being of good behaviour, the rest of you I'm seeing separately, ending up with the worst. All I can say to you at this stage is that you seem to be the best of the worst.'

This assessment of myself amused me and a smile came over my face which was soon wiped off with a further comment: 'You can go home now, you have all lost three and a half days' pay for your trouble.'

From then on there was hardly any misbehaviour, only a reluctance on the part of the worst ones to get on with their work.

By the end of 1937 nearly half the senior cleaners were promoted to firemen and the numbers made up with new entrants, pushing me well up the ladder. The past was put behind with Dick and work was no longer a chore, the locos in general were respectable and with the exception of a few took very little effort to keep clean. Less was expected of us and we got caught less often making tea, even then the warning was to make sure the foreman didn't catch us.

Moving up also made a difference to status. Not only did I take a better place in the cabin, the work was cleaner. I was able to keep myself comparatively clean which showed against the newcomers, just as it had been with me at the start.

With seniority my turn came to go calling up on nights. This wasn't a job to be envied in the winter; overcoats were not issued until a cleaner had totalled twelve firing turns and at this stage it was impossible. For wet weather a voluminous cape was supplied which made cycling very hard, in fact it was easier to get wet. During the summer when the nights were fresh and short it was quite a relief to be away from the run of the mill work and out as my own boss. The nights were quiet and lonely. Occasionally a footplateman could be seen either trudging along carrying his food box or perhaps pedalling his bike with a little oil lamp flickering in the dimly lit streets. Other than these there were only police constables on foot patrol, always ready to stop and have a natter. Some took advantage and had a smoke asking before they did 'Have you seen the sergeant round yet?' Or they might say 'Keep a look-out for the sergeant while I have a smoke.' They were always a bit of company to break the monotony.

There was often the old-fashioned night watchman to call on. In those days when roads were dug up a man was employed to trim the red oil lamps protecting the excavations and to maintain them during the night, also to protect the tools and equipment. In the winter he was a blessing with his brazier of red-hot coke to get warm by and more often than not a cup of tea. Later in the morning the Co-op bakery had its attraction in the form of new bread cooking. The smell of fresh bread first thing in the morning drew us all, police as well. A fresh new roll went down well, even without butter.

On average about fifty to sixty men had to be called between midnight and 6 a.m. To cover this number three lads were on duty, the areas being divided into the Rainbow Hill nearest the shed; the Town, which covered calls a little further away; and Outstations being the farthest of all. The Hill had most calls with short distances to ride, the Town less calls but farther to ride, and Outstations only perhaps about six calls taking between 20–25 miles between them. I hated the Hill area. I didn't care for knocking doors all through the night, I preferred riding and normally did the Outstations. We booked on at 11 p.m. and took stock of all the men in our areas, booking a call one hour before their time on duty. Most men were up and answered the first knock but some were dead to the world and it was easier to wake the street than them.

One such character lived on the Hill. My mate Doug had the privilege. We ragged him so much that in the end he challenged us to knock the man up. 'It's all right for you to talk. I'll bet you a pound you can't wake him first time.'

We both backed out with the excuse that we had calls to make. Doug looked at my sheet and soon spotted that I had spare time. 'Come on,' he said, 'have a go.' Why not, I thought. 'All right, I'll try but I won't take on the bet.' Perhaps I was too sure of myself.

Number 18 Belmont Street was a small terrace house, one of many which lined this side of the street. The street was dimly lit with three or four gas lamps, one of which stood almost opposite. Doug and the other call boy directed me to the right door and retired to the area of the lamp to watch the fun. I walked the four or five yards to the door and turned to look back, to see they were highly amused. What did they know that I didn't? The normal procedure was to rap the knocker gently and wait for a reply and then if none was heard to give it a hard knock. I realised that a rap would do no good so gave it a fair bang, bang, bang. No response so a second attempt with the same result. Looking across to the others I saw they were laughing their heads off. Doug said 'Go on, give it a good bashing, you've got to wake him.'

I turned to carry out his order and as I did so the window next door opened and out poked a female head. 'Why don't you bloody hop it! It's always the same the morning after his pay day. Waking the street.' I took no notice, she disappeared from the window so I gave it another hard knock and at the same time my mates disappeared into the shadows to watch the fun. The driver slept on but the face reappeared at the window. This time, amid a tirade of abuse, a container of water was thrown my way. Fortunately I was able to dodge it by skipping down the path, never to return. I often wondered, considering this was a terrace house with no upstairs bathroom, what sort of domestic utensil this was.

I was calling every other week for the next six months before returning to my regular turns again.

During the summer of 1938 when almost all of my seniors were promoted to firing duties I was often in line to do firing myself or to do shedmen's work such as ash loading, shed sweeping or assisting the boiler washers in washing the lime and sludge out of the boilers, each loco needing this once a week. A messy job which no one liked. It did at least increase the pay each day I was upgraded. The job we all detested was emptying wagons of coal at the emergency coal stack, or worse still loading them. The work was hard and back-breaking with no let-up until sufficient had been loaded. In addition it was the dustiest of all the things we did. We were well away from the shed with no facilities for tea making or washing and if it rained, no cover. We all got very tired and fed up but twelve hours a day at 7s 2d a day basic made the burden easier to bear. A big improvement on my 5 shillings a day.

As the summer wore on the management realised that there was insufficient cover for spare firing duties and arranged a system whereby the top six cleaners were paired to work three turns round the clock to be on hand to cover any emergency turns that might crop up. At this stage I was fourth from top and was mated with number one. He was often booked out firing leaving me next available on duty. Dick was now showing quite a changed attitude: I had become a blue-eyed boy, could do nothing wrong. He found me as much work away from cleaning as possible, and in between running errands I was at leisure to sit in the cabin for short periods – in general I was able to keep out of the way.

The same cover extended to the late turn, booking on 2 p.m. Dick usually left us to sit in the cabin until the day cleaners had gone home before giving the simplest of jobs, then he went home leaving us in the care of the afternoon firelighter. We made the work Dick had given us last to teatime and had as long as we liked for tea. All that was expected of us then was that we kept out of sight of the shift foreman. That presented no problem at all, we wandered off out by various routes and often finished up at the fish and chip shop, returning to the cabin for more tea. Although our day was not up until 10.30, the night firelighter nearly always let us go home soon after he booked on at 10. At that time the pair for the night turn came on, once again to do very little. The shed at night took on a different aspect. It was dark and dingy, the gas lamps gave off a yellow light trying to cheer the gloom, leaving areas of darkness in between with the odd lump of coal to trip the lethargic night worker back to reality. Trying to clean under these conditions was hopeless. The chargeman recognised this fact and didn't bother us much; he often turned a blind eye when we curled up on a footplate for a little snooze.

After midnight the shed was as silent as an elephants' graveyard, the only sounds being creaking boilers as they gradually heated up with their newly lit fires, or the sound of the firelighter's shovel as he brought more to life. From then on the silence was unbroken until the men turned up at about 3.30 for the morning mail to Moreton-in-Marsh.

On the late turn I was often given the job tube cleaning. A certain number of locos were allocated to be examined by the boilersmith each day and to have their boiler tubes cleaned. Clean tubes played an important part in a loco's steaming qualities. First, I opened the smokebox door, removed the spark baffle plates and fitted a steam lance to a cock on the side. By placing the lance in each tube in turn and blowing a jet of steam through it all the deposits were cleared, if any doubt arose a long rod with a corkscrew end was used to clear any blockage; then round the other end and into the firebox to get off all the scale known as corks from that end of the tubes. If these were left the tubes would block very quickly. The last loco I had to do came in about 8 a.m. and it was normally after 9.30 when it became available to me. One evening it was so late I thought I would give it a quicky. A quick blow through of the tubes and a glance in the firebox led me to believe that it was clean enough. Pleased with myself I made my way towards the cabin only to come face to face with the boilersmith.

'Have you done it already?' he asked.

'Yes, all the tubes are clear and the inside is clean.'

'Come back with me and let's see,' he said.

Together we returned. He was such an easy-going old chap and I didn't want to upset him so I faced the music without trying to make excuses. The first thing he did was to get his acetylene lamp which was far brighter than my flare lamp and look in the firebox. 'You had better go back in there and knock those few corks off,' he said, not even suggesting that I had dodged it in the first place. I took my lamp and crawled in, feet first. As I entered my fears of a very hot box were confirmed, it took my breath away. The loco being a 'Castle' had a long brick arch and I was compelled to lean over it to reach the tube plate. In a very short time I smelled smoke and attributed it to the flare lamp. As quickly as I could I finished and got out. The boilersmith was sitting on the fireman's seat. He looked at me in horror, exclaiming, 'Crikey, lad, you're on fire. Come here quick.' With his cloth cap as a beater he soon had my smouldering overall jacket put out. 'I didn't realise it was as hot as that,' he said. Then, without using a light, he looked in the firebox to see the brick arch glowing a dull red.

'If you find another as hot again don't go in without seeing me first. Don't worry about your jacket, I'll get you another one.' Then I admitted, 'I knew it was too hot, that's why I didn't go in.'

Because of the more relaxed attitude I was enjoying being able to talk to the crews as they prepared their locos. As well as assisting the firemen I listened to their tales of express running, of how they often slogged up the bank at Honeybourne, sometimes with a banker to assist them if the load was too heavy. There were the yarns of running down at breakneck speed with the speedometer on 100 mph. Tales were related of picking up water at speed on the troughs and how they raced other trains on adjoining parallel lines. As most of their work was carried out in the day in full view of enthusiastic passengers and with locos looking every bit the masters of their work they had no difficulty in holding my imagination. The run to Paddington was only 120 miles but they made it sound as far as eternity.

Many times I heard of a wonderful diesel loco shunting in Acton yard. It was described as looking like a large box on wheels; inside and out of sight there was a diesel engine spoken of as if secret. It had a chimney so short that it could hardly be seen and, above all, the cab was completely closed in with windows to keep the weather out and furthermore the fireman had no work to do at all. The stories of its enormous power seemed grossly exaggerated to me. I dismissed it all, perhaps it was because I could not comprehend it or more likely the steam shunters in the yard were calling. I seem to remember thinking they had no future, that steam was here to stay. How wrong I was. They were developed so successfully that they are with us today with only slight modifications.

It was in the summer of 1938 when my first opportunity came to act as fireman. One day, half-way through an early shift, the foreman came to me and asked 'Are you the senior cleaner on duty?'

'Yes,' I replied.

'Then go with Frank Pomeroy over there on that 72xx, be his fireman for the day.'

Frank was one of the many firemen whom I had assisted in preparation and had got on well with. This particular day he was upgraded to act as driver. I went over to him, not believing my luck. He was standing at the side of a huge tank engine oiling the side rods.

'Have you got to come with me?' he asked.

'Yes, what have I got to do?'

'We're taking this one light to Stourbridge. Go and get your things from the cabin.'

I was down to the cabin in double quick time and back.

'Have I got to get it ready?'

'No,' replied Frank, 'the fire's all right, just tidy up the footplate.'

This was the first time I had been on a tank engine of this size; they had passed by on the loop line often but never near enough for me to appreciate their size. This type, built for work on the South Wales valleys, strayed to our shed very rarely.

Frank soon came up to the footplate. 'Take the hand-brake off, Jack, we're moving up for water.'

Then with tank full we waited for the shunters to move aside while we moved to the signal to leave the shed. Frank blew the whistle code for this end and the signal was lowered. As we slowly passed the box Frank came over to my side to tell the signalman our destination. We slowly approached the tunnel and I reflected that I had never been through it before, but had only seen it from my meanderings when I should have been cleaning. When we emerged Frank turned to me and asked,

'How many firing turns have you had, Jack?'

My answer of 'None' brought a slight look of dismay to his face. He looked at me querying the wisdom of taking me on the main line for the first time.

'I know you well enough, I expect it will be all right. That is if you do as I tell you.'

'Just tell me what to do. I don't really know how to go on by myself.'

Soon we were passing the factory where I had previously worked and seen the diesel rail-car passing. I stood back in pride, inwardly hoping that someone would see me. Frank saw me and said 'Don't stand back there, the draught will catch your back and give you a chill.' The fresh air suited me but his suggestion could not be ignored.

The trip turned out to be an eventful one. We were stopped at every signal box and shunted into every siding there was. It seemed the foreman was not the only one that didn't want the loco.

On my first day out I went into practically all the signal boxes on the route which the rules required me to and gained a good insight into Rule 55, often referred to as the firemen's rule.

After much delay we eventually arrived on the shed at Stourbridge only to be told by the foreman there that he had no use for it. 'Will you take it on to Wolverhampton?' he asked Frank.

Frank turned to me. 'We've managed well this far, might as well go, it's not far.'

We dumped the loco and obtained a ticket from the office to travel home. In those days the ticket was a metal tablet with the two names it was valid between stamped on it. Riding home talking to Frank made me feel quite grown up as regards railway work. I was itching to get home to relate my experience to my father.

My next turn cropped up in a similar way. This time the foreman's question was, 'Do you think you can work a passenger train on the branch to Bromyard?'

With visions of glory I replied, 'Yes.'

'Then go with Harry Plum, he's on that 45xx over there.'

My enthusiasm dimmed on hearing his name, as he was one of the old brigade. His life seemed to be set on making firemen's lives miserable, even cleaners got on his nerves. He was forever moaning at us and telling tales to the chargehand or foreman if we upset him. This in turn made us annoy him further, not giving any consideration to the fact that we might have to work with him some day.

I made my way towards him, only to be greeted with, 'Have I got to put up with you, then?'

'Yes, I'll fetch my things from the cabin.'

'We haven't got time for that, we're off shed soon. Just get and tidy up. Don't touch the fire, it's all right for now.'

I wasn't in any position to dispute anything he said, firstly I knew so little about what I was embarking on and secondly he would play hell with me if I failed to comply. The footplate was just about tidy when he came on board to move for water.

He groused immediately. 'Come on, get some waste on this cab, I don't want to stand in dust all day.'

I made an effort to wipe his side off first only to be chided with, 'Not now, get out of my way. Get on top of the tank.'

Having taken water we moved off to the station with me under strict orders not to touch anything until he told me to.

The shunter coupled us to a train of three small coaches. As we stood in the platform waiting time I tried to study Harry. He was very short, lean faced with thin, pursed lips and beady eyes darting about all over the place. I felt I was under surveillance all the time.

Eventually the guard blew his whistle and waved his flag. 'Right away from the guard,' I said. Harry was not prepared to take my word and pushed me to one side to look for himself. The train trickled out of the station without much effort on the falling gradient.

'Shall I open the damper and put some on now, Harry?'

'No, leave it alone until I tell you. Who said you could call me Harry?' he replied sternly.

Even in my ignorance I could tell the fire was in a poor state and should have some attention. I had no choice but to stand and wait orders.

We drifted down to Worcester Foregate Street station, then on to Henwick before leaving the outskirts of the town. The line was still falling and very little steam had been required yet but I was still barred from doing anything to the fire. Just before Bransford Road halt we turned right on to the branch line. Harry came over to my side to take the single line staff, our key to the section. Looking at the fire he said, 'Better get some on there,' in a manner that suggested I had been at fault in not doing so before. No sooner had I made a start than he interfered by shouting, 'Throw it straight down the middle.'

By this time the fire was so dead that it didn't burn as it should, the coal remaining black and lifeless. 'More up the middle,' said Harry which did no good at all. The fire looked even worse, turning into a black pancake. The gradient of the branch changed to uphill quite sharply and the steam pressure responded by going down.

'The fire's not burning at all, mate. Shall I pull the pricker round?'

'No, put some more coal on. I'll tell you what to do.' The steam crept back and the boiler level dropped. If it had not been for the station stops and Harry putting the blower on each time he shut off I don't know how we would have managed. It could be said that we were getting along and managing but with the steam pressure about 100 psi instead of 180 I was disappointed at not doing better. I followed his instructions with disastrous effect until he eventually looked at the fire. 'Good god, what a mess!' he exclaimed. 'What did you want to do that for?'

I got cheeky and replied, 'If you had let me alone I would have done better.'

Harry didn't like that and raved at me saying, 'You'll never come with me again.'

I returned the compliment by retorting, 'I don't want to.'

As it happened we had reached the summit and had a

freewheel down to Bromyard where we took water and ran round the train for the return trip.

Before we started Harry began to interfere again so I said, 'You'd better do it yourself. It's no good me trying while you keep on at me.'

'Damn it, just do as I tell you.'

The time came to depart, the fire still looked black and hopeless. The line ahead rose sharply and I could see no way but to poke the fire. While Harry was busy looking ahead I took the poker out and gave the fire a stir up. He turned on me again but it was too late. I returned the poker and turned away pretending he wasn't there, looking out of the window the bunker end. Then I turned back to look at the chimney; the black coal that had blocked the fire was now smoke up the chimney, the steam pressure was rising. It was like magic, I didn't care what Harry thought now, we were winning. As we went over the brow we were in the best position we had been in all day. As I opened the fire-hole doors the heat that came to greet me was so much more than before, I knew I had succeeded. Very soon I was in trouble again. After going over the top and turning downhill steam was shut off and the safety valve blew off. This brought the immediate response, 'Now look what you're doing, wasting steam.' Simply by controlling the steam I kept out of further trouble.

We were relieved at the station on arrival and walking back to the shed I asked in a cheeky way, 'Will you take me again, Harry?' After a pause he said 'You'll be all right, son.' That was the best possible comment from him.

Years before my time the London Midland & Scottish Railway had a shed at Worcester with running powers over the Western line from Norton Junction through to Droitwich where it turned off to rejoin the Midland again a few miles from Bromsgrove. The shed had long since been demolished, the sidings laid in its place known as the Midland sidings. Two turns remained and one loco was stabled each night in the Western shed. One set of men worked it out in the morning to Derby and on return was relieved by the other set to work to Bristol in the afternoon.

The men were self-sufficient, being administered from Gloucester. This worked well until one morning the fireman failed to turn up. The driver hung on as long as he could before he told our foreman that he hadn't got a mate. The foreman searched round for a fireman and came up with me. I was the last resort.

The Midland driver was a miserable old man but he did claim to have fixed the fire saying, 'No need to do anything yet, I'll tell you what to do.'

My immediate thoughts were 'Here we go again.' I climbed aboard the small o–6–o tender loco and took stock. All our own footplates were on the same pattern, this one was different. When the driver came I asked him to tell me where some of the controls were such as the injector valves and the blower. He grumbled and said, 'I suppose I've got to nurse you all day.'

He was one of the real old brigade, epitomising the driver of the past, those that were dirty simply because they believed that locos were dirty and they were part of it. There was no real attempt to keep clean. Overalls and serge jacket alike took on a sheen with the regular smudging of oil. This particular one was no exception, he buttoned his jacket at the top only and wore an old-fashioned cloth cap which glistened with oil. To complete his appearance he sported a very large bushy moustache which hung down over his top lip.

With hardly a word to me he took the loco off shed to the old Midland yard to couple to three small coaches. 'Put the lamps right,' he said. 'I suppose you know how to do that.'

I thought I could humour him by asking as politely as possible, 'Shall I lift the damper and put some coal on now?'

'Only lift the damper on the first notch, it's a front damper, we might get a blowback.'

'How about coal?'

'Leave that until I tell you.'

From then on I might as well have been with Harry Plum; it was a repeat of my last trip with him.

The aim was to work to Birmingham New Street stopping at all stations. At this stage it seemed far from possible but as this was a complete stranger to me I was happy to let the driver tell me how to go on.

'Shall I start firing yet?' I asked.

'There's enough in there for now, leave it for a while.'

'It's not burning, I think I ought to pull the pricker round.'

He didn't take kindly to this suggestion, just grumbled. As we stopped at the intermediate stations I was able to recover some steam. Leaving Droitwich the line rose and a repeat of the fiasco with Harry loomed up. Soon we were at Bromsgrove, the foot of the famous incline. Once more I pleaded with the driver to let me poke the fire with the same negative response. Looking ahead I could see the bank rising sharply in front of me, 1 in 40 for nearly three miles. My mind went back to the Bromyard trip and without more ado the poker was in the fire and doing its work. The smoke flew and so did the fury. I opened the damper wider, steam rose as it had before and after firing we reached the summit with flying colours. The driver said nothing more, just sat on his seat looking miserable. The seat on this one, in common with all Midland locos, was on the left-hand side to match the driving position and this added to my difficulties firing. Not having seen this route before I was compelled to ask the driver for information which annoyed him even more. A trip which should have been pleasant was again miserable. Relief at Birmingham was most welcome.

Also in the summer of 1938 I was booked on the duty sheet for the first time as a fireman. Even now, I can still recall my excitement at booking on and mating up with a driver to start a day's work officially as a fireman.

The turn started at 1.40 in the afternoon, to walk to the yard and relieve a shunting pilot in the middle yard. The driver was George Bishop, a man I knew well as a top link fireman on the expresses to London. I had helped him on many occasions to get his loco ready and we got on well together.

When we met in the time office he soon asked, 'Have you had many firing turns yet?'

'No,' I replied, 'only a few odd ones.' I continued to relate the few bits I had done.

'Then you'll be new to shunting work. I'll have to show you the shunter's hand signals, it's important that you get those right.'

We walked over to the yard with George asking me details of my background, I'm sure only to put me at ease, for by the time I got to the loco I was quite relaxed.

The tank had been filled and the coal bunker trimmed ready for a fresh start for us. The bunker was easy to get at because the cab was open backed: little cover for the crew was a feature of Great Western locos. It was quite a small tank engine and the footplate gave very little room for manoeuvre; there were two rear sand boxes fitted to the bunker, one each side of the shovelling hole. The distance from the bunker to the firebox was so short that a normal-sized shovel was too long and the shed carpenter had the job of shortening the handle. In the floor of the footplate two damper handles stood up and the front sand lever kept them company. Where to put one's feet when firing was the big problem.

'Now let's see what you know about hand signals,' said George. 'Later on you'll be looking out for them yourself.'

We went through everything over and over again until George was satisfied. I found myself engrossed in his instructions. Here I had a driver who was as interested in me as in his own work, so different from my previous experiences. For the first couple of hours the shunters were on the driver's side but George kept me looking out to watch them and expected me to take their signals and pass them on to him; under his watchful eye I learned quickly. Later in the day it proved valuable when I had to take them all my side. I was also allowed to get on with the firing without any interference although I found it was not so easy to cope with the varying demands for steam.

Tea was taken in more civilised conditions in the shunters' cabin; a sit-down in comfort with a strong cup of tea was enjoyable.

At 9.30 we finished work and left the loco in the condition it was when we took over, clean and ready to do another shift.

Several days with George helped to improve my education, so

much in fact that he was heard giving me a good name. To me that was music.

The summer of 1939 brought my first real move: I was promoted to fireman for the three months of the summer service on a temporary basis. I had no regular turns or driver but was booked out week by week or even daily according to vacant turns. With the exception of a few main line local trips my time was spent on the yard pilots of which there were five. A great variety of experience was to be found under these conditions. The whims of the various drivers were hard to understand: some wanted plenty of steam and others were satisfied with a moderate amount; some were happy to help a young man while there were those that barely spoke. While learning firing in this way was good for me I also appreciated that there was far more in learning about drivers, for they were the ones that could make or break a fireman. Learning to bend in the wind was equally as important as providing steam. Working nights and doing everything in the dark was a new experience, shunter's hand signals were by lamp and had to be learned over again. Main line signals gave a different aspect, showing lights instead of semaphore arms. Keeping awake seemed much harder than when cleaning. Making sure of the lamps of the buffer beams was more important than I thought; the right colours had a meaning.

Perhaps the most interesting turn was working the pilot shunting in the loco shed yard; there was always so much activity to maintain interest but above all it worked a trip to the vinegar works down in the town. To get from the yard the line ran at right angles across the main line curve and down a very steep incline to the main road just outside the station. There was quite an unusual feature here: to stop the road traffic while a train was crossing two main line signals were placed in the road, one each side of the line. Both were placed to Danger by the shunters and one stood each side with a red flag before signalling the driver to cross. Two other roads were crossed but without any signals before arriving at our destination. After shunting for a short time the trip for the return was made ready.

Because of the very severe gradient the load was limited to six small wagons, each loaded with casks of vinegar. The steepest part of the incline was after passing over the main road up to the main line. To make this possible the driver waited a little way back from the road and when the signal was given he opened up and went like a madman, sparks flying all across the road and amongst the factories until the top was reached. It was always a relief to everyone when the trip was safely over the top.

During this spell of temporary firing I was also fortunate in having several trips on local main line goods trains, mainly on the 'Dean' 0–6–0 tender locos. These were by far the simplest to fire and manage, unfortunately for every mile worked in the forward direction there was an equal amount of tender-first working – lovely in good weather but not to be envied in rain. In all, I had a wonderful experience of a fair variety of work but all good things must come to an end. By the end of August I was returned to cleaning duties, standing third senior for promotion on a permanent basis. Not expecting anything until after the winter I resigned myself to cleaning and any other shed work that might come along. Dick had mellowed even more, treating me more like a mate. I was quite happy to let things drift along.

A week after returning to cleaning, war was declared. This put everything into a different perspective. I knew that I would soon be eligible for army call-up and that at my age I could expect to be placed in a fighting unit. It was a case of wait and see.

After about a month of watching men going off to enlist and wondering where my fate lay I was working with my two seniors Jim Hewlett and Doug Bennet when our now friendly charge-man came to us.

'I've got a note for each of you,' he said as he handed them to us. 'You're all going to Banbury on Monday.'

We read our notes and looked at each other in amazement. We were all promoted to firemen from the following Monday.

Dick left us to talk it over, we couldn't believe it, particularly as we had already concluded that this would not happen until next year.

On the way home I bought a large suitcase. My mother asked, 'Whatever have you got that for?'

When I told her the news, she asked, 'Have you got to stay there, then?'

'Yes, Mum, it means staying there. Anyway I'll be in the army soon.'

I went back to work the next day, Saturday. This was to be my last day as a cleaner at Worcester.

During the morning Dick came to me again. 'Your trip to Banbury is cancelled,' he said.

'I'm not being made a fireman then?' I asked.

'Oh yes, but at Didcot instead,' he replied as he handed me another note.

THREE

A young fireman

MY MEMORIES of Didcot were vague. I'd only heard of it once on the way back from my medical at Swindon.

I asked Dick, 'How do I get there?'

'I don't know, it's up towards London. Come down to the office, we'll find out.'

Everyone was full of help with service books out, almost as if they wanted to get rid of me.

Mr Elms came in. 'Well, you're leaving us at last. I hope you get on well, keep up the good work.'

Dick looked at the time, it was just turned noon. He said, 'You might as well go home now, no point in staying here. I expect you have some packing to do. Give me your check, I'll book you off right time.' Then like the good chargeman he proved to be he shook hands and wished me luck.

Monday 16 October 1939 I was on the 8.55 a.m. for my transfer to Didcot. I took a long look at the loco, it was one of the best-looking of our 'Castle' class, 5063 *Earl Baldwin*. I thought, well, I won't be cleaning you again.

I stood at the carriage window talking to my father, who had taken time to come along between his work to see me off and to give some fatherly advice.

Presently the guard gave 'Right away' followed by a sharp blast from the loco whistle. The bark from the 'Castle' as it got under way emphasised its power as it quickly got into its stride and gathered speed. Soon it was whisking me away at a speed which I was not accustomed to. My memories of this short stretch of line were of the few local goods trips which had come my way as a cleaner but I was able to imagine with some accuracy what was happening on the footplate up front and could quite easily have related this to my fellow passengers. As it happened I sat back and considered my own immediate future as the countryside sped past. The loco's exhaust ripping through the fresh morning air as it hammered its way up Honeybourne bank reminded me of my excursion trip to Weymouth. My dreams came back to reality as the train reduced speed to run into Oxford. Here I was to change into a stopper to complete the journey.

'Change for Didcot and Reading,' came the call from the porters as they busied themselves attending to passengers and their luggage.

Ten minutes elapsed before the express departed and was replaced by a local train consisting of five non-corridor coaches hauled by a 51xx class tank.

'Didcot train, Didcot train,' came the repeated call. About ten of us in all boarded, myself in the rear coach near the guard. Expecting to alight at the next stop I was surprised to see Radley and popped my head out. The next stop at Culham caused the same concern and another peep, so when we stopped at Apple-ford Halt I felt obliged to ask the guard, 'Am I all right for Didcot, please?'

'Just round the corner, about three minutes' run.' Then he asked 'Why are you going there?' not considering running time and quite prepared to have a chat.

I told him my story quickly of moving to be made a fireman.

'You'll like it here, they're a good bunch to work with. Good luck to you, lad.'

From Didcot platform I could see the shed beyond the carriage sidings. A porter directed me via the subway and lugging my heavy suitcase I made my way along the ashpit road to the office. It was just turned eleven o'clock, no one stirred. It seemed the morning shift had squared up for the day. My first impression was of deadness: only one loco stood outside and a few more inside in the darkness. The newness of the shed struck me, so much cleaner than the one I had just left. It had not yet got its full covering of grime, having been built only a few years earlier.

As I tentatively entered the shed a voice from behind the door asked 'Looking for the office, mate?'

'Yes, please, I'm lost.'

'It's just on your left inside. Through that archway.'

Although the shed was new the layout didn't vary. Inside, the lobby was the same: familiar notice cases, roster sheets and the glass panels with the small window. I knocked and was surprised to be answered by a lady, it had never occurred to me that a lady would be working in a loco shed.

'Come inside,' she said.

She took my particulars and then introduced herself as Mrs Bray, adding 'Everyone is surprised to see me.'

The foreman, Fred Webb, came in. 'Have you got your turn for tomorrow?' he asked.

'No,' said Mrs Bray, 'I was coming to ask you.'

He looked at a list. 'You'll be with, now let me see. That'll be on at 1.25 in the afternoon on a depot pilot.'

Then he asked, 'Have you got anywhere to live?'

'No, I've never been here before.'

'Come along with me,' he said, and led the way along a passage behind the duty sheets to the stores.

'Wait here, I'll find the call boy.'

A few friendly words with the storesman helped to cheer me up. The foreman came back with the call boy. 'Take this new chap and see if you can find him some lodgings,' he said.

The young lad about sixteen humped my case on to his bike and half-heartedly said, 'I don't know where to start looking.'

As we left the shed a fireman was putting his bike in the rack. The call boy turned to him. 'Does your landlady want another lodger, Stan?'

'Well, I don't know,' he said eyeing me up and down. 'She did say she would rather have another lodger than have a refugee billeted on her. Perhaps you could go up and see.' As we moved away he called out 'Tell her Stan Webb sent you.'

So it was I had found a good lodging companion with a first-class family.

Within ten minutes I was sitting down to a meal with the landlady firing questions at me to make me feel at home and of course to get my background.

I asked her, 'What do I call you?'

'You can call me what you like but I'll clip your ear if I don't like it.'

'I think I'll call you "Ma" if you don't mind.' Not realising it at the time I had christened her with a name that stuck, even her family used it – 'Ma Haynes'.

Soon after two o'clock the landlord came home. He was a signalman just finished off early turn. After the usual introductions and a little talk he suggested I should have a walk round to get my bearings. 'It'll be dark when you come home tomorrow night.'

That was the first of much good advice that was to follow during my stay.

The next day I booked on at 1.25 spick and span in my new overalls and cap. I had made the transition from top cleaner to bottom fireman but who cared, I was here and already feeling quite happy.

As I waited a rather short man came to me from the office. 'Just come here have you, kid?' he said.

'Yes, came yesterday.'

'So did I. Ain't it a bloody hole.'

Soon after this a driver came to me. 'They tell me you're my new mate. Just got to go to the cabin. I'll be back in a minute.'

In no time at all he was back and, after speaking to several other drivers and firemen, said 'Are you ready then, mate, we'll make our way to the depot.'

The word 'mate' sounded good to me. He looked a decent sort although a bit stern.

On the way to the government stores depot I chatted to the two firemen, who were very friendly. I could see what the guard meant when he said I would get on well with them. Everyone I had met so far had been so kind that I felt quite at home.

We passed through the depot gates and the guard post, parting company with the two other crews. My mate said little until after we had settled on the loco then opened up by asking 'What's your name, mate?'

'Well, it's John really but the cleaners called me Jack.'

'That's it then, Jack it shall be.' He then introduced himself as Bert East.

He interested himself in my affairs, asking much the same questions as Ma Haynes had, only to get to know me he assured.

'Do you know who that little man was who spoke to me in the office?' I asked.

'Aye, I saw him. He's the new shed foreman, came from Cardiff yesterday. Bill Young's his name.'

'He didn't think much of the place by the way he spoke.'

'Don't take any notice of him. You'll like it here.'

Further questioning followed. 'Have you done any driving at all when you've been out firing?'

'No, at home they don't trust their own mates much, let alone a cleaner. I had over a hundred turns but no one suggested having a go.'

'Well you're going to now, I don't intend to do all the work while you sit on your backside. Make no mistake, you're going to work with me.'

Bert was a thick-set man about forty years old, clean-shaven with a square jaw and a ruddy complexion but quiet mannered and considerate. He was my first regular mate and by now I knew that we would get on together. This new venture into a strange world needed a man of his calibre to guide me; something which I have always appreciated.

'Have you just been made a driver?' I asked.

'Oh no, almost a year ago. Got sent to Llanelli,' he said trying to get his tongue round the Welsh name. 'This is my first day back, glad to be home again.'

The time came to start work. Bert said, 'Come on over here, Jack. You do the first part in daylight, I'll take over after tea.'

The shunting was easy, taking loaded wagons out of the

sheds and replacing them with empties. All movements made at a slow speed took little steam; it seemed ages before Bert needed to put any coal on the fire and when he did he made it look so simple. For a big man on such a small footplate he was very agile. He also knew how to keep clean – not one of the greasy ones, who were by now a dying breed.

After quite a long tea interval Bert took over the driving. The daylight had gone and everything changed in the blackout, it was easy to see why I was asked to do my stint in the daylight.

Our day's work was over at ten o'clock and as we waited, coupled to two more locos ready for shed, the air raid sirens sounded. No one knew what to do, the depot wardens scurried about shepherding everyone to the shelters. We were left alone to tend our locos with strict orders to close the fire-hole doors and to put out all lights. We lay low for over an hour before the all clear. Nothing had happened, there wasn't a raider within a hundred miles.

Finding my way back to my lodgings in the blackout was a nightmare. The road seemed so much longer than when I went to work and when I arrived at the neat row of semis I didn't know which one it was, I had failed to take notice of the number. I walked up and down getting increasingly anxious, until I found a house that looked promising. I was very relieved when my latch key fitted the door.

Bert and I had struck up a good relationship immediately, a fine start to my career. We were together in the bottom link. Every depot had its turns split into links of usually twelve turns, those twelve sets rotating round the turns, only leaving them if on a spare turn. As a man progressed in seniority he moved up to the next link and so on. My link consisted of several shunting turns in the ordnance depot, some in the yard and three turns in the shed moving locos before and after servicing. Among these were several night turns.

My second week's work was on a pilot in the depot on early turn. We went off shed coupled to two others, the reverse of the previous week. Bert decided to do the firing to start with, in little more than an hour we were stopped for breakfast.

Bert asked, 'What have you got for breakfast?'

'I've got a fry-up, Ma insisted on me bringing it. She says, "No one goes to work from this house without a proper breakfast." '

'That's good, so have I. You can cook them both.'

I was horrified. I had never tried before and seen only a few drivers do it. My first start was to make a hash of cleaning out the shovel. Bert wasn't at all impressed and soon said, 'Come on out of the way, mate, let's show you how.'

With the dexterity of practice he soon had the bacon sizzling and smelling appetising. Some are appalled at the thought of cooking on a shovel in the firebox but done with the care that Bert had shown it was delicious – and I swear tasted better than at home. Unfortunately a cup of tea to complete the meal was missing. The practice was to take a bottle of tea and keep it warm on the loco. Above the firebox there was a tray – we called it the dish – right in the influence of the fire. Both bottles resided there and above them a lubricator valve for the cylinders dripped oil and lime-laden water. It was the unwritten rule that the fireman kept the dish clean. Occasionally a lethargic hand reached out for a bottle nicely timed for a spot of hot oil. I soon learned not to laugh. Bert thumped hard.

Another part of the ritual was the inevitable food box in the shape of an old sea chest with a curved lid under which was a flap to carry books in, particularly the driver's log-book in which he recorded the day's happenings to later transcribe them to his daily record.

Shed shunting involved moving dead locos after they had been washed out or repaired. To make life easier one of us worked the loco hauling, doing both the driving and firing while the other coupled and shunted. One day I had a particularly stiff coupling and being not quite tall enough to reach it from in the pit I heard Bert, in his usual friendly way, say, 'Come on out of it, I'll be glad when you grow up.'

The coupling was almost too stiff for him and in his struggles the adjusting handle dropped down hitting him in the mouth, breaking several teeth and subsequently having the rest removed by his dentist. That was the only time I heard strong language from him.

Another shed chore was shunting the coal stage. The stage was elevated to raise the level above the tenders with a rather steep ramp rising to it. Our job was to take the empty wagons down and replace them with full ones. On one occasion when I was driving I shoved a raft of six up, this needed a fair run to be sure of getting to the top. Just as I got to the top and stopped at Bert's signal the coalman let some full ones down from outside the other end. They bumped into mine giving me a nudge which set me off down the bank. I was in a hopeless position, the brake was on and the wheels were sliding; slowly the loco increased speed. I pulled the rear sand lever but nothing happened. I looked back at Bert, who was waving his arms in despair and shouting something which I couldn't hear. Looking down the bank I was aware of the trap point getting near at an alarming rate. Bert was running but stood no chance of getting to the point before the loco. A dramatic derailment was imminent. Without further ado I abandoned ship and raced down to pull the point in the nick of time, watching in awe as the runaway vehicles trundled past me and came to rest at the bottom.

'What the hell happened there, mate?' Bert asked.

'I don't know, there was a bump just as I stopped.'

'By God, you were nippy there,' said Bert. 'Don't know where that lot would have finished up.'

Before we were able to congratulate ourselves the foreman came across, having watched the episode in horror, and gave Bert a fair ticking off for not having a man on the points to cover such an emergency.

The night turn was casual, all we did was run the locos down for coal and run them away afterwards. Normally we were finished by 3.0 a.m. One morning as we were getting near to the last move Fred Webb, the foreman, approached Bert. 'You know the road to Swindon, don't you, Bert?' he asked.

'Aye,' answered Bert.

'There's a train at Foxall junction, the driver is asking for relief, he's running several hours late. Will you relieve him and work to Swindon?'

'Yes, that's all right, Fred.' And turning to me Bert said, 'See you tonight then, mate.'

'Hang on,' said Fred, 'you'll have to take your mate.'

Bert turned to me. 'Come on then, if that's all right with you.'

We wended our way across the yard picking our way in the darkness to the junction. Waiting for us was a 43xx 2–6–0 tender with a train of fifty empty coal wagons. On the way over Bert had spent most of the time assuring me that there was no need to worry, he would look after me.

True to his word, the first thing he did was to look in the firebox to assess the fire for me.

'Take a good look at that, Jack,' he said pointing out the shape of the fire. 'That's just about right. Try to keep it like that, if you can we should manage all right, it's not a heavy load.'

With that last direction he blew up for the signal. When it lowered Bert said, 'Take the handbrake off.'

We steadily eased our way off the curve with its rising gradient and off into the night, the loco heaving from side to side as it took steam alternately. I began firing and was quite delighted to see the steam being maintained. So much more satisfaction to succeed without being told every little move and being interfered with. Bert looked at the fire now and then, passing his opinion in the way of hints. After a while he said, 'Better ease up a bit now, you're beginning to do too well, have a sit down.' I sat down and opened the fire hole doors a little. Although by now it was about 4.30 Bert got a bit anxious. 'Don't leave the doors open, Jack, there's plenty of time yet for stray German bombers.'

On hearing that I lost that lovely comforting glow over the footplate and tender. In fact it was better in the one respect that I was able to see much better when looking forward, the oil lamps of the signals giving welcome green lights as we trundled through the fresh night air.

The journey had been only twenty-four miles non-stop but it

had given me great satisfaction even though the train was light and the loco in good condition. Bert's gracious congratulations as we rode home on the cushions boosted my self-confidence.

One afternoon when we were shunting in the centre yard it came on to rain. The little cab without a back gave no protection at all, we were soaked. At the window of the refreshment rooms close by stood the young lady attendant. She seemed to be offering us a cup of tea. Bert was quick to say, 'Now's your chance, go and see what she wants. If it's a cup of tea bring me one.'

Licence to visit a young lady was good enough, I was soon there.

'I noticed you getting wet,' she said. 'Thought you might like a hot cup of tea.'

'Yes please, can I take one out for my mate?'

I took Bert his cup. He asked, 'Where's yours, then?'

'I'm going back for mine, better company in there.' While comfortably drinking my tea a young fireman came in and rudely asked, 'Where's my free tea then?'

'Mind your own business, it's nothing to do with you. Besides you're not wet.'

'If they can have free tea so can I,' he retorted.

With no more ado she lifted the soda siphon and levelled it at him; her aim was spot-on. The room was too small to allow him to escape; he got soaked. He turned to let rip at her but was met with a disarming smile. 'Now you're wet you can have a cup of tea. Don't get cheeky with me in future.'

Almost a year and a half passed by working with Bert before my turn came to move up to the next link. I had become senior in the link and had to leave him. Bert had been a good mate and guided me well through what I now know to have been my formative years, a good basis for the future.

I knew I was going to miss him but at the same time there would be a change in the type of work I would be doing – very little shunting but a fair amount of local freight and some light passenger trains.

The arrangement of junior work for junior men was in itself a good, sound system of training, every man being brought along steadily, learning in stages as he went. My move up really made me feel that I was progressing.

My new mate Frank Wheeler had been in the link for some time and knew all the turns which would be a big help to me settling in. Frank was another man of the more enlightened type, made a point of greeting me with 'I hear you're good at keeping clean, can't stand dust flying about. Keep the pet pipe on the coal, I'd rather be drowned than dusted to death.' (The pet pipe was the name given to the pipe used for washing down.)

Frank was a good mate and also a very good engineman, a good swap as far as I was concerned. He seemed to have the ability to get the best out of any loco and above all he left me alone to get on with my own work without interference. 'That's your job,' he would say. 'If you can't do it, I'm not going to.'

That was the pattern of things to come. Although I had learned a lot from driving with Bert I knew that I now had a different set of standards to acquire. Frank never let a fireman drive, not even in the shed if he could avoid it. I didn't wish to drive on the main line, too much to learn yet, besides my turns as a fireman were interesting and various. There were weeks when we were on spare turns and parted company which gave me the opportunity to work with other drivers and gain more experience.

My time with Frank was not without incident. One of our regular turns was the 5.52 p.m. passenger to Newbury. The train usually had eight coaches worked by a 22xx 'Collett' design; on this occasion we had two extra coaches on. Winter was upon us and the evening was dark as we left Didcot and slowed up to take the single-line token at East junction signal-box. The signalman came out with the token and instead of putting it in the stand for me to take he stood at the side of the track and held it up – quite a normal thing to do. Frank, aware that the extra load would take some extra pulling, didn't ease up too much. I looked out and saw the signalman but not the token; his light was shining in my eyes.

'Whoa Frank, I've missed it,' I called out.

'What the hell did you do that for?' he bawled out, as he shut off steam and applied the brake. 'Now look what you've done. Made us stop right across the junction. It's those bloody owl-catchers you've got on. Cissy firemen wearing gloves.'

'Come and take the token yourself if you think you can see it better in the blackout than I can. I couldn't see it with the signalman's lamp shining in my eyes.'

The train had stopped as he said it would, right across the junction stopping all traffic. 'Now you can go back and get it for your trouble,' he said sarcastically.

I hurried back to the signalman, who was full of apologies, saying, 'I didn't see your hand, mate.' Not realising that all he had to do was to hold it up and let me take it rather than put it into my hand. Too late to explain, I had to get back to the loco. Frank carried on at me again about the gloves so I threw them straight into the firebox. 'Are you satisfied now?' I asked.

'You'll work for it now. How do you think we're going to get this lot up over the bridge?' referring to the sharp pull over the road bridge.

Not feeling inclined to take the blame I answered, 'Nothing in that, this loco will take twice this load. Don't know what you're worried about,' I added.

Frank didn't like that too much but later relented and turned it into a joke. A few days later he presented me with a new pair of gloves.

The Newbury branch was the basic training ground for Didcot firemen and like many others this was where I cut my teeth. Often when shunting in the yard on nights I had watched the 4.30 a.m. goods leave double headed weaving its way through the crossovers and out on to the relief line then across the main lines to the branch, firelight from the open doors shining on the men as they stood on the sparse footplate with the fireman tending the fire. They watched intently as the two locos tugged away in unison, wending their way through the rows of poplar trees lining the branch and disappearing out of sight soon to be lost to sound in the darkness.

Working this line was an education in itself. After that initial heave up the gradient over the road bridge the line eased off and speed picked up with a gentle run to Upton where the token was changed before tackling the 1 in 106 gradient to the top of the downs. To change the token it was necessary to reduce speed to 15 mph through the station. This called for skill from the drivers who had to co-ordinate their movements without having any communication between them. Not only did the braking need to be considered carefully but picking up power with a loose-coupled train on the varying gradients through the station was also tricky. The guard using his brake to control the rear of the train also had to be taken into account.

The climb was tackled with vigour, the two locos sounding their crisp exhaust as it reverberated from the high chalk cutting, diminishing gradually as the train slowly wended its way through the gentle curves to where the cutting eased to become little more than a grassy bank before giving way to the flat expanse of the downs. The locos' crisp bark levelled off to match the lay of the land until steam was shut off for the undulating run down to Compton. It was here where the firemen came into their own. The drivers never used the power brakes on this branch if it could be avoided; much better control could be maintained by the firemen using their tender handbrakes with assistance from the guard. This was probably the first insight a fireman had of controlling a train, the first step in his ultimate goal. A noticeable rapport existed between front and rear, very necessary when working this type of train. From here on the branch twisted and turned, rose and fell all the way to Newbury, the eighteen miles taking almost an hour to cover.

One never knew which of the small locos to expect. The most likely was a 'Dean', of which Didcot boasted a fair number; they had escaped transfer to the army solely for use on this branch. There was also an equal chance of a 22xx which pleased everyone; the large comfortable cab and the excellent steaming made them very popular. The heart dropped out of anyone who was unfortunate enough to be booked on a 'Dukedog', a 32xx class which were put together in 1936 from the frames of the old 33xx 'Bulldog' and the boiler of the 32xx 'Duke'. Apart from the old-fashioned cab they were renowned for being the most reluctant to steam. Every fireman hated them.

I was working on such a crate, 3215, one morning with a spare driver on the 4.30 across the branch. We were second loco and it was therefore my duty to take and exchange the tokens. Not only were we struggling for steam we were also working in a thick fog. Approaching Upton I was standing on the framing outside the cab scouring the vicinity of the token stand with very little hope of finding it. The fireman on the leading loco allowed his safety valve to blow off steam which drifted down my side to completely blanket out any chance of my seeing the token. My electric torch failed to penetrate the fog. Once again I was compelled to shout out 'Missed it, mate.' Stopping this train was quite a different matter from the first time it happened. The loose-coupled train of 44 wagons on the varying gradients needed careful handling. When we came to a stand with the front end on the incline the driver said, 'You'd better go back and see what's gone wrong. Are you sure it wasn't there?'

I had already told him it was missing but he wasn't convinced. 'We wouldn't have had the signals off unless the token was out,' he said.

As before I met the signalman coming towards me with the token. Once again he was full of apologies. 'I'm sorry, mate, I forgot to put it in the stand.'

'I doubt if my mate will believe that, he's already blaming me. I expect you'd dropped off to sleep.'

Ten minutes later back at the loco my mate again tried to blame me but gave himself away by being insincere. The other fireman had been back to explain that the token was in fact missing.

Getting the train away this time was much trickier. The 'Dukedog' was renowned for bad rail adhesion at the best of times and the fog damping the rails made matters worse. The wheels spun madly although both drivers dropped sand. We slipped and slid, slowly clawing our way to the top. Two sets of very grateful men limped over the top that morning, relieved, even though the fog was much worse up there.

Often during the winter the summit was reached with some trepidation, crews having been forewarned of the conditions by the canopy of snow hanging over the top of the cutting. The snow blew across the downs and swept into the cutting giving some idea of what to expect. Once over the top in the open the wind blew directly across the footplate; the small cab, giving no protection, allowed the wind to whisk the small coal off the shovel as it was being swung towards the firebox, adding to the snow as it whipped round our ears.

On a clear quiet summer morning it was quite different. The staccato beat of the two locos – particularly the 22xx working hard on the bank – changed their rhythm as they climbed over the top, quickening their pace as the wheels turned faster. The clatter of the side rods blended with the chatter of the motion while the wheels tapped out their tune on the rail joints. Looking over the tender one could see the train following, each wagon waltzing to its own timing and the guard's van making up the rear with a wisp of smoke from its stove pipe. The footplate carried its own cosy red glow from the light of the open fire-hole doors. Sights and sounds of the past, only memories, never to be experienced again.

The branch joined the West of England main line at Newbury. From here another little old-fashioned and most interesting branch line went off to Lambourn. Many experiences have been related by men working this line. Mine are limited but I well remember my first trip, which was with Frank on a horse-box special. The racing stables provided a fair amount of extra work and it was partly because of this that the 'Deans' were retained, these being the largest locos allowed over there.

On this particular day we went light to Newbury to take forward a train of twenty empty horse-boxes. Leaving Newbury the line rose steeply alongside the main line. I watched it getting lower until the branch veered away to the right and out into the country to find the pretty valley of the river Lambourn. We wended our way through short sharp curves and cuttings, up hill and down dale and after only a few miles climbed a sharp rise into a small tunnel. About 50 yds outside Frank stopped the train.

'What have we stopped for?' I asked.

'We don't want to knock those gates down in front.'

About another 100 yds in front a pair of level-crossing gates were closed across the line. There were no signals to protect them, just a fixed distant before entering the tunnel which I had not seen.

'It's your job to open them,' Frank said.

'What, me?' I queried. 'You're pulling my leg. Who's going to close them then?'

'You go and open them. Make sure there's nothing coming along the road first. Be sure to latch them open and then get up on the platform, I'll pick you up there. The guard will close them.'

'You're making me walk a long way.'

'It won't hurt you. If I stopped any closer on this bank I might not be able to get away again.'

I opened the gates and went up on to the little halt platform, just long enough to hold two coaches. The name Speen was new to me but it has always stuck in my mind. Many years later when I worked over there I took more notice of the signals at this crossing and saw that as the yellow paint was peeling off with age it revealed a previous coat of red. Those signals must have been some of the original wooden arms used in the days when distant signals were painted red with a red light at night. The only way to identify them then was by the fishtail ends. Drivers were required to pass the first red signal and be prepared to stop at the next. I know for a fact that these signals were in use right up to the time the line was eventually closed.

Several more crossings of the same type were negotiated in the same way as we slowly weaved our way through some of the tightest curves I have ever encountered before eventually arriving at Lambourn.

Another relic of the past on this line was the use of the old-fashioned wooden staff, the forerunner of the later electric token. The staff was the original method used to ensure that only one train entered the single line at a time. The driver was responsible for seeing that he had it in his possession before proceeding. A large key was fitted to one end to lock points into sidings where necessary. The staff for the section from New-bury to the half-way crossing point at Welford Park was still in use also until eventual closure. This was surely a line rich in history.

Sunday afternoon provided a very interesting trip in the way of the 3 p.m. passenger train from Didcot to Lambourn. The day normally started by preparing 1335, a small 2–4–0 tender loco, an ex-MSWJ which joined the Great Western at the time of the grouping in July 1923. One could always rely on this one being on the job, the light train and stopping service was about its capability. It always steamed well and was light on coal. I worked this train one Sunday with a driver named Bill Champ. He was a stoutish man, a bit out of place on this small footplate. His round red face always had a stubby pipe in it, quite often not alight.

We stopped all stations to Newbury and shunted to the up side. It was only from here that we could get on to the branch to Lambourn. I immediately uncoupled the loco and we dashed off to the racecourse to turn on the turntable there and back on to the train. This always made us late departing but we gained the advantage of only travelling tender first to Lambourn then it was engine leading all the way home. The train was usually packed with service personnel who were quite amused at the ancient method of working, particularly when we stopped to open the gates. On arrival at Lambourn I uncoupled again and Bill took the loco into the siding close by instead of, as I thought, round the other end of the train to recouple.

'What have we come in here for, Bill?' I asked.

'We've got to pump water up for the station.'

Standing by the siding was a mushroom water tank which held water for the station domestic supply, not for loco pur-poses as I thought. Each Sunday it was the job of the Didcot men to pump up a fresh supply.

Bill said, 'Get up on the firebox while I move into position. Shout when we're in line with that pipe there,' pointing to a long steel pipe like a jib. As he moved the loco I toppled a bit in the strong wind. I shouted, 'Whoa.' It was a bit too far. 'Back a bit, Bill.' After several attempts at getting it right Bill shouted up, 'You'll have to shout louder, mate, I can't here you with this strong wind.'

When the pipe was lined up he handed me a spanner. 'Take a whistle off now and couple the pipe in its place.' Bill pulled the whistle chain down but instead of the whistle blowing a donkey engine started to chug in a hut on the ground to pump the water up. Ingeniously Bill hung the coal pick on the chain to hold it down while we had tea. The water-level indicator was out of order so Bill climbed the ladder to look inside. As he did so a strong gust of wind blew, the ladder rocked causing Bill to wobble and in grasping hold he dropped his beloved pipe only to see it smash on the paving below. He came down shaken, looked at his pipe and said, 'I haven't got another, I'll be miserable for the rest of the day now.' He was too; he thought a lot of his pipe. I was glad to see the day over, if only for him to get home to his spare.

My first trip through to Southampton was more like a day's outing. I was on an early turn; my pal Doug Morton was also early, on spare. In great delight he told me, 'I'm on the Southampton passenger in the morning.'

This particular turn was in the top link and was considered the cream, mainly because it was a simple train and the booking on and off times were ideal. As usual the branch train was only three coaches worked by a 22xx. On his return that afternoon he related his experiences of the day knowing quite well that he was whetting my appetite. Then he said, 'I'm booked on it again tomorrow. I wonder if you'd like to change turns and have a trip?'

'Do you mean it?' I asked.

'Yes, of course. Why shouldn't I?'

'Well, yes, I'd like to, that's if it's all right with the foreman.'

'Leave it to me. I'm going down to the shed, I'll fix it with him.'

I turned up for the 7.38 to Southampton the next morning and found to my horror that the dreaded 3215 was booked on it, the 'Dukedog' that was renowned as being a bad steamer.

'That's why Doug asked you to change with him,' the driver said.

Here fate took a hand. A boiler washout plug was leaking badly, so badly in fact that the boilersmith refused to touch it. The foreman changed the loco for 2282, quite the reverse in character, considered one of the best. This particular loco had one of the old ROD tenders fitted, a huge thing for such a small loco, it held so much coal that the tender didn't need trimming all day. The day's work went well, the driver being a friendly man taking great pains to make my day interesting. The line had many historic features which he related as we went. To him it had more significance than the nicknames it had been given such as the 'Gold Coast' or the 'Linger and Die' – names which reminded me more of the Yukon trail which, in bad weather conditions, it probably resembled. Its other name, the 'Alps', was most certainly derived from the arctic conditions in the winter. Here on a lovely summer day it was a treat to be alive and working on this casual line.

That night Doug couldn't wait to hear of my struggles not knowing what had happened with the locos. I went along teasing him for a while before I let on. I must say that he was a very good mate, except when he got me arrested at Blackpool for alleged spying, taking photos of local scenery, but that's another story.

My mate Frank would be leaving me soon but not before we had a few memorable incidents. Late one afternoon we had worked to Swindon. The control asked him, 'Will you relieve the Neyland passenger for me?'

'Yes,' said Frank, 'how far do you want us to go?'

'I'll tell Reading you're on it, leave it to them.'

The train duly arrived at the station with steam blowing off from its safety valve.

'Looks like we've got a good 'un here, mate,' said Frank. The retiring crew left after giving details, twelve coaches for nearly 400 tons. I took stock of the loco and noted that it was 4920 *Dumbleton Hall*, the first time I had worked an express passenger.

We departed almost on time at 2.20 a.m. Frank got stuck in with gusto, the sharp blast shattering the silence of the night. The train soon made good speed with me bending my back and shovelling hard without a break, not even for a breather. The night was dark, after looking in the fire I was lost when Frank shut off steam about twenty minutes later.

'Where are we?' I shouted above the din.

'Steventon,' he replied.

As we were running the last few miles into Didcot I remarked, 'Not bad for a 49xx, Frank.'

'What?' he exclaimed. 'I thought it was a "Castle", I wondered why all the vibration and where the speedometer had got to. Must have been doing at least seventy.'

My thoughts returned to the days of cleaning when the firemen used to say 'You don't take any notice of the speed, you're too busy shovelling.'

Frank made my day by saying, 'You did well there, mate, I'd have taken it a bit steadier if I'd known.'

My first express run ended at Reading when we had relief. A cup of tea outside the station at the Church Army hut and a ride home passenger made my day.

Also on an afternoon turn we were working a goods up from Swindon with a raft to put off at Steventon. We stopped on the main line and after the guard had uncoupled he said to Frank, 'You've got eighteen twenty tonners on. Go ahead over the points. Come back quietly when I give you the signal, the siding's empty.'

When he received the signal Frank gently pushed the wagons back towards the siding. The loco was one of the North Eastern on loan. It was a big clumsy thing, one of those with a large straight-barrelled boiler with no noticeable firebox, just the boiler shape continuing back to the cab. After a short while he said, 'I've lost sight of the guard, mate, can we see him your side?' I looked out in the darkness but the wagons snaking in through the crossover obscured my view.

'Can't see a thing here,' I replied.

Just then Frank said, 'All right I've got him. Red light.' He casually put on the brake and stopped, then sat waiting events. After some time we began worrying. 'What's happened to the guard? He should have shown up by now,' said Frank. 'I think I'll go back and see if he's all right.'

He had just reached the ground when I saw the guard coming up my side. 'All right, Frank, he's coming up this side.'

We breathed a sigh of relief, the guard was all right but the tale he had to tell about the train was quite different. Although he had said there was an empty siding there was in fact eighteen already in there which he had failed to notice. This brute of a loco pushed them back without so much as a murmur and kept pushing. The result was dramatic to say the least. Sixteen of the empties were derailed, five of them had travelled over the stop blocks leaving their wheels behind and three were on end on the main line behind our train. Frank and I simply could not believe it, we had no idea at all that the loco had even met any resistance. That minor error shut the main lines for the rest of the day and made us very late booking off. As a result, and because we had to have a minimum of twelve hours off duty before booking on again, we were accommodated on a yard pilot the next night. The casual work suited us both, we were more certain of finishing early. Unfortunately as we were making the last shunt of the night we again became derailed, this time the loco as well. It came to rest at an acute angle, too uncomfortable to stay on board.

'Frank,' I said, 'they'll be giving you that supervisor's job a bit sooner if you carry on like this,' knowing full well that he had nothing to do with either incident. He had already been interviewed for a supervisory post and was waiting confirmation.

'It's not my fault, I didn't do it either time,' he said in a self-effacing manner.

'It doesn't matter about that, you'll have to go,' I joked.

Quite by coincidence he was called to his new post to start the following week. The reason for creating the supervisory section to which he was promoted was to take the train crew relief arrangements away from the shed foremen; they had enough to get on with. The war effort was building up to such proportions that trains were running as and when they could, schedules for freight were virtually non-existent, only hopeful starting times. The new supervisors had the job of juggling men for relief purposes even though the depot strength was doubled.

The single line branch had been doubled as far as Newbury with improvements all the way to Winchester in readiness for the coming big push. Work over this line increased daily with numerous trains of government stores and fighting equipment in readiness for D-Day. Whenever we were given a job in that direction we could not expect to get finished under about fifteen hours. I suppose this was my only tangible contribution to the war effort.

Frank had gone, and in his place came another very good mate by the name of Harold Gasson. A short cheerful chap, always had a ready smile, never seemed to get ruffled over anything. He smoked or sucked a briar pipe endlessly, lost without it. Much the same as Bill Champ. I used to say it was like a baby's dummy, a pacifier. He only grinned.

The first day we were together we booked on at 2.10 in the afternoon for relief as required. The supervisor, who happened to be Frank, gave us a job to relieve at Foxall junction on the curve – the spot from where I did my first main line trip with Bert. Walking out to the train Harold asked, 'Did you do any driving with Frank?'

'No, he preferred to do his own work. I've been quite happy watching him,' I said.

'Well I like to do some firing so I hope you took notice of what went on.'

'Of course I did, learned a lot from him.'

As we drew near he tossed a coin. 'Call,' he said.

'What's that for?' I asked.

'To see who's doing the first driving today.'

'You carry on, I'll watch for a while.'

'Not likely,' he replied. 'I'm watching you. You lost.' We relieved a medium-weight goods train with an almost brand-new 28xx on the front. I was quite relieved to see the good loco because I felt guilty at letting an older man do my work for me. I need not have feared, he did it so effortlessly that I knew instinctively that there was still much more to learn. From the start I got the feel of the loco, it pulled away from the curve on the rising gradient with such ease and ran so freely that I felt completely relaxed, no doubt because I was aware that Harold was there to keep an eye on me.

When the distant signal for Wantage Road loomed up at caution things were different. I turned to Harold with a look of doubt on my face. He casually turned away, gazing across the fields, sucking the pipe alternating with whistles and I could see all the time he was grinning, deliberately making me use my own judgement, forcing me into using my own initiative. It set me up for the rest of my time with him and for ever, come to think of it. The remainder of the trip went well, arriving at Swindon after nipping in and out of a few loops on the way. I set about trimming the coal ready for my relief only to be chastised by Harold. 'Get down off there, I'm fireman until we get relief.' Then he added, 'Put some oil on the bars and glands. That's your job.'

FOUR

Effects of war

THE EXPERIENCE with my new mate compelled me to look at driving through a different pair of eyes. It's easy to be critical until it comes to your turn. I was always aware that the only way to learn my future skills was to watch for the best in all drivers and to combine these things to create one's own methods. All drivers by necessity followed a basic principle of train handling but each had developed his own techniques to apply personal judgement. To try to emulate any one of them would be like looking for a carbon copy situation. This was impossible resulting from the varying circumstances which prevailed daily. The only alternative was to search out the highest standard and aim to equal it, if not better it, in one's own career. Until now I had seen only the very best in my regular mates. Harold gave me the opportunity to put my thoughts into practice while under his supervision.

On spare turns I often worked with other drivers on trains to Southampton, both passenger and goods. Although at times the docks suffered heavy damage from enemy bombings I was never involved, never even affected by it.

Conversely, the turn I often fell for on late turn took me to London for a week at a time. It was the 3.45 in the afternoon from Didcot usually with a 43xx and ten coaches, all stations to Slough then fast to Paddington. There was an occasion when I worked this train for two weeks consecutively due to link alterations. Every night for the two weeks without fail the air raid sirens blew about eight o'clock. I sat uneasy on my seat waiting for the 'Right Away' signal at 8.10, glad to be on the move, albeit at the restricted speed of 15 mph. Luckily I was never held up long enough to witness any of the serious bombing, though I saw it in the distance and often heard the patter of shrapnel falling from our own anti-aircraft shells and heard the boom of guns firing from Wormwood Scrubs as we passed. By then we were getting away from it all, back to the sheltered life of Didcot. Overtime and the privations that accompanied it were the worst of our troubles.

There was a long period when overtime took us right round the clock, having taken only enough food for a normal day. This could not be attributed to bad planning, rations didn't allow more. I was hungry many times before the situation improved with the provision of canteens at some of some of the main line stations. At least it eased the pangs of hunger some of the time. Being cold, wet and hungry in the frost of winter and shivering even with an overcoat on with a fire in the box seemed unlikely but it was true. When standing in a loop waiting our turn to go it was necessary to keep the fire low to avoid blowing off steam to conserve water – cold comfort with a low fire. I can recall one particular night when I was stopped at the 'Intermediate Block signal' between Wantage and Challow. There was just a signal and telephone, no actual signalbox for warmth. We were enveloped in a blanket of freezing fog and a foot of snow lay on the ground. The east wind blew in from the back, the little heat which came from the fire-hole doors was lost. The continuous trek to the phone had cut a rut in the snow, the only sign of any movement. After several hours the inside of the cab was covered in white frost for about a foot up from the floorboards. Eventually we took the smokeplate out of the firebox, turned it upside down and pulled some hot coals on to it; a few selected cobbles placed on top and the blower on a little soon gave us some warmth and comfort. I well remember standing in those conditions that night for over eight hours. Later when full blackout sheets were provided and fitted correctly the cab was home from home.

Fog was undoubtedly the worst condition to work in. Even a

light fog created some problems by distorting distances. The thicker fogs caused havoc making normal working impossible. As can be expected the driver took the brunt of it all. Even in a marshalling yard his head was over the side listening for the shunter's whistle code, straining eyes and ears, trusting implicitly in the shunter. On the main line he was alone, except for his fireman. At these times the value of a good mate could not be underestimated; two pairs of eyes being better than one but what really mattered was teamwork.

Great Western signalling was good with well-maintained oil lamps but there were drawbacks. Signals were placed where drivers could see them from the right-hand side. In fog when signals could not be seen from the usual distance the sighting angle and relative position changed which seemed to place them in the most awkward places. The majority of signals were placed on the left, mainly for convenience, others on the right solely for better sighting on curves or to avoid obstructions such as bridges in the line of sight. This arrangement worked better for other companies with their locos having left-hand drive. It was not so good on the Western right-hand drive, even in good weather conditions when the driver was often forced to search for his signals with an occasional call to his firemen to look out for a particularly awkward one. In thick fog both men would be peering, searching into what seemed infinity but often seeing only as far as the chimney or a little further. When searching for a stop signal in this manner it always seemed to be further away, anxiety growing as the train crept nearer, wondering all the time whether it would be possible to stop when a stop signal loomed up. Fog in the darkness caused signal lamps to lose their crispness to be little better than a glow-worm. The fog was compounded by steam and smoke from the chimney together with the usual leakage from the cylinder area. Woe betide the fireman who allowed the safety valve to blow off steam adding man-made fog. If only a wisp of steam escaped it developed into a large volume spreading like a spectre to envelop the cab, to blot out any hopes of vision. The glare of the firebox contributed to the problems by reflecting back from the steam over the tender, to shine in the cab windows and turn them into mirrors so that the only things seen were a reflection of the tender and the man's own outline. To obviate this the fire-hole doors were kept closed, which in turn made it more difficult to control the boiler. When the loco was working hard the steam and smoke lifted out of harm's way only to settle along the track to add to the next driver's problems. The development of larger locos added to this problem by making forward vision even more difficult. The poor driver had his head over the side all the time. Steam engine design had this particular drawback, the boiler and chimney protruding out in front with its inherent problems. The men accepted this as part of the unalterable design which was part of the job they had elected to do. No grumbles about the locos, cursing the weather but always taking it in their stride.

Great Western men enjoyed the assistance of the 'Automatic Train Control' (ATC), particular to this Company. There was no doubt that its contribution to our enviable safety record was by far the greatest single factor. This does not detract from the dedication of the footplate crews who coveted their own application of safety.

Knowing the route in clear conditions where ups and downs could be seen was comparatively easy, every undulation having a meaning and a consequence. During darkness and fog everything changed. My mate Harold was one of the most confident men I ever worked with, never getting ruffled even in the thickest of fogs.

At about this time a number of locos had been drafted in from other companies to help cover the loss of our 'Deans'. Needless to say none of them parted with their best, each sent several types, a poor sample of large and small. All were complete strangers to Western men, the versatility of all was tested in coping with the various differences. Almost all these foreigners were left-hand drive giving a totally different outlook to the crews. Signals which were difficult to sight before came into view but familiar ones were harder to find. Firemen also had to change their firing position to the other side or try to manage in their usual way with the driver directly behind them. I personally found this was the only way to manage; if I tried from the other side the fire-hole door needed to be twice the size. Probably the strangest thing to get accustomed to was the lack of the ATC. Drivers had been brought up with its use and had come to rely on its assistance. The men adapted themselves to the various anomalies, accepting the smaller cabs of the Southern as being similar to our own but enjoying the comfort of the larger Midland and North Eastern ones, some of which seemed to be the largest part of the loco.

Later the American locos arrived – quite powerful but on the clumsy side – with a lovely cab, padded seats and full side windows completing the cover with a high tender; comfort unheard of before. It took some time to get used to the changes but we still found such things as brakes, reversers and regulators not so easy to manipulate as those we were brought up on. The regulators varied, some lifted in the same manner as the Western while others pulled out vertically, hinged at the top. The most difficult of all was one of the North Eastern which traversed right across the footplate pivoted in the centre to allow the loco to be driven from either side. This was dangerous for the firemen; when it was pulled out on the driver's side to open up the fireman's side went forward and when the driver shut off steam the end on the other side came out in line with the fireman's head likely to cause an injury. The fireman's problems were not confined to dodging regulator handles. He so often had to puzzle out how to work the boiler water injectors such as on the 'Yanks' where they should have been automatic but invariably needed coaxing. Others had steam valves which worked in reverse and many other small innovations which were discovered by trial and error. No form of instruction was given or even contemplated except that given after two boiler accidents with American engines; it would have been beneath the men's dignity to expect it. With team work the 'immigrants' were tamed and coped with but not missed when they were repatriated.

It was during this initial period of getting used to strange locos that Harold and I worked the Swindon 'Fly' (a name given to all local goods trains which stopped at all stations to shunt yards and goods sheds). Wantage Road always had a little more work than the others because in the evening the 'Wantage Tramway Company' had a service which terminated in the yard. It was worked by a very small 0–4–0 well tank which usually arrived with about fifteen or so wagons, after running the three miles from Wantage alongside the main road all the way until it passed the Volunteer Inn on its right before turning into the yard. It left its train for us to shunt with normally an ancient LMS 0–6–0 tender loco, quite a good match for the WTC loco. Harold had a system which worked out to his own advantage, he always did the shunting to start with and when the WTC driver had tended his loco he gave Harold a nod and they both ambled off to the local to quench their thirsts. Harold took his sandwiches with him and left me to finish the shunting. In addition I was asked to keep an eye on the toy loco. It is interesting to note that WTC loco No 5 *Shannon* was placed on Wantage Road platform on display for several years after closure of the line until Wantage Road station succumbed to the same fate. It was then taken over by the Great Western Society and preserved in working order at Didcot, where I was the first to move it again under its own steam after all those years.

My period with Harold came to an end all too soon when I moved up to the next link. Until now I had enjoyed the company of three excellent mates, each of them also being very good drivers from whom to learn.

The bottom dropped out of my little world when I found out that I would be working with a driver named Jack, one of the heaviest at the depot. On top of that he didn't enjoy the best of health which made him miserable as well at times. My whole outlook on footplate work changed overnight. The good times and pleasantries were over, perhaps this was the norm anyway. Others had suffered before me. I would just have to live with it. The link contained much the same variety of work except that we worked farther, the few spare turns being a welcome change, good for both of us. I had many quarrelsome days due to the way the loco was handled, not just for my own sake but because it was so unnecessary. I could not reconcile myself with such a poor engineman. I was well aware that he was entrusted to drive as he saw fit but Harold had spoilt me. I was able to compare too easily with Harold, and Frank for that matter, without using my judgement to assess his actions. Jack was a difficult man to work with but when the day's work was over he changed completely. So often when returning home passenger with no more work for the day he tried his best to make amends, doing his best to be polite and helpful. I'm afraid I was guilty of thwarting his attempts, still sore at losing Harold. Months passed before I came to reasonable terms with the situation, accepting that it was not for ever and in any case because of the congestion of traffic we only normally worked one way. I was in no doubt that Jack knew the routes well and didn't seem at all unsettled, he simply had no confidence in loco power.

Some of our heaviest work was across the branch to Newbury and on to Westbury. The branch had been doubled for some time and larger locos were now allowed over there; 28xx and 49xx classes were quite common. For me a 28xx signalled more work. They were such perfect locos for the heavy coal trains to Westbury or the government stores to Southampton that everyone looked forward to them. It hurt me to watch one of these being worked up the banks in full fore gear when others I had worked with managed with almost full cut-off. One thing that could be said for this method was that there was no doubt about getting over the top.

Our time together provided some unusual and serious incidents, a typical example of which occurred one day when we were sent to Oxford to work a train. It was early in 1944 and troops were on the move ready for D-Day and we were to take a train to Westbury. We went to the shed for a loco. The foreman said 'Take that one over there,' pointing to a 43xx, a 2–6–0 with a small tender. 'It's all ready. Go off shed when you're ready.'

As we walked over Jack said, 'There's got to be a catch, they don't get them ready here for nothing.'

When we arrived at the loco his words were proved correct.

The tender was stacked as high as possible with coke, a board had been placed across the front between the tool boxes to enable the maximum loading, much more than usual, the highest heap I had seen.

'That's no good to us, Jack. I'll never be able to fire with that.' I was thinking more of the way he would be treating it than whether it would make steam. Jack's protestations to the foreman yielded no results.

'I've got nothing else,' the foreman said.

'Why didn't you put some coal with it?' Jack asked.

'It's nothing to do with me what they put on at the stage. Can't do anything about it,' he said as he walked away. We went off shed to the Midland siding to couple to ten coaches forming the troop train, a load of Americans on their way towards the south coast. On our way over to the train I became even more despondent as to the steaming possibilities; the fire settled down to a large pancake, glowing a dull red with little blue flames flickering and dancing on the top. The steam pressure held steady, not a sign of making any more.

Opening the doors and turning to Jack I said, 'Take a look at this, it's positively hopeless.'

He shrugged it off. 'We'll just have to wait and see.'

Now for the moment of truth I thought as I shovelled piles of coke in. The red glow was submerged but here and there a little blue flame signalled the fire to be still alight. Neither of us were too concerned, if we couldn't get along we could always stop and change locos. For once Jack took the train away steady. I'd already closed the doors and waited for the results. Normally with coal a black plume of smoke would rise to herald the fire coming to life. I didn't expect this to happen, don't really know what I was looking for. Not a sign of life did I see, not even a blue haze. By now we were going through Oxford station, Jack had no alternative but to open up. Westbury was the next booked stop, some ninety miles away. What was I to do? Nothing was happening. My curiosity overcame me, I opened the fire-hole doors while there was a fair blast on the fire. Whoosh! That big pile of coke inside the doors leaped in the air and disappeared towards the front of the firebox.

'Christ, Jack. It's all gone,' I exclaimed. I bent down to look closer and saw that it had mostly leapt on to the brick arch. More was needed, I turned to the shovel and just kept piling it in. Within minutes the steam began to rise but the coke was disappearing at an alarming rate. There was no chance of scientific firing; as soon as the coke got anywhere near to the fire hole it popped off the shovel and into the box on its own. It piled up against the brick arch and over the top completely covering the tubeplate. The blast ripped through it turning the fire into a huge blast furnace, the heat was phenomenal, so hot that I was glad to close the door. Unfortunately it was necessary to keep feeding the brute. Although the worry about providing steam was resolved Westbury was a long way off. Where was the coke coming from to keep going that long? We were getting along in real fine style, managed to take water on the Goring troughs and were surprised to be signalled right away round the curve at Reading. I had hoped for a stop to shovel more coke forward but we kept on the run. I took water again on the Aldermaston troughs and set the scene for a non-stop run with about twenty-five miles of hard pulling in front of us, the last eight or so being very stiff. By the time we had reached the summit I was walking right back into the tender for fuel. As I got further I came across some small coal in the bottom of the hole. This should mix a bit I thought but I was wrong, the coke kept rolling down insisting on being burned. All this time Jack had been mute, a casual glance now and then was his only contribution. Not even a bit of encouragement or a word of praise for me or the loco. The run down from Savernake to Westbury was light, not taking too much fuel. When we eventually arrived I breathed a sigh of relief and scrambled more coke forward while the tank filled. I was surprised when a driver arrived alone.

'Haven't you got a mate?' I asked him.

'No, I've come to conduct your mate to Yeovil.'

Jack didn't mind, he was able to stand back and let the conductor get on with it while I carried on as before, well not quite. This man had a lot more consideration; although there was a fair gradient to face as far as Brewham signalbox he took it steady.

'We're not booked all that fast,' he observed.

Eventually we arrived at Yeovil Pen Mill station where the troops alighted. Our problems weren't over yet, we still had to turn the loco for the return.

The conductor took us to shed; leaving us he said, 'Don't do anything to the tender yet, I'll see if we can get some coal on.' He came back with the foreman. Full of apologies he said, 'Sorry I can't let you have any coal, don't get enough for my own use.' He looked at the tender and gasped. I pointed out, 'There isn't enough to get past Westbury. We'll have to go in for some.'

'Don't do that, you'll never get out again.'

'Well, if it's too congested we won't,' I replied.

He relented and let us have two boxes, that was one ton. The real fun started then when we tried to turn on the table which was too small for this size loco. Ramps were fitted to one end to allow the tender to run up specially to accommodate a larger loco. This was a loco with a full tender which would balance properly. All Great Western tables had to be finely balanced on a centre pin before they could be moved. With very little coal in the tender the situation was hopeless. The shed men and coalmen were called to assist without any success. A driver and fireman turned up, yet still the table stayed firmly where it was. Then I saw a face at the office window. 'There's some more help,' I said to the foreman. Without hesitation they were recruited. There were now eleven of us heaving and at last it moved, only to stop half-way round. There was quite a panic, but eventually a pinch bar was produced to ease the wheels round and the reluctant table completed its half-circuit.

The start of the run home was quiet by comparison but when Jack took over again at Westbury we were back in the rut; he had not learned from the conductor's casual handling. This trip was a one-off job, interesting but not one I ever wished to repeat.

Even when working ordinary everyday turns some sort of

event turned up, such as the occasion we took a light loco from Didcot to Newbury at 3.30 in the morning. It was a pleasant summer morning, the air was still and warm. Dawn was rising as we were stopped at Hampstead Norris by a red light from the signalbox. The signalman, quite amused, asked, 'Will you stop at Hermitage? Mary says she's got a rat in the box.' Mary was in charge of the box there.

A sceptical pair of knights sallied forth up the bank expecting to find Mary sitting up on the instrument shelf and the signals left in the 'On' position. We rose over the brow at Pinewood, from where we could see Mary walking about the box and the signals 'Off'. Jack said, 'We'll stop and see, might get a cup of tea.' He stopped outside the box and said to me, 'Pop up and see what's happening.'

As I opened the door Mary said, 'Shut the door quick, he might get out.'

I did as I was told thinking she was having a joke on me.

'Well, where is it then? You're pulling our legs a bit I think.'

'No I'm not, there it is, behind the air raid shelter,' she said pointing to the floor where a narrow gap separated the shelter from the wall. Sure enough a pair of beady little eyes were looking up at me. I opened the window and called 'Come on up, Jack, there's one here all right.'

He came casually in and was also told to close the door quickly. Mary was certainly a cool customer, considering most women are scared of mice.

'How are we going to get him out of there, Jack? The shelter's too heavy to move.'

I suggested to Mary that she should put some clips on her trousers but she wasn't bothered. Without any more fuss she set about trying to whack it with the poker. It made a bolt for the other side only to find Jack waiting there with a flag stick. Back it came, surprised Mary and ran wild round the box. Jack let fly and broke his stick and took another which quickly suffered the same fate. Mary was charging about with the poker but still failing to make contact. The rat in panic squealed as it raced about, up the signal levers it went and on to the instrument shelf, dashing back and forth pinging the telegraph bells as it went. Here I took up the chase and knocked the poor animal off to see it dash across the floor and up the broom handle in the corner. As it reached the top I hit it down again and grabbed it. In my youth I had done quite a bit of serious ratting and with my fingers in the right place round its neck I said, 'It's got to die now.' Mary at this stage suddenly became compassionate. 'Don't kill it, poor thing.' Mary's plea went unheeded and the rat was dispatched and cremated in the firebox.

The expected cup of tea was then taken before moving on. The Western had a number of the class 30xx 2–8–0s, RODs as they were known, having been acquired from the government. As far as I was concerned there were far too many of them, they were the bane of my life when I was working with Jack. The boiler was big and clumsy; fitted with a GW safety valve which sat on top of the firebox, it could be considered redundant when working a train. One was never able to get enough steam to need it; it was about as likeable as the 32xx as far as firemen were concerned. Their one redeeming feature was that they would keep on plodding along even with a ridiculously low steam pressure. The sight of one on the front was enough to make a man go sick.

Jack and I had several incidents with one. One caused a bit more quarrelling. We had worked a train down the Worcester line and had relief at Honeybourne. The supervisor said to Jack, 'I want you to work that one back standing in the "Garden loop".'

I had noticed when we went down that a horrible 30xx was on it and no crew. 'How long has it been there?' I asked.

'Several hours, the men just left and went home.'

Jack said, 'Come on, mate, we might as well get on with it. There's no other way home.'

'Do you want a banker?' the supervisor asked.

'Yes,' I replied quickly before Jack had a chance to say no. We found the loco in a shocking state, the fire was full with clinker and as dead as any I had ever seen. It looked much worse than the coke fire but this time I knew without doubt that there was no hope at all of it ever coming to life. It was well beyond redemption.

'I'll take me ages to get this thing going, mate.' At this time the banker came on the rear and blew up. Without any consideration for me or whether there was any chance of success he answered the banker's whistle. The signalman immediately pulled off. I called Jack a few idiots and the like, he had not even taken the trouble to look in the firebox. Before we had gone the length of the train we were in trouble. The gradient of 1 in 106 faced us for over two miles and steam was already down to half-pressure. It was too much, even a loco in good condition needed a better start than this. We came to the expected stop half-way up the bank, out of puff. Jack spoke for the first time since starting: 'It's all your bloody fault, you're useless.'

'Perhaps so,' I said. 'Now we can find out just how good you are. I'm going to light the lamps and then go back to the guard and banker while you have a go. If you'd given me a better chance we would have done much better.'

'You come and do your own work, I'll do the lamps.'

'The lamps are my work. I'm doing no more to the fire until you put it right.'

The guard had gone back to protect the rear of the train in accordance with regulations so I stayed and talked to the banker crew who were not too happy at being put in this situation. Being Worcester men they let me off but said 'Can't understand what your mate was thinking about. You couldn't have been anywhere near ready.' He continued, 'Look at the state we're in trying to help you out.'

I watched from the rear and could see smoke rising from my loco and knew Jack was at least having a go. Repenting a little I took my leave and returned. I knew there was still plenty of time, the guard would have to be called in before we could move off. I found Jack flustered and ready to capitulate. It was enough for me to say, 'Come on get out of the way, I suppose I'd better do it.' I wielded the long poker, it was like stirring porridge. When I returned it to the tender it was glowing red hot for three parts of its length. We had been standing threequarters of an hour by the time the effort was made to climb the rest of the bank. With a tremendous struggle the two locos heaved the train away up through the tunnel and down the dip through Blockley and up again to Moreton-in-Marsh. We halted here for another breather while the tank filled. The run to Oxford was easy and to our surprise we were relieved. Jack got off the loco and immediately became friendly, completely forgetting the trauma of the last two hours.

A much more serious event took place shortly after this, again with a ROD. We travelled to Newbury to relieve a train coming up from Westbury. While we waited tea was brewed. Before it was finished the supervisor came in. 'Your train's just coming up the middle line. Will you work it as far as Kingham?'

'Yes, we'll be all right,' said Jack.

We finished the tea and went out to be taken aback by the sight of the loco. The look that passed between us was sufficient to remind us both of the previous trip.

The guard said, 'Don't go until I've had a chance to look round the train, we're going over the branch.' He returned later and said, 'That's it, Jack, you've got thirty-six class threes* on, just the full load for this loco. It's a train full of bombs.'

The departing crew gave the loco a good name, the fireman saying, 'It's one of the best we've ever had of this sort.'

'I'll take that with a pinch of salt. I've heard those tales before,' I replied.

When we set out across the branch I realised he was telling the truth, it wasn't a bad one after all. It soon proved that it needed to be a good one. The sharp rise out of Newbury almost brought us to a stand. Either the train was very heavy or there were some brakes on. For once I maintained the steam and the old thing kept plodding on, dragging hard all the way up to Hermitage where Mary was hanging out of her box to cheer us on our way. For our part every exhaust beat was the last. The slight easing of the gradient through the station gave just enough respite to be able to keep moving. We struggled over the top at Pinewood with great relief not knowing the worst was

* The lightest loaded vehicles up to but not exceeding three tons' load.

yet to come. The loco had been in full fore gear and full regulator all the way; we should have known that we were grossly overloaded.

As speed picked up a little Jack said, 'I think I'd better try the brake.' He applied it and there seemed to be little effect. 'These steam brakes take some time to warm up. Put the tender brake on, mate, we don't seem to have much of a brake here.'

I tried to wind the tender brake on but it would not budge, even with the steam brake operation to assist me. 'It's useless, Jack, can't get it on.' Consternation crept in, the steam brake was on and the hand brake wouldn't work. The train was gathering speed as it made its way down the steep gradient of 1 in 106, the ruling gradient for all the steep ones on that branch.

'We're running away, mate,' I said to Jack but he just looked nonplussed, turned pale and said, 'What if the fly is shunting at Hampstead Norris? It's about the time that it should be there.'

This was a sobering thought which prompted me to reply, 'Put the engine in back gear. Don't forget the train's full of ammunition, we'll get blown to bits if we run into anything.'

Jack carried out my suggestion but with little effect and when the distant for Hampstead Norris loomed up at caution he didn't hesitate to open the regulator fully while in reverse. The rattle and clatter that followed was tremendous, the engine and tender crashed into each other banging away like a machine gun. Coal was shaken off to fall on to the footplate and then trickle out through the gangway. We were still doing about 20 mph when I sighted the home signal at stop. 'Jack, I'm getting off,' I bawled. 'Might as well break my neck as get blown to bits.' There wasn't much chance of surviving anyhow. I was surprised to see Jack follow suit on his side. The moment of decision was on and to my great relief I saw and shouted, 'All right, mate. There's nothing here.' We both pulled ourselves back on board. Jack shut off steam and let the reverser go back to forward and sat back waiting for the train to come to a stand in the bottom of the dip.

To make matters worse the guard admitted that he had given no assistance with his brake. Jack refused to move until we had assessed the train for weight. The previously fussy guard had been a total let-down; in checking the train at Newbury he hadn't checked the loading on the wagon labels and had also miscounted by ten. The thirty-six turned out to be forty-six and each of them had more than double their intended load. In all, the total train weighed twice as much as the load given to us. Before we descended the bank from Churn down to Upton, Jack insisted that the guard come forward and pin down side brakes on the wagons to assist us with braking. It was strange how soon that unpleasant episode was cast from our minds and working normally as if nothing had happened. I was getting on rather better with Jack by this time. My rebellious attitude was curbed and the whole situation accepted.

Light-hearted incidents were not quite so common, nevertheless there were times when one could sit back and think did this really happen. One such incident with Jack comes readily to mind. We had worked the 1.45 p.m. stopping passenger to Swindon in the afternoon and were returning with the 5.20 back to Didcot. No one seemed to care what sort of loco we had on this turn, it was only a stopper with plenty of station time to recover lost steam. With this in mind the foreman often booked an old crate on the job. On this particular day we had the dreaded 'Dukedog' 3215. On the rear of the train we always had a box van for Challow goods shed. The usual arrangement was to stop in the station in the normal way for the passengers and in the meantime the shunter uncoupled the van. When all were ready we pushed it back inside the shed. The station work was completed and the shunter called us back from my side. 'Right, Jack, shove back inside,' I called. Jack opened up and kicked off in the usual way. 'Whoa, mate,' I called as the shunter gave me the stop signal. Although Jack stopped quite gently the safety valve which was blowing off lightly made a different sound than usual. Jack looked at the boiler level then at me and said, 'I thought you had too much water in the boiler but I see it's all right. Sounded as if we had shot some out.'

I said, 'There was a little went out. The water must have swished back as we stopped.'

The guard waved his flag. I turned to my mate, 'Right away,

Jack,' then as usual turned to look ahead to check the signals. In doing so I saw a man on the road bridge in front waving his arms furiously.

'Better hang on, mate, I'll see what he wants.'

Above the sound of the escaping steam I was unable to hear what he was saying. One thing was certain, he was in rather an irate state. I placed my hands round my mouth and shouted 'What did you say?' With my cupped hand round my ear and him shouting I was still no wiser.

'I'll put a drop in the boiler. That will quieten it down for a few minutes.'

I did so and returned to the man on the bridge. Again I shouted, 'What did you say?'

'There's a part of your engine up here.'

'Did you hear that Jack? There's a part of our engine up there.'

'Get away. How can there be?'

'Half a minute, the safety valve did make a funny sound when it shot that water out,' I said as I looked out through the oddly shaped front window to where the safety valve stood on top of the firebox.

'That's it, Jack, the cover's gone.'

We gazed at each other in total amazement. The silence was broken by my mate saying, 'You'd better go up and see.' I climbed the fence alongside the platform and scrambled up the grassy embankment by the side of the bridge buttress. I wriggled through the typical wire strand fence on the side of the road to come face to face with a very bad-tempered farmer type. In the centre of the road stood our cover not very far from his nice shiny car. Before I was allowed to remove it I was subjected to a tirade of abuse. I gathered through his vehement attitude that it had come hurtling over the parapet narrowly missing his car as he braked hard to stop. He concluded by threatening me with all kinds of retribution if anything like that happened again.

'Never likely to happen again,' I said chuckling as I heaved it over the fence to roll down the bank with me slithering down behind it. With the cover on the back of the tender we departed while the man on the bridge still vented his fury.

Interspersed with these episodes there were many days of working long hours particularly leading up to D-Day and for a while afterwards, sixteen, twenty or even longer hours on duty were not uncommon. We couldn't grumble too much, not in our comparatively safe reserved occupation.

There was a day when I worked a train of four American locos to Southampton docks. We also used a 'Yank' to haul them being told to leave that one as well. The military transport officer in the docks had other ideas.

'We need you to work a train out of the docks with that one,' he said.

'How long will that be?' my driver asked.

'Don't know yet, they've only just started unloading it. You'll have to wait.'

I said to him, 'That'll be ages before we can get away. Can I go over to the canteen for a cup of tea and a bun?'

'No you can't, you're not allowed in there.'

Trying to plead with him I said, 'I haven't had anything to eat for over six hours. You can't expect me to work on an empty stomach.'

'My job is to keep these docks working, not to feed you.'

'Well, if that's it I'll walk out and try to get some.'

Without hesitation he blew his whistle and several soldiers with fixed bayonets emerged from the guard room. 'Now see if you're going to walk out,' he said as he walked away.

That day ended with being on duty twenty-two hours.

The management adopted a diehard attitude towards the age-old principle of working double home as it was called. This was when a set of men worked outward one day and booked off duty at another depot to work home the next day. The principle was continued to the bitter end although none of the men ever liked it. One day I was booked to work our one and only double home turn. The journey out on the 5.15 a.m. to Birmingham was pleasant enough. On the day in question I was booked with a driver named Sam Morton. He wasn't keen on young firemen calling him by his Christian name but I was honoured, his son Doug was my pal. Sam belonged to the old-fashioned diehards and firmly believed in keeping a fireman in his place. 'Only one gaffer on this engine,' he would say. He was always well turned out, wore the old cloth cap as did many of them of that era. A small moustache helped to identify him. Above all he was noted for chewing tobacco. This in itself repulsed many but when he spat juice on the footplate almost every fireman fell out with him. For myself I bit my tongue, better to keep a happy relationship especially as I often visited his house.

The loco that morning was one of the LMS 'Black 5'. A nice comfy cab with side windows, not that they were necessary that particular day. It was late summer, just breaking daylight as we left the yard. I put my foot in it straight away by saying 'Being a left-hand drive, Sam, I suppose your left-hand spit will go over the side.'

Looking at me rather severely he said, 'That's enough of your cheek. Get on with your work.'

The loco was in a good condition, the nice clean fire shone through the open ashpan to reflect on the ballast as we gently trundled along. The route took us via Oxford turning at Wolvercote junction on to the Worcester line. By now it was daylight and the trip was going well. Sam couldn't resist interfering. 'Don't get too much in there, we stop at Moreton for exam.'

I was doing quite well by myself so I said, 'I'll have to keep it going for a while, haven't got much in there.' Knowing from experience that the line was on a rising gradient I added, 'I don't think I've got enough in there to manage.'

'Just leave it alone and do as you're told.'

Sam was one of the best enginemen one could ever wish for but even with his gentle handling the steam dropped back. I felt I could get a bit cocky and said, 'When I get back I'll tell Doug and your missis how you've messed me about.'

Well, when he came down and saw me grinning he also broke into a little smile. 'You'd better get on with it then,' he said and left me alone.

It was unfortunate that on this sort of train we were booked to stop about every twenty-five miles to have the train examined. The old-fashioned wheel tapper came round to check the axle boxes, the miserable fat used as lubricant so often failed to do its job that bearings got hot, any doubt and the wagon was put off. On this occasion we were all right but Sam told me to expect to stop again at Stratford.

Leaving Moreton I asked Sam, 'When do I get a chance to cook my breakfast?'

'Why didn't you ask before, there's not much chance now.' Then he said 'I suppose you can cook it going down the bank when I'm shut off.'

It wasn't a good idea, the fire was too hot. The back of the shovel was too cold while the front frizzled the bacon. I managed to eat it but not with much relish. The rest of the day went well, arriving at Tyseley almost on time soon after eleven o'clock. After relief Sam took me to the office to report in then off to his favourite club. Not wanting to drink I sat around while he had a couple and chatted to the locals. This was probably the highlight of his trip, he originated somewhere north of here and felt quite at home.

Later he led me to the lodge. This was an ordinary house that took in men on this sort of turn. We arrived and Sam introduced me to Annie Tolly, a wizened old crone. About 2.00 p.m. she directed me to a little back bedroom, 'Sam will come and call you when it's time to get up.'

It was dark from the wartime blackouts hanging at the windows. When my eyes became accustomed to the darkness I could see that for curtains she had used old hessian sacking. I got into a very uncomfortable bed and failed to sleep. Within two hours I was up again and down in the back kitchen to have a wash. Sam had been trying to doss in the armchair. The rest of the day was long and dreary, glad to go back and book on again at 11.30.

We made our way to the relief cabin to wait for our train, the 10.45 from Stourbridge. While we waited in the cabin the air raid sirens sounded. No one seemed to bother. Sam said

'The shelter's worse than this,' referring to the small smoky cabin.

Presently the supervisor came in and said to Sam, 'Your train's out on the loop if you want to relieve it and get away.'

'Might as well,' said Sam, then asking me, 'what do you think about leaving in the raid?'

'It's all right with me. We might as well be on the move as stay here. Let's make the tea and get going.'

The Stourbridge men were glad to get off, they had filled the tank and we were soon ready to go. The blackout sheets were fitted so we felt secure from being spotted by enemy aircraft. As we wended our way through the junction and out onto the main line for the Leamington road I looked back to see our search-lights playing on the clouds and the orange flashes of bombs as they fell about four or five miles to our rear. Although the blackout sheets were very good Sam said, 'Don't open the doors to put any on yet, no need to take any chances. It'll be all right soon, we're going away from it.'

This was my first time on this road and I had no idea of where I was except that it was obviously a rising gradient, not much but I thought the fire needed some attention. The train was not too heavy and the almost new 28xx made light work of it. About ten miles had passed under the wheels before Sam said, 'You can put some on now, not too much and don't leave the doors open too long.'

I got stuck in with big shovelfuls thinking he wouldn't notice. He did and promptly stopped me.

'Don't get too much in there, we'll most likely get stopped at Leamington. They'll play hell if we blow off steam there in the middle of the night.'

I sat down. 'Sam,' I said, 'you'd better tell me how to go on, I've no idea where I am.'

The night was dark with no lights anywhere but I felt the gradient easing. Sam said, 'It's downhill all the way to Leamington now.' His casual instructions seemed to be right after all.

We had been drifting downhill for a little while when Sam

stood up peering forward and then started to swing his arm to and fro.

'What's the matter?' I asked.

'Get some in there, lad, we've got the road right away through Leamington.'

As I shovelled away he added, 'It's a long hard pull from here, get stuck in.'

After politely telling him he was mucking me about again I got on with it. The loco cruised up the bank with no effort at all. Sam had known best.

In common with others I refused to go double home again.

In no time at all the war was being won; our successes reduced the load put on the railways and overtime gradually fell off. The chance of air raids had become very remote. The whole atmosphere was much more relaxed and then – at last – in May 1945 victory was announced.

We all had a day off work. It had been the first day a call boy had come to me and then only to tell me not to go to work that day.

FIVE

Branch lines to 'Castles'

DURING MY HAPPY STAY at Didcot I had met my wife to be, she had been called to service as a member of the Auxiliary Territorial Service. Our paths crossed by a mutual interest in dancing. She was no stranger to railways. Already she discovered the inconvenience of shiftwork from me but her previous connections were with her family on the Southern Railway, ranging from guard, fireman, several office clerks to a police sergeant through to her father who was no less than costing accountant at Brighton loco works.

All this was left behind and I started afresh when I arrived back on Monday 21 January 1946.

Having been away all this time I soon realised that I had become a stranger. Few men remembered me at first, it took some time to get accepted again. I was a stranger and needed to prove myself. Taking up residence, in the enginemen's cabin this time I was quite alone, not exactly ignored but not greeted with open arms. Perhaps my return to automatically take my place in a higher link in preference to a junior fireman caused some mixed feelings.

Several months passed before I was established in number three link. In the meantime I did all sorts of spare work, usually with a different driver each day, a cross-section of the mundane work at the depot. This suited me quite well, and enabled me to get myself known.

After the austerity of the war men now showed a more relaxed mood. In general there were signs of getting back to normal, whatever that was – I don't think I really knew. It seemed the old ways, particularly the acceptance of dirt, were gone. The stale tea bottle was out of date, cans of freshly made tea had long since taken their place. The pride in the job so evident before the war was returning slowly. Locos that were grubby and uninteresting gradually came back to reveal their livery, once again standing proudly at the head of a train. I don't know who cleaned them, I was too occupied being a fireman to notice. All the borrowed locos returned to their home depots, we reverted to GWR once more.

The heavy traffic of the war had ceased but passenger traffic was heavy. There were plenty of service men and women still on the move and volumes of people travelling for the first time in many years. The railways, particularly the passenger side, was inundated. It was good to see so much life in the way of people instead of wagons. People brought the railway to life – it was them and express passenger trains that created the interest. I had my sights set on working passengers after so much loitering about on goods.

When I eventually moved into number three iink I found it had an unusual arrangement of turns: ten drivers but only five firemen. It was referred to as the 'car link'. We, the firemen, worked round the five turns solely on the 'auto cars' with a driver and when not with one of us the drivers worked turns on the diesel rail-cars.

Auto car was the name given to the push-and-pull trains where both men worked on the loco when hauling and the fireman was left on his own while the driver drove from the vestibule end of the leading coach when running in reverse. When working with only one trailer the driver had little difficulty operating the regulator connection rodding but with two on the amount of play made it almost impossible for him to move it. The fireman was expected to assist from the footplate. This was all very well but he had other things to do such as look after the fire and boiler; true it was small and didn't need undivided attention but with such close station stops and assisting with the braking the job could become very busy.

Most of the drivers asked me to take full control without having the regulator rodding coupled up. This was even more busy but at least I knew where I stood. It was strictly against the rules so a sharp eye had to be kept open as well. On the Saturday service with two trailers each end the driver didn't work on the footplate all day, but only said a few words as he passed by changing ends at the terminals. The 48xx as they were originally numbered, and later renumbered 14xx, were a very efficient machine for the job they were designed to do, not very big but with a good turn of speed, quite economical on fuel and water and comfortable to work on.

The rail-cars worked by the drivers were the same as the one I had seen from my factory before my cleaning days; no change in design at all. Three of them were stationed at Worcester, numbers 4, 5 and 6. My only experience of them was when I was cleaning and had to assist in the fuelling. I remember the drivers not having much feeling for them, taking their turn as they came with little interest. The rail-cars worked only on local stopping trains, much the same as the auto-cars. Most of the drivers said they would rather be on a loco particularly the auto services we worked such as preparing a 48xx and taking one trailer empty to Kidderminster at 6.5 in the morning, then loco leading round the branch to Bewdley, reversing ends and running engine first all stations via the loop line at Worcester, through to Ledbury, and back through the very small tunnel up the gradient of 1 in 80 to get over the top round the Malvern hills and a free wheel almost all the way back, once again with trailer leading – fifty odd miles' casual work. Other turns followed a similar pattern, all simple relaxing work. This lasted a couple of months before I moved up to number two link with a driver named Alf Sommers. I had never worked with him before and approached my job with caution. He seemed on the face of it to be a miserable type. Within an hour or two that was completely disproved, I had impressed him with my effort, as a result of which we had an excellent relationship.

Our first day together was on the 6.22 a.m. passenger from Worcester over the Severn Valley line to Shrewsbury. I was on unfamiliar ground, never having travelled in this direction before. With the unknown route I asked Alf to give me some indication of how to carry on.

'We've got a good engine and only three on. I'd like to see how you manage. I'll tell you why later.'

The engine was a good one, an almost new release from Swindon, one of the 43xx class. As was usual all branch passenger trains stopped at all stations. We jogged along quietly, turning off the main line at Hartlebury on to the branch via Stourport to stop at Bewdley for a spell of twenty minutes waiting for a connection from Kidderminster. The morning was cold, early winter, and as we stood at Bewdley Alf commented on the lovely warm fire keeping us cosy.

'Tell me. How do you manage to keep the fire so nice and red just inside the doors?'

'It's simple, Alf. I just select cobbles to put there and burn the rubbish up front. I find it helps to keep the fire burning evenly.'

'My last mate was useless. We would have arrived here with steam low and a black fire. I'd have sat here freezing.'

'How far is it to Shrewsbury?'

'Not very far.'

After about twenty minutes the connection arrived and we soon left together, side by side, the Kidderminster going away on our left to turn across the river out to Wooferton Junction on the Shrewsbury to Hereford line while we carried on for a while to cross the river further up by the famous Victoria bridge and to hug the valley of the Severn for many miles, an attractive and interesting trip, especially in the summer months.

On we went stopping at Highley to drop off the miners for the local colliery then wending our way through trees with an occasional glimpse of the river to a major stopping place, Bridgnorth. After working with single-line tokens and staffs we worked through the station on double-line arrangements with a signalbox at each end. Out through the tunnel at the other end of the station and away out on to flat country for miles.

'How far is it now, Alf?'

'Just round the corner.'

We went round several corners and eventually stopped at Buildwas where there was a connection on the right from Wolverhampton; another branch went off to the left for Craven Arms. A little old refreshment room adorned the up platform.

'How many more corners have we got to go round?'

'Not far now, only a couple more stops.'

That turned out to be four and a long distance between them by comparison. Eventually we joined the main line from Hereford and ran the short distance to Shrewsbury. That station was quite impressive with several bay lines this end. We ran into either platform 7 or 8 to unload then did an unusual shunt by pushing our train out and then via the loop at Abbey Foregate, back to the junction to form a triangle and then propelling back into bay platform 1. Along the platform side there were windows from where I could look down over the river Severn. This end of the station was built over the river itself.

After a wait of almost two hours we made our way back the way we had come. The little refreshment room at Buildwas provided a watering hole for Alf in the way of a glass of beer. The run home was ordinary to Hartlebury when we uncoupled and ran light to Worcester.

These little branch lines were often the most interesting to work on – almost working themselves – always lovely country scenery with a casual way of life. The war scars were not quite healed and rations were still a bit tight. Townies such as ourselves were always welcomed with fresh farm eggs and an occasional rabbit to help us along. I had a couple of turns to Hereford, one being the 7.15 in the morning, the train I first travelled on when I went to Swindon for my medical. It wasn't far, about thirty miles, with the rise up the Malvern hills and through Colwell tunnel to gradually fall down and enter the exceedingly narrow single-line tunnel at Ledbury. We often had a 'Castle' on this service and the sides of the cab were only six to eight inches from the walls and the chimney missed the roof by about the same amount. Falling down the steep bank towards Ledbury was not too bad, no steam or smoke from the chimney to worry about but if the tunnel was still full of smoke from a previous train it was not possible to see the signal at the exit, nor even the exit. To give drivers an indication of getting near a large clapper gong was placed in the tunnel about 100 yards inside, which nearly shattered the ear drums.

Coming up the other way always caused great concern. It was a wonder that men survived the terrible ordeal of the sulphur fumes. I avoided firing anywhere near the tunnel by having a massive fire beforehand and giving it a stir with the poker leaving Ledbury. By the time we entered the tunnel there was no smoke and little sulphur. I then lifted the fall plate between engine and tender to allow some air to come up from below and then stood in the corner with my hanky over my face until we emerged into daylight once more. When we did so the cab and front of the tender was almost white with the effects of the sulphur fumes. All the way through the blast of the exhaust steam had been hitting the roof and rebounding down to completely engulf the cab. Colwall tunnel had plenty of room and presented no problems.

With Alf I worked the 6.52 stopper to Wolverhampton, normally with five coaches. Occasionally we had a 43xx but usually a 'Hall' class. It was an easy and casual trip with a generous break in Stafford Road shed after we had turned. The job was one of those everyday turns where nothing normally went wrong. The only time that I found anything amiss was early in the new year of 1947. We set out as usual; away in front in the region of Droitwich the sky was extra dark while overhead it was quite clear. Daylight was some way off but the sky looked ominous. By the time we arrived it was snowing and a blizzard was blowing, a remarkable contrast in such a short distance. The farther we went the worse it became, snow was falling thick and heavy. The two middle lines at Stourbridge were full with drifting snow and unusable but the bay lines were open. Somewhat delayed we carried on but at Round Oak we came to an abrupt stop. A snowdrift had covered our line to a depth of about a foot on the off side and three feet on my side. We didn't have enough speed to keep going and the packed snow in front of us brought us to an amazingly quick stop, I wondered what had happened.

'We'll never get out of this,' said Alf.

'I don't know, let's go and have a look.'

I returned to Alf and said 'It's not too bad. I'm going to have a try at digging us out.'

The firing shovel is not an ideal tool for the job but it was all I had. Using the coal pick to loosen the solid parts I was making some progress when along came two platelayers, one of them a woman. They joined in with a will and in about fifteen minutes we were on our way. At Wolverhampton things were decidedly worse, the blizzard was raging, no trains were running. We were fortunate in being able to turn the loco but in doing so we now had the full fury of the storm blowing in behind and only the smallest of storm-sheets to keep it off. After several hours of indecision we were eventually sent home light to arrive back six hours late.

I had not worked in the link covering the branch through to New Radnor. This was a quaint little line which carried through beyond Bromyard. My only trips there were when I was spare, once for a whole week at a time. I knew where I was as far as Bromyard but again I was on strange ground beyond. The day started with a train to Evesham and back to Worcester, leaving there again at 8.5 to Radnor. This was no ordinary trip, it was one from the past. We had taken water on shed, again at Evesham and filled up again at Worcester. In the ten minutes at Bromyard we filled up again and away up the bank to the summit at Fencote where we crossed a train coming in the opposite direction. Then we almost freewheeled all the way down to Leominster. As we always had something in the way of a shunting tanky the coal was low by this time so it was a case of unhook and into the shed sidings for coal at the tiny coal stage where I had to wind up the coal tub by hand. The bunker invariably had no back so that when the tub was tipped quite a lot of it fell on the footplate and had to be cleared up. What with the mess and the dust to get rid of and take water again we were hard pushed to get on our train and away in twenty minutes and into the bargain we turned as well. Bunker first with fresh dusty coal and no back on the bunker was a rare treat.

At Kington we again took water. From here we were in a land of our own, one train only working. That meant that until we returned no other train could enter the single line. The line left Kington with the small loco shed on the right, it was about large enough to house two small tanks. Passing here the line rose steeply through very tight twists and turns through trees and skirting a little rippling stream with kingfishers darting about until it made its way out into the open to a little halt called Stanner. From here eagles could be seen swirling and soaring among the crags of the rocky hills. On to the next little stop at Dolyhir. From a position nearing here three distant signals came into view all at the same time, odd for this type of line, they were only for level-crossing gates. Further on the line weaved through mountains climbing all the way until it came to its end at the foot of a mountain.

At the terminus we were booked five minutes in which time I had to uncouple and run the loco forward over the points. Then I walked to the ground frame, unlocked it, turned the points and, after the driver had run into the loop, then had to close the points, get back on board to go to the other end and open the points for the driver to come over and return to the train. After locking the points I had the pleasure of recoupling the loco. With a fast driver one day we tried to see how long or at least how quick we could do it. The shortest time was nine minutes, a guaranteed five minutes late start back. The run back was very interesting, the driver opened the regulator and after a few puffs shut off to freewheel for what seemed miles. Leaving Radnor the view was spectacular, mountains everywhere, valleys filled with trees. I gazed on several occasions trying to find which way we would eventually go but I never did sort it out, we were soon in the trees with no hope of seeing anything. Back to Kington for water and again at Leominster where we had our first break after six hours on duty, water again at Bromyard to take us the rest of the way home. In all we had travelled some 130 miles, taken water seven times, stopped fifty-five times,

1　The view of Worcester shed as seen by the author on his first day of cleaning, 3 August 1936. (This photo was taken in 1962.) The separate passenger and goods sheds are seen with what remains of the shunting yard in between

2　The author (*r*) poses on the front of 4007 *Swallowfield Park* after cleaning it on his first day as a cleaner; his colleague cannot be identified

3 The author (*r*) with cleanin colleague Ted Wigley on 5092 *Tresco Abbey* outside Worcester shed, August 1938

4 Fireman Tidball of Readin on a 43xx 'Mogul' 2-6-0 in Reading station, 1939; not the shiny shoes, rather tha stout boots

5 The driver of 5085 *Evesham Abbey* tries out his new issue of gas-mask and helmet at Paddington on 21 May 1942

6 4040 *Queen Boadicea* departs from Paddington in the evening of 23 May 1942
with the crew no doubt glad to get away from the nightly bombing raids;
all is quiet except for a pilot pulling another train into the station

7 5955 *Garth Hall*, the first of the passenger locos to be converted to oil burning.
The photo, taken in August 1946, shows fireman Len Chillingworth attending
to the oil filling; he is now a High Speed driver

8   GWR dedication: seven members of the Hall family at Kingham, who all
worked for the railway (*l-r:*) John, retired station master; Charles 'Chippy',
fireman; Fred, foreman; Walter, relief signalman; Cecil, bricklayer; Charles
Arthur, ticket collector; and Harold, relief signalman. The fireman of a 43xx
class looks down from the tender in the sunshine of October 1946

9 6018 *King Henry VI*, with the '100 mph' look, at Chippenham after working the down Bristolian in the early 1950s; driver W. Pithers and fireman Stan French in charge

10 Southall shed in 1950, shortly before its demolition to make way for the new shed

11 'Mogul' 7319 at the front of Reading shed in 1958 with the author oiling, ready to work a Sunday afternoon train of empty coal-wagons to South Wales

12 6003 *King George IV* at speed on the up Bristolian passing through Chipping Sodbury with the dynamometer car next to the loco

13 'Hall' class (*foreground*) ascending Whiteball on the up line with the second part of the Torbay Express in the early 1950s about to pass another 'Hall' on the brow of the hill with the distant for Burlescombe in the off position

14 The author drawing issue of oil from the stores at Reading shed for preparing 5076 *Gladiator* ready to work the 'Continental' forward to Oxford, February 1961

15 The author moving off Reading shed towards the station on 4921 *Eaton Hall*, February 1961; note Automatic Train Control equipment against window and the cylinder lubricator sight feed glasses

16   GWR rail-car W20 with trailers attached approaching Bromyard from Worcester in 1961; note the guard with single-line token in hand ready to give it up to the signalman

17   Didcot shed with a mixture of steam and two diesels – a shunter and a 'Hymek' – in 1963

18 'Warship' class D603 *Conquest* starts the Cornish Riviera Express from Penzance, 1961

19 7027 *Thornbury Castle* waits at the down main signal at Reading with a Paddington to Bristol in the summer of 1962 for a west of England express, headed by a 'Warship', to clear the junction

20 4086 *Builth Castle* passing through Sonning cutting on an up express – one of the author's favourite locos when firing at Worcester on the 'runners' (footplate term for express passenger trains)

21 7007 *Great Western* at speed through Pershore with a Worcester to Paddington express in 1962 – not looking in the same pristine condition as when the author first worked it in 1947

22 5090 *Neath Abbey* departing the down main at Reading for Bristol with the lower distant arm for West Junction at 'Caution'; this photo was taken in May 1963 from the old West Main signal-box

23 'Warship' D845 *Sprightly* (*l*) departs from the down main at Reading in May 1963 signalled towards the west of England with the lower distant for Oxford Road Junction in the 'Line Clear' position. A DMU waits at the bay signal to follow to Newbury as a stopper

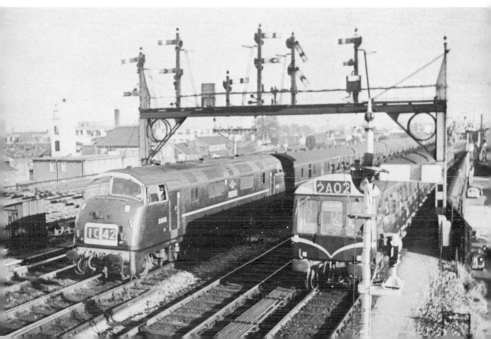

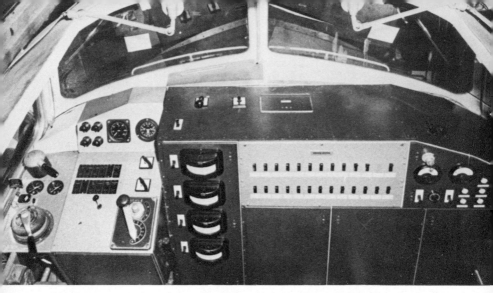

24 An unusual view of the cab of 'Warship' class D800 *Sir Brian Robertson* taken from above with the cab roof removed soon after its delivery. The array of switches and controls can be seen, showing the confusion facing drivers used only to steam

25 Diesels 1023 *Western Fusilier* and 1051 *Western Ambassador* at Spetchley, near Worcester, on 27 April 1975 heading the 'Western Enterprise' tour; the author is in the front cab as inspector

26 Great Western Society enthusiasts' special near Culham on a Didcot to
Hereford train, headed by 7808 *Cookham Manor* and 6998 *Burton Agnes Hall*
with the author on the leading loco, 14 June 1975. The 'vintage train' used
was completely restored by the GWS

27 A preserved 'Hall' class working a regular service on the Severn Valley
Railway on the climb out of Bridgnorth

28   Square cab 'Mogul' 7331 eases gently into the bay at Reading station shunting parcels traffic at the East end with the 'up line' pilot in 1962. Reading driver Wally Farr pays serious attention; soon after this he was among the early Reading drivers to be 'Warship' trained

29   6000 *King George V* at Knowle on the return of the commemoration special on 25 March 1974. The specially made plate is mounted on the side of the smokebox. Driver Percy Talbot of Didcot looks out over the side while fireman Tony Neale works at the fire and the author, as inspector, looks out on the other side

taken on coal and turned. That was real old-fashioned railway work. Into the bargain there was always the eggs and farm produce to gather.

As the severe winter of 1947 wore on my mate Alf left me to move up to the top link. In his place I had a newcomer who had only recently learned the routes for the link. His name was Clarence Turvey, quite a decent chap but somewhat erratic. His political views did not endear him to me and my first hurdle was to make him clearly understand that I was not to be one of his converts. After that we worked well together. The first week's work was on the Severn Valley and for the first time we had a 51xx tank. The enclosed cab was ideal for the harsh weather. About the middle of the week the thaw set in with a vengeance, floods rose everywhere, and as we travelled alongside the river it was noticeable how quickly the level rose. While we were standing at Buildwas a ganger came hurrying to us from the direction we were heading.

'There's a lot of floodwater between here and Cressage. Don't know if you'll be able to get through,' he said.

'What do you call a lot of water?' asked Clarence. 'It couldn't have been very deep if you've walked through.'

'There's more than half a mile of it and it was rising all the time.'

'How deep was it when you walked on the sleepers?'

'It was almost up to the top of my wellingtons, had to walk steady to stop it going over the top.'

'There's no fear of the ballast being washed away, is there?' Clarence asked. 'Anyway, thanks for telling us, we might as well press on.'

The ganger walked back to the guard and station staff. It was obvious that he was trying to persuade them not to let us go.

Clarence turned to me. 'We've got big wheels. That amount won't come half-way up the spokes. No point staying here.'

With that he beckoned to them to get us away.

We left and, passing through the first bridge, saw a sight which made us look at each other in disbelief. As the ganger had said for at least half a mile there was a vast stretch of water with a tree dotted here and there. The fence posts along the lineside were only just standing above the water at the deepest part.

'Too late now,' said Clarence.

We entered the water with the line gradually dipping lower and the loco getting deeper. Steam started to rise from the firebox sides where water was touching the ashpan.

'I'd better close the ashpan, mate. The next thing we'll have the fire going out,' I said.

As the connecting rods turned their big ends splashed down into the water to add round ripples to the very prominent wash from the front end as we surged forward. The bow wave swept right across the flooded fields to be lost in the flow of the river.

Clarence had ploughed along regardless, water was splashing everywhere, quite a sight to behold. Out on to dry land again he said calmly, 'I told you there was nothing in it.'

We turned in the usual way at Shrewsbury and waited in the bay for time to return. A loco inspector came and asked, 'Can you tell me how deep the water was when you came through?'

'I would say about up to the axles.'

The inspector replied, 'The water's still rising, they tell me. It'll be too deep for you to go back through.'

Clarence was prepared to have a go and replied, 'It can't have risen that much more.'

In the meantime I had been watching the river rise down below us and added my comment, 'I don't know about that, mate, it's risen about four feet up this lamp post on the path down here in the last hour and it's still rising.'

'I'll send relief out for you and you can travel home via Wolverhampton,' the inspector said.

I had some experience with 'Star' and 'Castle' class locos while I was with Clarence, mainly on stoppers to Oxford but also on the 8.10 a.m. to Birmingham via Stratford-upon-Avon and Henley-in-Arden, terminating at Moor Street. Clarence always dashed off from the loco to see what he could find cheap in the Bull Ring market, leaving me to go forward on to the traverse table and back for water. The traverser was a platform on which the loco was taken across from one line to the next instead of using the usual crossover points.

One particular day we were a few minutes late. The loco was a small 40xx, a 'Star' class, 4017 *Knight of Liège*, and in his hurry Clarence wound the reverser into back gear, opened the regulator to ease the coupling for unhooking and dashed off shouting, 'It's all yours, mate.'

The shunter called out 'Right, on the table.' I opened the ejector to take the brake off and at the same time spun the reverser to forward not noticing that the regulator was still slightly open. The loco shot forward with no hope of stopping and hit the metal plate across the end of the blocks with an almighty clang. The noise brought people running from everywhere including Clarence.

'What the hell's happened?'

I tried to explain that he had left the regulator open and that it was his own fault but I still carried the can. The two broken buffer springs were conveniently forgotten.

About this time oil burners were introduced, a number of 28xx and 49xx locos were modified to burn oil instead of coal. At this period oil was comparatively cheap and coal was getting dearer. I never had any experience of these myself but those who did formed two quite separate bodies of opinion. There were those, particularly the firemen, who found that operating a few valves skilfully saved them an enormous amount of work and thought they were marvellous. Diehard steam men had different ideas, particularly the drivers who got frozen, because the permanently closed fire-hole doors gave no comfort. The experiment didn't last long, the failings soon showed themselves up. Firemen were getting too enthusiastic with the fuel and spraying too much in and it ran out of the dampers to catch alight round the wheels and axle boxes. It also dripped on to the ballast when standing in stations and caught sleepers alight. Another problem with them was they heated up very quickly and also cooled down too rapidly. This caused extreme stress on the boiler and very soon the tubes and firebox stays were leaking like a sieve. On the road they were probably good on a run but for stoppers they were more of a loss.

A milestone in my career was passed about this time too. I can't remember the date but the occasion sticks in my mind well enough. It was the day I was sent to Swindon for examination for driving. Normally a man was given a week to prepare himself for the exam. I found out by accident on a Saturday that I was to go on the next Monday. This visit to Park House had a different meaning. When I went before I was hoping for a job, this time I had a job which I could lose if I failed the examination. Each fireman was expected to prepare himself and acquire the necessary knowledge to become a driver. There was never any official instruction given, each man attended his local Mutual Improvement Class in his own time. The instructors were mainly drivers who were prepared to give up their own time to help to teach men the rules and give them instruction on the workings of the various types of engines. Their only reward was the success of the examinees. After several years attending at Didcot and Worcester I felt reasonably hopeful; the penalty for failing was a reduction in seniority and the stigma that went with it. Three chances were allowed and should a man fail the three he was taken off footplate duties and offered alternative work as a shedman. I was delighted to pass first time, thus giving me the title of passed fireman, authorising me to take charge as a driver only on a spare or temporary basis. Before appointment as driver I would have to undergo another similar test, even more comprehensive if that were possible. My spare driving was not as lucrative as the firing I did, only eight turns.

In the summer of 1948 I moved up to number one link to mate with Doug Battersea. Until now I had never had the opportunity of working with him. Others had said how well he handled locos but no one seemed to want to tell anything of his character. I had no idea of what he was like. My first day with him sorted that out. We were booked for our first trip together on duty at 8.40 a.m. to walk to the station to relieve and work the 8.55 fast to Paddington with 4086 *Builth Castle*. I met Doug in the time office on time to be told that I should have been there earlier to get on the loco and make certain it was ready. I replied

'As far as I'm concerned it should be ready if it's already on the train.'

'That be blowed for a yarn, you'll see,' he replied.

As we walked to the station I felt I had already got off on the wrong foot. This feeling was reinforced when Doug started to lay down the standards he expected.

'I've been in this link for nearly two years now and haven't kept time any day. My mate has never been able to keep enough steam. I'll tell you now, I don't intend to lose any more time. It's up to you.'

Discretion was obviously best, at that moment we were getting on the loco. Everything seemed to be looking in shipshape, though I thought the footplate needed a better tidy up as regards dust and quickly washed down.

'Don't get too much water over this side. I don't want my feet wet all day.' Then, just with a few minutes to go, he added, 'Don't you think you'd better get some more in there?'

'Doug,' I exploded, 'if I thought I needed to put some more in there I would have done it without you telling me. I'm the fireman on here and I'll do it my way. You just do your job properly and leave me well alone.' Pointing over to the down platform I added, 'When we get back there this afternoon you can criticise if you can find any justification but you must allow me to say what I think.'

I surprised myself at being so forthright with a senior driver but my mind had darted back to those first turns where I was harassed because I was a greenhorn. Things were different now, I felt I knew enough to be left alone.

Doug was taken back a little and merely retorted, 'All right then, have it your own way.'

The whistles started to blow and looking out I took the right away signal and passed it on to Doug.

He had been sitting on his seat cross-legged and quite casually rose to open the regulator. With a determined movement he lifted it giving me the impression that it was going to be opened all the way. Instead he carefully opened to what he thought was the necessary amount for the job then sat down resuming his position with one leg wrapped round the other and gradually winding the reverser up to obtain the best performance with cut-off. With twelve coaches on the exhaust was sharp and crisp. I took another look in the fire and decided to lift it a bit with the pricker. Doug was taking full notice of my every movement and sat on his perch saying nothing. The fire burned up nicely and steam was soon forthcoming. I put the injector on to maintain the boiler and set about firing. Up the slight rise we went and past Norton junction in fine style rising to 75 mph before shutting off for Evesham.

So far excellent, I was feeling already that Doug was happy and I felt a little cocky myself. We left Evesham right time with Doug getting stuck in a little more. The rise over the river bridge justified this anyway; just the same Doug explained, 'Got to get stuck in from here to the top of the bank, it's timed too tight. Nobody ever keeps time up here.'

Not knowing any different I carried on with firing and enjoyed the run. Twelve coaches was the normal full load so we were not troubled with a banker. As we sped through Honeybourne at 63 mph Doug looked at his watch and then at the steam pressure still on the maximum 225 lb and the boiler full. He said nothing but his look of pleasure said it all. Doug was happy. The bank seemed to present no problems, we were running well; after all I had stuck half way up here once. As we neared the tunnel Doug judiciously played sand on the rails to save any possibility of slipping when we got on to the moist rails in the tunnel. We emerged from the other end with flying colours and passing through Campden Doug looked at his watch and started jumping up and down with excitement.

'We'll do it, we'll do it,' he repeated.

'Do what?' I asked.

'We'll be right time at Moreton-in-Marsh. Never done it before.'

With Doug's superb braking we did in fact stop at Moreton in the exact twenty-one minutes allowed.

'Got to tell everybody about this,' he said. 'They all reckon it can't be done.'

'Perhaps they've never had the steam to do it,' I said in a manner to remind him of our dubious start.

Doug kept quiet, we weren't home yet.

The rest of the day went just as well arriving right time at Paddington at 11.28.

Into Ranelagh Bridge turntable to find a dinner laid on. Doug had arranged this for me the previous week.

Our return trip with the 1.45 p.m. and the same train was just as interesting. While I was eating my dinner a labourer had shovelled all the coal forward on the tender for me and once again Doug had given him some cigarettes to encourage him to make a good job of it.

At 4.48 we arrived back at Worcester right on time. I reflected that although this was an achievement looking at the tender, what had I got to show for it? An empty coal hole – about eight tons had departed from there and gone up the chimney.

We had relief and walked back to the office, both feeling quite satisfied. Doug said, 'I wish I'd kept my mouth shut.'

I replied, 'So do I.' He grinned and that cemented what was to become an excellent working partnership.

As most of our work was on the Londons the rest of the odd turns seemed a bit mundane but there were some very interesting trips to record while dashing about on the expresses.

Honeybourne bank might have been stiff to climb but it provided the glory running down. All drivers enjoyed the thrill of seeing the speedometer needle on the peg. That was 100 mph plus any excess speed that couldn't be recorded because the needle couldn't go any further. The bank twisted and turned gently all the way, just enough to make the loco dig into the curves and roll drunkenly as it righted itself ready for the next in the opposite direction. Firing down the bank was impossible; I stood in my corner and held on to save myself from being buffeted about. Honeybourne station went by in a blur with steam shut off to run the rest of the way into Evesham.

One day someone approached us at Moreton. 'Driver, I'm

from the civil engineers' department. Can I ride with you down the bank?'

'What's that for?' asked Doug.

'We want to see if we can raise the speed limit.'

'What do you want to put it up to?'

'Hundred mph.'

We both stayed dumb. Neither of us knew there was a limit of 75 mph.

'How fast do you want us to go?' asked Doug.

'As fast as you like, a hundred if you can.'

Doug set off vigorously, down the dip through Blockley, up the rise to Campden and over the top to the tunnel and away down the bank. Unfortunately we had the worst possible loco to create an impression. It was 5017 *St Donats Castle*. The loco rode perfectly on the straight and steamed very well but down the bank it had a completely different character. It rocked and rolled at the slightest curve, the back waving to and fro from side to side snatching at the tender draw bar and jolting back in line. We were used to this and took little notice. The engineer was in my corner in a place of safety and when I looked at him half-way down the bank he was as white as a ghost. He was so shaken when he got off at Evesham that I had to assist him down.

'What did you think of that?' Doug asked.

'You must be stark raving mad. As far as I'm concerned you'll never do more than seventy-five again.'

What a hope he had.

I don't know why it was that Doug and I seemed to get more than our fair share of the small 40xx locos as we called the original 'Star' class. They were lovely in the sense that they were very economical on fuel as were all 'Churchward' locos. They ran well and rode comfortably but lacked that little extra strength of the 'Castle' class. It always seemed that when we had one of these we also had extra coaches on. Getting a banker on was such a nuisance. After the station stop at Evesham I uncoupled and we ran forward; the banker, usually a 22xx 0–6–0 tender, backed on then we came on top again. Then we had to pull forward to get the rear of the train in the platform.

Ten minutes lost already and then our run was impeded by the fact that the small banker was not suitable for the high speeds through Honeybourne and the driver didn't push it too much because of the rough ride. It wasn't until we were approaching the top of the bank that our assistant came into his own, then he was invaluable. The run down through Blockley must have been hair-raising for them; Doug took no mercy on them and raced through at 75 mph. Looking back at the poor little banker sandwiched between us and the train it seemed to be suspended by the draw bars. The same delay occurred at Moreton when we had to uncouple. In general twenty minutes were lost for the sake of one extra coach. After a while I kidded Doug to go without a banker and created some nail-biting pulls up the bank, but we always managed.

On one occasion we were working the 6.5 p.m. semi up to Oxford when we were delayed by a diesel rail-car failing in front of us. This was likely to cause problems later because we had to get to Oxford and have relief to catch another train back to Kingham and relieve it there. If we arrived too late no one would know and the train would be at Kingham with no one to work it forward.

Doug said, 'We'll have a mad dash, mate, it's the only way.'

We scrambled along as fast as we could and ran into Kingham on the up road in fine style. The normal practice was to run several of the front coaches off the platform to save pulling up. Doug did this relying on me to give him a signal when to stop. At the precise moment I stopped him. Very soon we were away again and proud to have made up sufficient time to get our service back.

Two weeks later an inspector came to us when we were about to leave with the same train.

Doug said to me, 'What's Reg Wade coming up here for?'

When Reg got on board he said to Doug, 'I've got a complaint about you and the Super's asked me to ride with you.'

'What's all this about?' asked Doug. 'I've never been in trouble all my railway life.' Doug was quite indignant and hurt which showed.

The inspector reassured him and said, 'You were working this train on Friday two weeks ago and a passenger has complained that the driver was a complete madman. Let me read out the important passage to you.'

He thumbed through the letter until he found the offending section, it read 'I was standing on Kingham station waiting to board the train and expected it to stop with the dining car on the platform to enable me to join it. The train ran in at an incredible speed, sparks flew off the wheels like a fireworks display and the train failed to stop in the station in the correct place. I was obliged to join the train farther back and walk through to the diner; in doing so I experienced a nightmare trip. The driver left Kingham as if he had the devil on his heels and careered towards Oxford at an alarming rate. In walking the corridor I was thrown about crashing from side to side cutting my face and getting a bruise on my ear which looked like the rising sun. I consider that this man is unfit to drive express trains and should be barred from doing so in the future.'

There was a simple explanation for everything. There was no doubt we hopped along well and it was well known that there was a very bad spot on the curve at Shipton. What no one knew until later investigations was that the passenger was somewhat the worse for drink. A letter like that could hang a man.

My day of triumph came one Sunday when we were working the 6.20 in the evening from Paddington home. The loco was 5092 *Tresco Abbey*, the train was heavy with fourteen coaches on. At Oxford the shunter said, 'I've got to unhook you, driver, and pick one up in the bay for Hereford.'

Doug replied, 'We've already got a full load on.'

'It's loaded with important traffic. It can't wait here until tomorrow.'

'I don't think one more will take much pulling,' I said to Doug.

'You're the one to do the work, it's up to you.'

We went into the bay and the shunter called out 'Ease up' for Doug to squeeze the buffers in.

The fire-hole doors were open and when Doug opened the

regulator a superheater tube split blowing into the firebox causing a massive blowback. A vicious searing flame blew out right across the footplate and into the tender fortunately missing both of us.

'That's torn it,' said Doug. 'This one's no good now.' We took the extra coach back on to the train with the doors closed and the blower on.

'I'm going to ask for another loco,' Doug said and off he went to the phone. He returned in about five minutes.

'They haven't got another one ready. We can have one but we'll have to take this one to shed and prepare another one for ourselves.'

'That'll take at least an hour and half and all that dust and mess to get cleared up,' I said.

'The foreman says he hasn't got a single man in the depot he can put to help us,' Doug told me.

I said, 'Working it out, mate, if we lost an hour's running time we'd still be better off. We could stop quite a lot of times for steam and not be any worse off. I'd rather have a go.'

'You must be mad,' Doug said. 'It's up to you, you've got the work to do.'

'Right, give me a few minutes to shovel that bit of good coal off the back of the tender and we'll be away.'

We left Oxford about ten minutes late, annoying to us, we were always keen on good time-keeping.

With a roaring fire and the boiler as full as it could hold Doug pulled away gently. *Tresco Abbey* was for some reason a very powerful loco, it seemed to have that bit extra, an asset on this day. By the time we reached Wolvercote junction three miles away we were both thinking I had made the wrong decision. The steam had dropped from the maximum 225 psi down to 150 and the boiler level down to below half; by this reckoning we were not even going to reach the next station at Handborough.

However when we reached there we were not much worse off which was surprising. On we struggled gradually getting worse, speed was falling, the gradient rises we encountered from time to time made their mark, each little rise taking a few miles off our speed. We started to bet on how far we would get before being beaten. I put my money on Kingham and rubbed my hands with glee as we approached but only doing 40 mph and the boiler water almost out of sight in the bottom of the gauge class.

Doug said, 'Shall we stop? You've won your bet. It's no disgrace to stop now.'

I could tell he was anxious and wanted to stop. The steam pressure was now down to 80 psi and with some bravado I said, 'How about if we try to get to Moreton.' This was our first booked stop and only seven miles on.

Doug reiterated his earlier assessment of me. 'You're totally mad but who am I to argue. I don't want to stop in the section.'

'Let's have a go, shame to stop now.'

'Look at the steam, we'll never make it.'

So that he couldn't see the steam pressure I put my cap over the clock and said, 'There you are, mate, nothing to worry about now.'

'You've got some cheek,' he said and carried on.

Still rolling through Kingham I was considering the wisdom of carrying on when it occurred to me that there was a sharp rise just ahead for about half a mile. That last hump was almost the last straw, speed dropped to 25 mph and Doug was forced to open the regulator wide and put the engine into full fore gear.

'Looks like I've let you down, mate, that rise took too much out of us.'

'Never mind, we can only hope now,' he said. Those were the longest seven miles of my career, we rounded the last curve to come into sight of Moreton. It was exactly two miles to our stopping point at the end of the platform and dead straight, the station seemed to get no nearer and by the time we were approaching our speed had dropped to 20 mph. I had no idea where the steam had got to. Doug shut off half-way along the platform and stopped as slowly as he could; he could not brake sharply or the small amount of water in the boiler would have run forward and probably damaged the firebox. It was our good fortune that the boiler water injector was still working. I left it on while I scrambled some more coal forward. I had shovelled almost continuously all the way from Oxford, there wasn't much left.

While I was on the tender Doug had a peep under my cap and just uttered 'Good God.'

Standing there with the regulator closed the steam rose rapidly and in about ten minutes we ventured to move. All the steam we needed was enough to get the vacuum brakes off and to start the train out of the station. It was downhill then all the way to our next stop at Evesham except for the rise up to Campden. In that fifteen miles we were able to recover full steam pressure. The run into Worcester was an anti-climax arriving twenty-six minutes late and well down on steam and water.

Although I had worked exceptionally hard I considered it worth while and well justified. When we left the loco Doug said, 'You did well there, mate, I didn't think it was remotely possible. Don't you ever do that to me again, I've sweat more than you with the worry.' Then he asked, 'Did you know we'd only just over forty pounds of steam when I looked at Moreton?'

'You weren't supposed to look,' I replied.

Most of the express running was glorious as could be expected. Heading such trains with majestic locos, hammering up the bank and tearing down the other side, scorching along the level line on the four roads between Didcot and Paddington snatching water on the troughs and running through Reading on the middle line gave me a thrill every time. I never tired of the work.

One day departing from Paddington with the 11.45 fast a sparkling new loco came alongside entering the station on a stopper. I stepped over to my mate's side to have a look at it and in surprise turned to Doug.

'Did you see that one just passed us? It was number 7007 and had the name *Great Western* on it.'

'Get away, you're seeing things. They've all got the name on the tender.'

'I know that. This was on the name-plate on the splasher.'

'I don't believe you,' he said.

The next morning we walked to the station to relieve and work the 8.55 and to our surprise were confronted with the very same loco. We found out later that this was its first day in booked service after undergoing its tests. I seem to remember it was not very impressive with its steaming that day.

Another one we had was unimpressive for steam – 'County' class 1017 *County of Hereford* – but its character sticks well. The story given to us was that it was swapped for 5017 *St Donats Castle*, a perfect beauty (except for its swaying down Honeybourne bank) by Wolverhampton to give us experience of this new design loco. It looked good with its big boiler and larger cab; the squat chimney and front end design gave it a powerful, majestic appearance. The larger cylinders and boiler pressure at 250 psi certainly gave the impression that it would be the master of the job. As it happened it was only the master of all the firemen who dared to think they would manage. The loco was so impossible that after only two weeks it was relegated to stopping trains only. This was not a one-off job, the whole series or at least those I worked on were much the same, the boiler having a mind of its own. It was possible to leave Oxford towards Worcester with a full head of steam and within a few miles be wondering where it had all gone. They all varied in one respect, some would be capable of maintaining perhaps 180 psi, others 160 but some about 200. On all of them as soon as the regulator was closed there was no trouble at all to recoup steam. On top of this the extra power available caused the axle boxes to knock. In general the loco was very uncomfortable to work on.

After just over a year with Doug my wife and I decided to settle in Reading and I again applied for a transfer. Within a few weeks I was to say goodbye, not only to the work I had enjoyed so much but to the mate that had made it all possible. No one could have enjoyed a spell of footplate work any more than I did. The 'Castles' on the 'runners' was an era to look back on with pride.

We worked our last trip together on a Saturday afternoon on the 2 p.m. up to Paddington. The train consisted of fourteen from Worcester and we picked up another four at Oxford making eighteen in all. The train was so long that we had to pull up in Reading to get the rear end in. They said it was never known before. Panic reigned at Paddington; trains were not supposed to convey more than sixteen. The return train was the 6.20 with seventeen on to Reading and twelve from there home. That last eighty-four miles was like running light.

What a way to end my days at Worcester.

SIX

Routes out of Reading

ON MONDAY 8 August 1949 I moved to Reading and lived with a relation very near to the main line right opposite the water troughs at Goring. From my windows I could see the trains passing every few minutes in one direction or the other. 'Hard hitters' as we called them on the main lines, stoppers and freight on the relief. A tinge of envy crept in as I often watched my old mate going by. I remembered his turns and often walked across the small field to the lineside to give him a wave and feel sorry for him when he wasn't doing too well with his new mate.

I was missing the 'runners' but took some consolation in having a chat with the Worcester men whenever I could.

My journey to Reading from home was twelve miles and for a long time I did this on my bicycle, sometimes being able to catch a train from Pangbourne. Quite often the service I caught had the original diesel rail-car No 1 working it. After many attempts by the various main line companies to experiment with alternative traction this was the first successful outcome. Made by AEC in 1933 and sold to the Great Western it became the forerunner of diesel main line traction – the basis on which the 'multiple units' of today are designed. Although it was based at Reading not many had the opportunity of discovering its secrets. It had a top speed of 75 mph but its main use was on local stoppers; with only one engine it was hard pressed at times, subsequent cars being built with two engines.

Arriving at the shed I found that I could not be accommodated in my correct place in the top link and, as expected, I roamed about all the odds and ends of turns with different drivers. I knew what this was all about, I had done it all twice before in changing depots. On each occasion I gained valuable experience working with a variety of drivers, once again doing my best to make a name for myself. After a while I found a driver, Tommy Atkins who, unbeknown to me, knew my parents. He was a very popular man, for ever telling yarns in the cabin. His references to me put me in good stead.

My first few weeks were spent on the pilots, not really surprising, there were thirty-six turns on them altogether.

I was soon out and about covering local passengers and finding quite a difference running on the flat most of the time. At this stage I experienced any gradient only on the Basingstoke road.

My six years at Didcot and running up from Worcester had given me plenty of knowledge of the area but somehow quite a lot seemed different. During the war years it was impossible to have a run in this area on a goods train, I was used to going into every loopline there was and waiting for a spell. Now trains were running more normal it didn't seem right, the old game of fire and boiler dodging I was used to in this area was no good any more. There was no need to work in the way I had on the 'runners' but I found I had to do more than I used to in the past.

The only snag in being spare under these conditions was not knowing when and where I was working from day to day, every day and Sunday being a surprise until I booked off to see the next day's turn. I had to accept this as part of the inconvenience of moving. I can look back now and see that it was one of the wisest moves I have made; from this I found complete job satisfaction.

During the next few months in number two link I tired of peddling my bike all that way; it was the trek home at night after a day's work that put me off so I bought a little car. Petrol was rationed but I heard that extra could be applied for if it was for getting to work in essential jobs. I tried and got far more than I needed, plenty for pleasure. At this time no one else locally thought of going to work by car.

Eventually I moved into number one link to join a driver called Arthur Millis. He was unknown to me and knew little about me himself. I booked on duty on the Monday afternoon at noon and met him for the first time.

'Have you got to come with me, 'erbie?'

'Are you Arthur Millis?'

'Yes that's me.' Then he said, 'Can we take a quiet stroll up to the station, I can't hurry.'

'Yes, we may as well carry on. By the way my name's Jack, at least that's what I've got used to.'

'You'll have to be 'erbie to me. I call all my mates that.'

We walked to the station at an easy pace which gave me the opportunity to ask him if he was unwell.

'Yes,' he said, 'I've got some tummy trouble. It plays me up some times. Shouldn't be back at work really but I was told you would take care of me.'

'Yes, Arthur, by all means, I'll do all I can for you.'

'If I go a bit quiet don't worry, it passes off very quickly.'

'How did you get on with your last mate. Did he help at all?'

'No, I'm afraid not. He was a bad one all round.'

I could tell by the way he evaded criticising him that he was a man of good character.

'Don't worry, Arthur, I won't let you down.'

The train from Weymouth arrived with Reading men on board having worked up from Westbury.

As the men got off the driver said to me, 'Look after Arthur, you've got a good mate there.'

The loco was a 'Hall' class with ten coaches. At 12.32 we departed with Arthur opening the regulator as if it might break off in his hands. He took the train away so gently I thought we were never going to make any headway.

'Arthur,' I said. 'You can open up, I'm used to it.'

'No need to rush. We shall get there just the same.'

I felt quite ashamed to think that anyone should be so casual about driving. He seemed to have no regard for running time. On the 'Castles' we had a speedometer and at a glance I could tell if we were keeping time; there wasn't one on here so I had no definite guide. It wasn't until passing through Slough when I looked up at Horlick's clock that I realised we were keeping reasonable time. Apparently there was more time allowed than on the trains I was used to working. Arthur's gentle approach to driving was something new for me to learn. What fascinated me was that he lost so little time.

We turned at Paddington and had tea while we waited our return, in which time we both found out much more of each other. The day was completed working a semi fast back to Reading, an example of the simple life I was to enjoy.

The link had a good variety of routes, perhaps better than most links anywhere with jobs to London, Banbury, Westbury, Henley on our own railway and runs on the Southern to Redhill in Surrey and to Portsmouth and Southampton with excursions to Bournemouth in the summer.

The route to Southampton was different to the one I worked from Didcot during the war. From Reading we went via Basingstoke and Winchester picking up my previous route at Shawford junction and on to Eastleigh and Southampton terminus, long since closed.

The early train to Southampton nearly always had a 'Grange' 68xx class on the front with five on, stopping all stations. For this type of service it was a perfect loco, it had been designed to replace the aging 43xx locos. A good replacement as far as the men were concerned, the modern cab was much more comfortable. The engine itself was very little better with wheels and cylinders the same as the 43xx, while the larger boiler and slightly higher steam pressure gave it a slight advantage. I must think of it with some respect, for it entered service in 1936, the same year as myself, but then, so did the infamous 'Dukedog'.

To Basingstoke the line rose in stages and for a few miles beyond as far as Worting junction then fell all the way to Eastleigh and level the rest of the way. Coming home the reverse was against us but the good loco and light train made the whole day a pleasure, never anything out of place. I got the impression that the Southern Railway, at least this section, ran very smoothly – perhaps because there was a regular interval passenger service. The boat trains were always interesting to see with *Lord Nelson* and *King Arthur* racing along, particularly on the down road. My thoughts regularly strayed to the glory of the ocean queens.

The run to Portsmouth followed the same route turning off at Eastleigh through Fareham to join the main line at Havant junction. Uncoupling at Portsmouth station was a bit hair-raising for me. I had the greatest respect for the third rail, not knowing too much about it.

We made our way back to Fratton shed and passed right through to turn on the triangle out the back and then returned to the station where we had two hours to wait for our return train before arriving at Reading to have relief. Nothing exciting ever happened on either of these routes, it was always the same happy-go-lucky trundle along except for one odd day.

As usual we relieved on a 'Hall' at the station and did the usual last-minute tidy-up and wash-down with a sprinkle of water on the coal. When I wet the coal it glistened a shiny black. 'This is some smart-looking coal, Arthur, looks like some-body's been polishing it, not a lot of dust in it though.'

As we were about to leave I took my usual look in the firebox.

'Have a look at this. The fire's as black as the tender, it's quite dead.'

Arthur looked, frowned a little then turned to the tender.

'Do you know, 'erbie, I reckon that's anthracite.'

'I've no idea, Arthur, never seen it before.'

'Right away.' Arthur opened up in his gentle manner. As I watched the fire it seemed gradually to go out. What little flame there was diminished and crept back under the black mass. It was obvious that putting more coal on would only aggravate the situation. Be patient, I thought, perhaps it will come round when Arthur shuts off for Reading West. No hope at all, the fire hardly came to life.

'Arthur,' I said, 'I don't think we ought to go any farther. There's no chance of this coal ever burning.'

He looked at the situation in dismay.

'Well, we can't stop here, 'erbie, we'll shut the railway.'

Neither of us wanted to do that so I agreed to carry on and see how it worked. The experience with the tender of coke proved in the end to be very successful.

I could tell that using the normal pricker to lift the fire would be no good so I heaved the big chisel bar down, this was a huge length of steel about an inch and a half in diameter and twelve feet long with a ring on the one end and the business end hammered into a chisel shape. The idea of using this was to drive it into the fire and slide it right down the bars to the front and lift the fire to allow air underneath. Normally this woke up the deadest of fires and the effort needed was well worth while. Not today though, the fire stayed as stubborn as ever. Right, I thought, try another method, pile a lot in there, I've got nothing to lose. Steam pressure was falling, the station stops helped very little to recover. The pile I threw in refused to burn staying as a black mass.

By the time we arrived at Bramley the steam was back to 100 psi and the boiler water low. Although we had only five on I couldn't see us ever getting up the bank to Basingstoke.

'We're in a fine state now, Arthur. I don't see how we can make it up the bank and staying here won't help, it won't make any steam at all. Don't know what to make of it.'

The old gentleman in his calm way said, 'We can but try, 'erbie, we'll get the Southern to take the train forward from Basingstoke.'

With that in mind we struggled on, my heart not being in my work for once. I didn't mind slogging providing there was some result or at least a chance. Sadly I tried and was surprised to arrive safely at Basingstoke.

Arthur left and went over to the supervisor to ask for another loco to take the train on. In the meantime I got on the back of the tender and shovelled good coal forward. This sort of fire was not much to hope for in getting a start with it but I tried. For some time it failed to show any sign of burning. I considered there might be some sort of fault with the blast on the fire and in desperation looked in the smokebox end. I opened the door just as Arthur returned. As soon as air entered the smokebox the anthracite gasses in there ignited and a huge ball of flame came out missing me by inches. From the platform a voice said, 'Shut that door up, 'erbie, you'll get yourself singed.'

'Are they getting another one out?' I asked.

'No, but we can go to shed for coal.'

'I've shovelled some forward now, mate, if that does the trick we'll see if we can manage. It'll be easier than going in for coal.' While we stood there a boat train was diverted on to the local line making us unpopular. When a steam loco stopped for steam the poor fireman always got the blame, particularly from those that didn't understand. It took about twenty minutes before we were able to take a chance on leaving, bearing in mind that there was only the few miles of rising gradient before a long run downhill.

We finally arrived at Portsmouth very late and in Fratton shed Arthur put his foot down and refused to return until they gave us some of their better coal. The next day we heard that we were not alone with our troubles, all the locos coaled from the same wagon met a similar fate. We were the only loco not to come off its train.

I doubt if any of the other firemen had experienced coke as well.

The Henley branch was an eye-opener to me. Until then I had worked only on branches that went somewhere, as it were; even though they were old-fashioned they were interesting. The Henley branch was only four and a half miles long with two intermediate stops. We worked it on a Sunday afternoon with a 61xx and three coaches. Leaving from the bay at Twyford we stopped first at Wargrave, then Shiplake and on to Henley. After the passengers had alighted we had to shove the train back along the platform, unhook the loco and run forward over the points to crossover and run round the other end of the train, then recouple and push back in for passengers to board and away again to stop at each station to Twyford. At Twyford we went through the same ritual and set forth again. The day's work consisted of eight trips in each direction with sometimes an extra one thrown in if a connecting service was late at night.

I would rather by far have worked the 'hard hitters', they were at least straightforward. This branch, apart from its pleasant scenery, had little to commend it.

The other Southern route which I enjoyed very much was from Reading Southern station to Redhill. This train was normally worked with a 43xx; the route was too restricted to use anything larger, cylinder clearance at the platforms was, I believe, the main reason. The loco size mattered little because the train was usually a fixed three-coach set of a vintage belonging to one of the old companies before grouping, usually a South Eastern & Chatham Railway 'birdcage' set. These sets had a guard's van each end with a little lookout window; inside the van had a raised platform where the guard rode and from his seat up there he could see over the top of the train and keep a lookout for the signals. He had a certain responsibility for seeing them as the train passed. The whole train weighed only 84 tons, quite a light weight for our loco.

Leaving Reading Southern at 6.50 a.m. we stopped all stations to Redhill and unhooked to turn in the shed on the vacuum-operated table and, as usual on these turns, hung about for two hours before returning.

The occasional excursion through to Bournemouth gave us a day out. Leave Reading, stop at Basingstoke and then carry on to Eastleigh to take a conductor on board for the rest of the way where Arthur didn't know the road. One particular day a very young driver came to take over. He started from Eastleigh as if he hadn't a minute to spare, regulator almost wide open. He didn't have much idea of how to use the lever for cut-off either. We hadn't gone far before Arthur moved in.

'Come on, out of the way, you can't work an engine like that.'

Elbowing the young man away he closed the regulator down quite a bit and wound the lever up to almost full cut-off.

The young driver said, 'That's no use, this little thing won't keep time, it's not big enough.'

'Never mind that, your not working it in that way.'

'We'll never make the running time to Southampton Central, it's only fifteen minutes.'

'Then we'll have to lose some and make it up later,' said Arthur.

We left Southampton Central station in fine style and once again Arthur said his piece before we settled down to steady running.

The conductor was afraid the loco wasn't man enough for the job and kept making remarks about having a job to get up the banks. He was unaware that Arthur had been over this route and did have a little idea of what it was like.

'If we get stopped at the bottom of the next bank we'll never get up the other side,' said the conductor.

We almost came to a stop at the bottom but before he had a chance to expound his theories Arthur stepped in again and quietly explained, 'I have got a little knowledge over here, do as I tell you and we'll be all right.'

The young man, younger than me by the way, carried on as instructed and was greatly surprised to see how easily we went over the top.

'Sorry, gents,' he said. 'This is a much stronger loco than I thought.'

It was 4920 *Dumbleton Hall*, one of the best of this class. I suppose one can understand his fears when the Southern locos which were expected to work twelve coaches on this route were considerably larger.

We took the empty train down to Hamworthy sidings and back to Bournemouth shed. The shed at the back of the station always gave me the impression that it was out in the road. After settling the loco we had hours to spare before the return so spent some of it on the beach, not suitably attired for that kind of thing in overalls.

We returned and took our loco light down the rather steep bank to fetch the train back. This time we had a different conductor, although young he said he had some experience of these locos. Leaving Hamworthy we were stopped at Poole by the signalman to ask if we needed a banker. There were three level-crossings at Poole and the length of our train covered them all, traffic was piling up while everyone was trying to work out the loading. In the end Arthur said, 'Put the banker on. It can't be wrong.'

'Right, pull up,' the signalman said. 'I'll get him out behind.' Presently the banker blew up and away we went. The conductor pointed out that it was rather stiff and made a definite effort. Half-way up I looked back out of curiosity and saw the banker, a little tanky puffing along about two coach-lengths behind; we had left him short of steam. Not enough to get up on his own let alone assist us. Always plenty of interest if you looked for it.

I felt sorry for Arthur one day when we became derailed at Basingstoke with the loco. Having worked over in the evening we waited for a train to arrive in the bay. We took a box van off the rear to shunt it into the bay siding with the intention of then returning to the train to work it back at 10.30. This was a regular shunt and usually it was carried out with clockwork precision. On this particular night we pulled back over the points ready to shunt but the signalman decided to cross another train in front of us before letting us shunt. He closed the trap points and signalled the other train. The shunter didn't look at the ground signal, he had seen all the movements made by the signalman and assumed that on completion the route was set for us and called us ahead. Unfortunately from the footplate we were unable to see the signal ourselves. Arthur opened up and we went ahead, straight through the open trap points and off the road with van and loco finishing up in a very awkward place and being lucky to stop the other train. At that time we had a young 'whizz kid' superintendent who insisted that Arthur should be held responsible. Under no stretch of the imagination should this have been so but Arthur accepted it philosophically saying that someone else would have to take the blame if he didn't.

'We know it wasn't me, 'erbie,' was his only comment.

I had an interesting night with him in thick fog once. We had worked up to Paddington in the late afternoon and turned to work the 11.3 down semi fast to Slough and all stations to Reading, arriving at 12.3.

About 10.50 we left the sidings to join our train in number seven platform. Even as we moved the fog was coming down at an alarming rate. The colour light signals on the ground were a blessing with their indicators to guide us. By the time we had travelled the few hundred yards into the station the fog had developed so thick and quickly that it wasn't possible to see the end of the tender. The big lights hanging from the roof gave an oasis of light where they hung but the lights themselves were not visible. We knew that normally we would have seven on and knew where to expect to find them but to chance that was asking for trouble. For safety's sake I walked along at the end of the tender calling out to Arthur to guide him back on to the train.

This was a real 'pea-souper', I had never seen one like this before, it was yellow and got in my eyes making them sting; as is known now it was more smoke than fog hence the coined name 'smog'.

To our surprise we were signalled away and left right time. As is normal we were intending to rely on the Automatic Train Control to assist us. Without any worries we departed with this aid and the bright colour light signals as far as Southall. Our dreams were soon shattered, every distant signal was at caution and every home signal at danger. The distant at caution gave us the siren as a warning, it was up to us then to look out for the stop signal. That was all very fine but we couldn't see as far as the chimney. It was totally impossible to stop with the loco the right side of the signal. We both looked out and craned our necks but each time we saw a red light it was too late and we passed it by a small margin, often finding it near the cab. Each time we set back to be inside the signal but this in turn caused the problem of not being able to see it, I either had to wait near it or go to the signalbox. This was dangerous if I had to cross any running lines, not being able to see and sound being deadened by the fog made the journey hazardous. In a normal fog the light from these intense signals penetrated to at least give some colour in the gloom but not in this at this range. We couldn't understand why we were being stopped so much, the last train preceding us had left eighteen minutes before us but still we stopped, ten minutes here, fifteen there and even thirty in one place. At our first stop at Ealing Broadway a porter came forward to give us 'Right away': 'It's all right to go, driver, the guard's in his van.'

In the first hour we had covered three miles to Old Oak Common; our progress after was not very spectacular. Eventually a signalman turned us out on to the main line and we were able to get some sort of movement. The fog thinned as we got farther away from London but it stayed rather thick even for an ordinary fog. Towards Slough we were able to run something like normal speed and eventually arrived at Reading at quarter to four in the morning, getting close on four hours late. A 'smog' was unique, it was almost tangible, one could see it, taste it, smell it and feel its effect in the atmosphere. The only sense that didn't register was sound and that worked in reverse: there was deathly silence.

Reading at this time had only two trains of any character: one called the 'Continental', a train which started on the Southern from places such as Brighton and Hastings. Such trains joined together at Redhill and came to Reading on to the Western where we changed locos to work forward as far as Oxford. Not much of a run, twenty-eight miles, but at least with a 'Castle'.

The other and more satisfying train was up from Westbury with the Weymouth. We had arrived there after working a stopper down, we turned and picked up several more coaches including a dining car and worked up at 10.50. We stopped at Lavington at the foot of the bank and found it was a fair slog getting away on the bank but nowhere near as rough as Honeybourne. Stopping at Hungerford and Newbury made it quite a simple job. It brought back memories of my days at Worcester with the wind in my face as we ran across the country; memories of the telegraph poles skipping past and the sagging wires dipping and rising to every post in a rhythm of their own. Glancing through the gangway as I bent to shovel and spotting the mile posts measuring our progress at barely over a mile a minute but thinking we were racing along much faster. The splendid mad dash down the bank and satisfaction at the end of the day. This was a poor substitute.

Arthur had a son cleaning, every now and then he would finish work at two o'clock, have a rest and come back to the station to have a ride with us on a stopper all stations to Savernake and back. This train always had a 61xx, a 2–6–2T, with five on. I was expected to teach young Pete the arts of firing, he was a strapping lad quite capable of the work involved and after only a few trips he was able to take over and managed quite well. As soon as Arthur was sure of him he stood aside and I did the driving. A good deal I thought: Pete learned firing and I got some valuable practice in under the watchful eye of Arthur. The practice I had been lucky enough to have with Bert and Harold at Didcot was being well supplemented with passenger runs.

Soon after this Arthur was taken off the main line and put to work on the pilots, his main work being on the diesels where he was not overworked. Before he went he gave some very sound advice to me.

'I know you don't need it, 'erbie, but to be successful as a driver you have to look after yourself all the time. Don't dash about in the shed and sidings, there's plenty of room for that on the main line. There are no medals for pile-ups.'

I can say that I always tried to heed that sound advice.

Through my firing days I can say that I was privileged to work with some of the best mates one could wish for. Even my old mate at Didcot bashing the engine like he did had his place in my education. The different ways of doing the same job came through, the attitudes of the men varied with each mate, every new one having to be analysed to be able to work in harmony. My simple principle was to do my job to the best of my ability and to provide steam as required, keep the footplate clean and to make the driver's work as straightforward as possible by assisting him as well as I could. This way he couldn't really carp on at me, we had to make a good relationship.

When Arthur left I was once again fortunate in getting another good mate, George Moss. George was another man with whom I had never worked before. He spent the usual time alloted to learn the routes for the link and joined me.

'I've learned the roads but I haven't bothered to study the turns. You'll know them, won't you?' he asked.

'I've been in the link nearly two years now, George, I've got it all sorted out. I know all the roads well if it's any help.'

'I was hoping you would, some of these routes are new to me, it's good to have someone to rely on.'

Our first day together was on the simple 6.50 to Redhill. My mind went back to the day I first went over there. The road was completely new to me but in my favour was the very light train and a very lively and able driver, a dapper little man, enthusiastic and ready to help in any way. We left Reading in fine weather but after leaving Guildford it became quite foggy. I was perfectly happy when I could see the line ahead and the stations looming up; it was easy to do what bit there was. In the fog I managed as well as I could and at the same time tried to keep an eye through the window for signals. This route being Southern was not equipped with ATC and all the signals were placed on the left, convenient for their left-hand-drive locos. We had just risen up a bank and I put the shovel down after splashing a few on and looked forward through the window to see a very short signal looming up at us in the 'On' position. Without hesitation I responded in a natural reflex manner. 'One on, mate,' I called out. He shut off and braked in one action. The train was not running much more than 30 mph and the good brakes on the Southern stock stopped us quickly.

The driver looked at me as if ashamed and said, 'Thank God you spotted that one, mate. I'd forgotten all about it, missed the distant in this fog. There's a telephone on the signal, I'll go back and have a word with the signalman. You stay here, it was my fault.'

I felt alone in a strange world while the driver went back to the Intermediate block signal. After a very short time he returned with apologies from the signalman.

'He wanted to take the blame, said it was his fault, he had the road for us but had forgotten to pull off. He sends his thanks to you.'

Passing his box on the way back friendly waves were exchanged.

The next day the driver insisted that I did the driving to repay me for my valuable assistance.

My new mate George was more portly than any of my previous mates, a quiet man with a confident manner. Through his whole railway career he had devoted himself to the railway 'First Aid' movement. He was a man of high regard, did a lot of good work. Often he would desert me to carry out first-aid duties. In return he insisted on doing at least one day firing a week on the lighter work. I always prepared the loco and he took over to go off shed. On turns where we finished our day's work by taking an engine to shed the fire had to be run down. George wasn't able to manage the pricker to rake the fire over so I swapped back to do heavy work.

Once again I had been fortunate with my mates, another chance to learn my future job under the guidance of a good tutor.

Days passed without incident, there was very little else for me in the way of experience unless I were to change depots again. Perhaps the only trip of special note with George was when we were booked to return from Redhill with a fast through to Banbury instead of the usual stopper. A 43xx 'Mogul' with ten on was a tall order, running non-stop to Banbury was about ten miles farther than the trooper with the coke, at least on this occasion the coal was good. George was a wily character and worked out that it was to our own advantage to arrive at Banbury about ten minutes early. The mileage bonus we received had to be worked within our eight hours on duty. By arriving early we would be able to get an earlier train back and also get extra pay for travelling home passenger after completing mileage.

'What do you think of that?' asked George.

'Are there any snags in it?' I asked.

'The trouble is getting out on to our main line at Reading, if we can get there five minutes early they'll probably let us go. The rest is plain sailing then.'

'All right, George, let's have a go. It's a long time since I had a challenge.'

The Redhill route is not an easy one at the best of times with a heavy train. There are plenty of rather severe banks and in most cases not much chance to have a run at them. One particular steep one from Dorking to Gomshall took all we could give at the best of times to get over the top. At the very summit a bridge crossed the line which was known to all who worked there as 'Welcome' bridge. It could not have been better named, particularly on this day. For some reason the loco went duff on the bank and we struggled. Our hopes of a spectacular run seemed dashed but just as it had jibbed up the bank it made exceptional progress on the flat. We managed so well that George's plans worked out to the minute. A non-stop run through to Banbury was achieved, quite a feat with this type of loco. I suppose this was my last bit of glory as a fireman. The rest of the time drifted by until I noticed that the new promotion system gave me a chance to apply for a vacancy as a driver and get promotion earlier than I would have expected normally. I felt this was worth exploring.

SEVEN

Problems of a young driver

SINCE NATIONALISATION in 1948 nothing much had changed to affect the day-to-day working of the footplate men. Secondary depots such as ours hardly knew it had taken place except for the changes in the promotion system. Instead of being placed at a depot by Swindon men were required to apply for promotion to the depot of their choice, the options being advertised monthly on a vacancy list. The main difference which affected all men from all regions was the opportunity to move to any depot of their choice anywhere in the country, providing they were the senior applicant or were prepared to wait until they were. There were several senior men to me at Reading who were reluctant to move, worried about the time it would take to return to their homes again. They had not read the small print which allowed a man to register his application for an automatic return when he became senior.

I spotted this and duly completed an application form; the chief was surprised that it hadn't been spotted before. Making my first option Reading and second Southall I automatically registered myself for a return when my time came and also filled a vacancy at Southall. There was one major difference: no longer could a man wander about from depot to depot as I had done. There was to be only one move in a lifetime except for promotion.

After what could only be described as sixteen years as an apprentice doing cleaning and firing I was finally appointed driver at Southall on 30 October 1952.

The first two weeks were spent learning routes which I had never seen before such as the local branch lines. I well remember pairing up with Tommy Smith – 'Crackers' they called him – a man who was appointed with me. By working together it passed the time away quicker and his congenial company made the days more relaxed. We were unfortunate to have arrived at a time of rather thick fog. I found it most awkward trying to learn something I couldn't see. The branches to Staines, Uxbridge and Brentford needed our attention and the yards at Acton and Greenford.

Taking on my responsibilities after two weeks in the yard at Southall was a new experience. The boot was on the other foot, my mate was almost as green as myself. He was a young lad away from home, never did any cleaning to get to know anything about firing, needed to be helped all the time. My thoughts were of my own first days and the harsh treatment I suffered at the hands of grumpy old men. Remembering those days made me give him every bit of help I could. I had started by bending to the drivers' whims and now here I was bending back again to the firemen's.

Most of my work was on shunting duties in the various yards mentioned; taking a loco to or from one of the yards was the only relaxation from continuous shunting.

Going down to Brentford docks was a bit of a tricky job especially to the uninitiated such as me. The morning turn started with preparing a 57xx class pannier tank and working a train from the yard down the bank to the docks. Sixty-five 10-ton wagons of coal was the stipulated maximum load. I'm certain that Jack the guard couldn't count, a good many drivers found themselves running out of hand. The branch fell but not too steeply as far as Brentford town sidings then levelled out until it passed over the bridge across the A4 Great West Road and then it fell very sharply towards the dock sidings. The intention was to stop at the shunters' cabin before entering the yard, sometimes when the load got out of hand it pushed against the brake with no hope at all of stopping. The driver, realising that he was in trouble, blew his brake whistle to draw the shunters' attention to his plight. They came racing to the rescue by turning the points to the longest empty road to allow the train to run itself out. At the end of all the roads there were stop blocks and beyond that the river Thames down a 30 ft bank. Whenever the brake whistle was heard anyone in the vicinity watched the drama to see if someone other than themselves was going to end up in the river. Fortunately the quickness of the shunters prevented this from ever happening. I suppose I was lucky, Jack did overload me once and I got away with it by running past only a matter of yards. The brake whistle mentioned was an extra whistle fitted only to GW locos as an additional safeguard. If a driver was in this sort of trouble or even if he needed to stop another driver for any reason he blew it. Any driver hearing it would automatically look out and stop if it applied to him. It must have saved many bumps.

The night turn at Acton was a snip: prepare the loco and run light to the yard, shunt for about two hours then go light to West Ealing and bed down for at least three hours waiting for the shunters to deal with the milk trains. I found no trouble to rest my eyes, one of my young mates got restless and unknown to me went for a walk. I knew nothing of this until a voice below, accompanied by the rattling of the cab door, shouted 'Is this your mate?'

A bit startled at being awakened I looked over the side to see two men in the darkness. 'Who are you?' I asked.

Without answering my question the repeated query was called out again.

I looked over to my mate's side and saw he was missing. 'I'd like to know who you are and who are you talking about. I can't see anyone.' With that I shone my torch down to pick out two policemen and my poor young mate cowering at the back of the bunker. 'Yes, that's my mate. What are you doing here?'

'Why don't you look after him? He's caused us a lot of trouble tonight.'

'Come up here, let's sort this out,' I said.

The two constables climbed up to explain that they had spent an hour watching him strolling up and down Ealing Broadway looking in various radio and television shop windows, thinking he was a persistent burglar they were after. My silly mate refused to tell them his name but they did come to the conclusion that he might belong with my loco. He was lucky not to have been taken in. After a cup of tea all was well.

Greenford was as near to the old-fashioned railway shunting as I got to in this area. The numerous factories all had their own private sidings and each had to be visited daily in order to take wagons in and out rather than shunt them. I personally found this to be of great interest, so often we waited for wagons and I used this time to explore such factories as the bath works to watch the making of an iron bath from start to finish, or the glass bottle manufacturers turning out their products.

A week of shunting at West Ealing on the late turn was enough to make any man weary, it was six days of real hard slogging. The young firemen were not able to assist with the work, not only because they were so inexperienced but because we normally had one of the 94xx 0-6-0 pannier tanks for the job. They had the same-size cylinders as the 22xx 0-6-0 but smaller wheels giving them an improved tractive effort. Although not designed as a mixed-traffic loco they did quite well on both types. Unfortunately for the driver the reversing lever wasn't balanced as well as it should have been and the pull into reverse was far too heavy for the immature young men. A whole day was spent heaving away and by the time we went to shed I felt very weary, worse than firing on the 'runners'.

I rotated round these sort of turns for nearly two years until I moved up to the next link. There was still some shunting work to do but also a little local train work. As with firing I was working my way up through all the mundane chores gradually getting to know more as I went. The driving I had been allowed to do with some of my mates helped me no end, I had an enormous advantage over those that were unlucky and didn't get the same chance. I had to face the fact though that it was different. While I have already stated that I was using the driver's confidence when they let me drive it was all down to me now. I needed this gradual progress just as much as anyone else.

I welcomed the trip via Greenford to High Wycombe shunting at Ruislip, Denham and Beaconsfield on the way. Much the same as the 'Fly' from Didcot but under better conditions: no war, no overtime.

There were other similar trips to Slough and one where we went light to West Drayton to work a train to Acton yard and back to Southall for another one to Acton.

The job was always worked with a 57xx pannier tank, the best loco ever built for shunting. Having just over half the tractive effort of a 'King', 57xx pannier tanks were fitted with a steam/vacuum combination brake the same as the rest of the shunting fleet – vacuum never being used unless they were needed to move vacuum stock.

One Saturday afternoon I was working up from West Drayton. My fireman was an efficient lad and we had plenty of steam. I had no difficulty at all in reaching 25 mph with the train of forty-five 10-tonners of coal. The road was clear ahead and the distant off for Hayes; running bunker first I had a good clear vision ahead. As we passed through the bridge approaching the platform I blew the whistle in the usual way and to my horror there were three men trundling one of the heavy four-wheeled platform barrows over the crossing at the other end of the station. I reacted quickly, shut off steam, put the brake on fully and even reversed the lever in what I knew was a vain attempt to stop. The steam brake always takes a little time to warm up, something we didn't have.

Fortunately the men scattered in all directions just as we were about to collide with the barrow. Still doing at least 15 mph we caught it with the bunker end on the fireman's side. The life guard did its job and deflected the barrow away to the offside on to the down relief line right outside the signalbox. The signalman came rushing to the window.

I shouted up to him: 'Stop all trains on the down relief.'

He darted back into his box and soon returned. 'It's all right, mate, everything's quite safe.'

I looked round for the men who were pulling the barrow and found three very frightened men looking pale and bemused.

'Are you all right? None of you hurt at all?'

They were almost too shaken to give a reasonable answer. Just then the station master came along, more concerned about the men than the damage. He rustled up some staff to gather up the debris from the shattered barrow while I checked round the loco for any possible damage. The life guard was pushed back a little and the injector waste water pipe attached to the bottom step was bent round. I turned to the waiting station master looking anxiously at me.

'I can cover up my damage if you can cover the broken barrow,' I said.

'That's good of you, I don't think these men need any more said to them. Are you sure you can cover up?'

'I reckon it'll be all right. Just tell the signalman and everybody that it didn't happen.'

I had made an effort to knock the pipe back to its proper position and thought it would do until I could get to shed. We resumed our journey towards Acton. We hadn't gone far when there was a crunch on the offside of the loco.

'What's that, mate?' I asked.

He looked over the side. 'I don't know, can't see anything.'

I had asked the signalman to turn me into the yard at Southall to see if I could get something done about the damaged pipe. As we slowly crossed over the points I asked my mate to look out to see if the pipe that was sticking out would clear the 'dummy' ground signal.

He studied it carefully and said 'Yes, it's clear, mate,' and in the same breath 'Whoa, it's going to hit it.'

Too late, another damaged 'dummy' to my credit.

In the yard I called up the signalman to say that we had hit the two ground signals.

'Hang on a minute, mate.'

After a few minutes he came back and said, 'I don't know what you're talking about, driver, it hasn't happened.'

With that we went to shed and a friendly fitter changed the offending pipe. After that there was no need to get anyone into trouble over something that was never likely to occur again.

It seemed that my footplate career was destined to be studded with incidents and none of them my fault. This particular fireman, although excellent, seemed to be with me whenever I had an accident.

One morning we went off shed with a 14xx 0–4–2T Auto loco and picked up the two trailers to run light to West Drayton to work the Staines branch. It was 23 December 1953 and the morning was very foggy, so bad in fact that I had a job to see past the chimney. On these locos the forward vision was excellent and as I pulled down the platform on the main line I searched for the new colour light signal, gradually some red glowed in the fog. I started to apply the brake and as I did so I saw what I thought was a red light in front of me. The brake went on fully. As I stopped a red light appeared again and receded into the fog. I gathered immediately that a loco had been standing at the signal as I approached and quite by chance it was signalled away and moved off just as I was about to hit it. I quietly pulled up to the signal. My fireman, who was quite unaware of what had happened, asked, 'Shall I go up to the box, mate?'

'No, you carry on clearing up here. I'll go up, I want to see him myself.'

I entered the box to find the signalman staring at me with a perplexed look. 'Where have you come from, mate?' he asked.

'I'm on this Auto on the down main.'

'You can't be, I haven't accepted you.' At the same time he looked at his instruments. 'Good heavens, you are. Whatever's he up to letting you down here. He's got two in a section.' He rang up the signalman the other end who had managed to make the error. 'Do you know that you've just put two in the section?'

The phone was clear and I heard the reply: 'Don't be stupid. How could I?'

'Now don't be stupid yourself, calm down while I sort this out. You may as well admit it, there's no way out.'

The signalman turned to me. 'What's your mate like? Does he know what's happened?'

'My mate doesn't matter, he's the fireman. He has no idea what happened, so forget him.'

The signalman turned to me full of apologies. 'I'm ever so sorry, driver, I thought you were the fireman, you look too young. I thought I hadn't seen you around.'

'That's all right. I don't mind that sort of mistake.'

He returned to the other signalman and explained that it was me in the box.

I heard the reply. 'What's he going to do about it? If he reports this I'll get the sack.'

Before I could be asked, I said, 'If no one else knows about what has happened then it hasn't happened.'

'Do you mean that you're going to forget it?'

'In this fog how could I have seen anything?'

I had quickly considered that if all was well why should I make a fuss and lose a man his job a few days before Christmas.

Over the phone I heard, 'Tell that driver when he comes back I'll have the biggest cigar for him he's ever seen.'

To the signalman I was with I said, 'Tell him to forget it and if he buys a cigar smoke it in celebration.'

I know I shouldn't have done that but I felt good at not having a collision.

I had worked the Auto cars as a fireman at Worcester and felt reasonably confident. My education came the hard way on my first day working the Staines branch. All was well going over loco leading. After changing ends at Staines and making sure my mate understood his responsibilities and instructing him on how to work the reverser to control the valve cut-off we left and climbed the stiff rise up over the Southern Railway bridge before levelling out to stop at Yoeveney Halt. The guard knew I was new to the job and casually came through to my vestibule end.

'The regular drivers normally shut off here,' he said.

I was deceived by the totally different outlook from the front end, no boiler to look along. The speed seemed to be so slow.

'You're leaving the brake too late,' he then added.

I had left it a bit late, not as bad as he suggested but

nevertheless enough to see the little Halt go slipping by with one of the two cars off the platform.

'I wish you'd spoken a bit earlier, guard. Thanks anyhow, that won't happen again.'

Shortly after I was on the branch again with a young but very efficient fireman. He had never worked an Auto before and it was very foggy. The day's work turned out to be disastrous. Because of the fog we arrived too late at West Drayton to run the first trip. The second was a bit of a nightmare. Not too much trouble finding our way to Staines, it was the return that caused the problems. Our first stop was at Poyle Halt on this trip. We had finished with the passengers and the guard had given me 'Right Away'. The inside of the cab was running with water from a leaking steam-heating pipe so I had the side window open. I was about to open the regulator when I heard someone running along the ballast. Thinking it was a passenger running to catch the train I waited. To my horror it was my fireman.

'What on earth are you doing leaving the footplate?' I asked.

'We can't go yet, there's no water in the boiler.'

'Why didn't you put the brake on before you left? You were nearly left behind.' To satisfy him I went back to see for myself. Apparently the pull up the bank from Staines had started the boiler priming and throwing water out with the exhaust steam.

'I didn't know what to do,' he said.

'Never mind. You did the right thing but if ever you need to leave the footplate again for goodness sake put the brake on.'

That trip completed we returned for the final one, which went well until we asked to pull towards the sidings to take water before running empty to Southall. The signalman authorised us to move up for water saying it was all right to come back into the platform when we were ready. I went back to the vestibule end while my mate took control of the loco to pull back into the station. Before moving I shouted up to the signalman, 'Is it all right to come back into the platform now?'

Although it was a dark winter night and thick fog I could make out his form at the window.

'All right to come back,' he said as he waved his arm.

My mate started to move back inside the signal ready to depart for home. The guard and I were in the vestibule and no sooner had the train started to move than there was an almighty clatter underneath accompanied by violent rocking of the car. I applied the brake fully. We came to a stand at a very awkward angle, the one bogie beneath us derailed. After a quick look round to see we were clear of all running roads I went to the signalbox. The signalman was quite surprised when I told him what had happened and looked at his levers.

'I know what I've done. I signalled you out on to the relief before you were back inside. It's my mistake, I shall have to answer for it.'

After some deliberation we decided to uncouple the derailed car and leave it while we ran to Southall with just the one. Because of the fog and the difficulty in getting the breakdown vans on the job the derailed trailer was left there for three days. Although I was not to blame I felt awful each time I saw it.

I was glad when that day's work was over.

The best Auto work was on the Windsor branch on a Sunday afternoon, tripping in and out many times. Quite a pleasant day's work.

At night we worked the staff trains with two trailers doing several trips between Paddington and West Drayton and also had some turns on the Uxbridge branch.

Southall probably had the biggest concentration of this type of work. It was all good experience.

After some local arguments about route knowledge I was allowed to work to Swindon. Some were of the opinion that a young driver should not stray far from the shed and local work; it took some time to convince people that my route knowledge was quite extensive.

Runs through to Swindon from Acton were a pleasure although they were mainly empty coal wagons trundling along loose coupled with only the loco brake to stop with. Austerity locos were very prominent at Southall – WD 2–8–0s from the Ministry of Supply. Very clumsy in all respects, not too easy to handle by Western men used to simple design. The left-hand drive and no ATC took some getting used to, that was without the brake which was of a strange design to us. The reverser was different and all the other little ancillaries were at odds to what we were used to. The cylinder lubricator looked as if it might blow up at any time, often bulging under pressure.

I worked one of these one Sunday morning with a fireman named Arthur Smith. We prepared the loco and ran light to North Acton via the Greenford loop. I ran into the sidings and on to the train or rather in to the train.

'You hit them a bit hard didn't you, mate?' asked Arthur.

'I did rather, the brake didn't seem to warm up in time. It's all right now though by the feel of it.'

With only forty-eight empty coal wagons on we set out for Swindon. Being Sunday there was very little to stop us and we ran quietly all the way to Reading down the main line. Reading East Main box crossed us over to the relief without stopping us. Normally these locos wouldn't run very well particularly when steam was shut off but this one was as free as one could wish for, perhaps it was because it had been having such a good long run. I cruised along down the relief to find the distant signal for the Intermediate block at Basildon at caution. I judged my shutting off point and applied the brake in the usual way.

'I wonder if the brake's going to be all right this time,' Arthur said.

'Why shouldn't it be. It needs time to warm up.'

'I don't reckon it worked properly at Acton. It wasn't your misjudgement.'

We watched the brake pressure gauge and to my surprise it didn't rise. I pulled the handle on fully but got no response. I snatched the handle on and off several times but to no avail, the brake would not go on. Arthur tried to coax it with a few taps with a spanner and still we rolled on towards the stop signal. The loco, which was normally sluggish, was rolling freely. Arthur exclaimed, 'Pull it into back gear, we'll never stop.'

'Too late,' I said. 'By the time I get this thing back we'll probably stop anyway. Might be a good idea if you put your handbrake on.'

That had little effect, the train slowly trundled past the signal eventually stopping with forty-five of the forty-eight wagons past the signal.

'Shall I go back to phone the signalman?' Arthur asked.

'No, I'd better go, we'll probably have to take the loco off if it won't work. You see if you can get it working while I'm gone.'

At the signal telephone the signalman blamed himself in the same way as the one on the Redhill road, saying he had forgotten to pull it off.

'There's no need to say anything about it, driver, everything will be all right.'

'I would like you to report the facts if you don't mind. I've had a brake failure which I must report. I can't let it go by, it's too serious.'

'All right then, I'll do as you say but I don't like doing it.'

I then told him of my intentions. 'When I get back to the loco if the brake won't work I'll go quietly to Goring and put the train in the siding and go to shed. If I've managed to get it working I'll carry on but don't forget to report it.'

Back at the loco Arthur was hitting it with the coal pick.

'Steady, Arthur, you'll break it altogether.'

'What are we going to do if it won't work?' he asked.

With a little cunning I eventually got the brake working normally. We toddled off to Goring to report that I intended to carry on and to reaffirm my intention of reporting the incident. I didn't experience any further trouble, all went well.

I had several turns where I worked this type of loco on what we called the Northern line. This was the line from London turning off at Old Oak Common to the north via Banbury. Our run was only as far as High Wycombe where we changed over footplates with a man from the Eastern Region to work back, either to Kensal Green gas works or to Southall gas works. Between them they had hundreds of wagons daily, nearly all brought in by these Austerity locos. They added another page to my book of experience.

The work in my link was quite varied and in general better than could be expected for a young driver. I enjoyed the opportunity to practise my skills on the main line even though the runs were of a limited nature. After three years I was getting restless for my return to Reading and watched with interest as one driver after another retired. When I was promoted I received a letter telling me there were twenty-one prior applicants, within a few weeks this was amended to twenty-nine. Eight drivers had been put back firing and would have to take their places first. It seemed a long haul back, I was in a rut, travelling every day to and from home. I had a room in the hostel, it was quite good but I found that I couldn't sleep there. My bed was not very far away so why not make my way home and enjoy the comfort? This unfortunately took an average of three hours a day on top of my working day, quite tedious particularly when I worked overtime. By now I was really looking forward to getting back although I knew that my work would not be so good for some time.

After three and a half years I eventually returned to Reading on 12 March 1956. The move back and being booked to learn the local routes for two weeks on regular days was out of this world. Every night in bed and office hours during the day was a different life to me.

Six of us were returned together so there was no shortage of company for the two weeks, after which the honeymoon was over. I was placed once again in a bottom link to start all over again shunting and with only a few little local trips to break the monotony. Several of the pilot locos in the yards were diesel shunters and quite a number of the drivers were in the link because of ill health or failing eyesight. Even then it was a large link and I anticipated some time before I got to the top. The general age of the men at the depot was rather high and they could be seen retiring at a quicker rate than in the past. The fact that I didn't stray far was no hardship, I had already exceeded my expectations of train working and the fact that I still retained my route knowledge to Paddington gave me the opportunity to cover a few spare trips on the stopping passengers. In all I was happy and contented to wait for the next link.

More than two years passed before my time came to move up to work to Swindon, Banbury, Westbury, London and Basingstoke. I'm unable to recall the name of my first mate but his image stands out well. He was of Welsh origin, well behaved and always cheerful. He liked his food rather and as a result was somewhat on the rotund side. I never knew whether he was too fat to bend down to shovel or whether he thought he could get away with being lazy with that as a pretence. Whatever the reason I was continually short of steam. It made me look back at my own firing career and to realise that my extra effort had a bearing on getting on so well with my mates. It's difficult to form a good working relationship with a chap that is for ever making the day's work more tedious even though his general manner was always pleasant.

This was where my previous experience driving for my mates as a fireman and my own responsibilities driving at Southall stood me in good stead. A newly appointed driver who had not been in this fortunate position would find it more difficult to take to his own work. While the driver can make or break a fireman the fireman can have quite an influence on the driver.

These small worries apart it was good to be rising in the ranks and to be considered a main line driver.

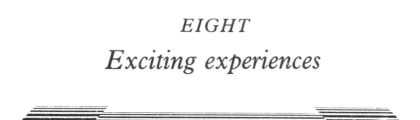

EIGHT

Exciting experiences

THE OPPORTUNITY had now arrived to put into practice the experience I had gained and to add to that experience by going further afield with heavier trains.

Until now I had never had the chance of working a freight train other than loose coupled, that is with the old-fashioned three-link wagon coupling slung over the hook of the next wagon. Trains fitted with through vacuum brakes were almost non-existent. Even trains with a proportion of their vehicles braked from the loco were scarce. Obviously where these trains ran they were booked to run at slightly faster speeds. The braked vehicles next to the loco had either a shorter link coupling or had the adjustable type as used on passenger stock. The rest of the train to the rear still had the loose couplings; a partly fitted train, as they were called, was quite different to handle from the point of view of braking. Most drivers were in the same situation as myself, having to learn the hard way. It's fair to say that I was quite fortunate with my mates who allowed me to drive fully fitted vacuum-braked trains in the way of passengers. Partially fitted goods were an entirely different matter, they needed to be handled with the utmost care. The extra brake force was capable of closing the rear of the train up to the front too quickly with the result that the guard often got thrown about his van and suffered injury. The fact that all partially fitted goods trains were inconsistent in their loading and also in the fitted head made each train different to handle, not that this didn't apply to the loose coupled trains also. If all trains were of equal loading, equal brake force and on the same gradients with the same loco, coal and fireman then the driver would have been able to acquire skills more readily. None of these norms existed, in fact not only each day but each train was different. In all my varied career I can say that no two days have ever been the same.

Passenger trains were much more consistent but drivers were nearing retiring age by the time they worked them regularly, not particularly needing all the experience gained from working freight trains. Between these two extremes lay years of often mundane work but it was here where skills were acquired, learning the value of the brake with various loads, assessing the running of the various trains on changing gradients, understanding the power of the many types of locos. There were very few locos which were fitted with speedometers and therefore drivers had the added difficulty of judging speed; it was only years of experience which enabled them to become reasonably adept. The various noises from the motion and the wheels on the rail joints with the ticking of the Great Western vacuum pump was a great asset but these needed to be used in conjunction with wheel sizes. In his early years a driver had little experience handling a freight train fitted with the vacuum brake, even a train with a braked head was a luxury. As he moved up in seniority these new experiences would follow, he relying on his memories of firing days to put his studies into practice. In fact driving skills were acquired working freight trains which were loose coupled with only the loco brake and some assistance from the rear. There was a noticeable rapport between these two men which combined to make the safe running of the train. The limitations imposed by the brake set the limits to the running speed, the driver being well aware that any excess would end up in disaster. To this end a driver is required to have a thorough knowledge of the route, every little undulation having a meaning and a consequence. The assistance of the fireman was always needed to apply the tender handbrake to 'buffer up' the train before the driver applied his power brake. This gave the firemen their first insight into the braking of freight trains. There were no professional instructors: only experience.

The route to Banbury provided quite a change with its gradients of varying severity, nothing serious but something different to think about. More often than not it was empty coal wagons for transfer to the Eastern Region at the junction and return with loaded coal. As I had done a lot of firing over this road as a fireman at Didcot it presented no problem, just another phase of learning.

There was an empty coal train I worked from Reading to Swindon with a difference. It started from the Low Level sidings on the Southern bank, because the siding could accommodate only forty-five wagons that was our load. The usual 43xx 2–6–0 was more than a match for this light train but to make up for this it was booked to run the forty-one miles in little over an hour. Taking into account the time to get them up the bank to the main line and get away, then the stopping time, the average speed running was just over 45 mph all the way – quite fast timing for coal empties but no trouble at all to bring the train to a stop. Almost the whole of the way was slightly rising, more a test of judgement when to shut off.

The other train at 10.10 in the morning was just a plodder, in and out of all the refuge loops taking three times as long to get there.

Whatever the service down the return was always different. The trains were nearly always well loaded, and in most cases with coal. Instead of pulling hard all the way the emphasis was on braking. Wherever a distant signal showed caution the brake was needed to hold the train back right up to the ultimate stop; quite different aspects with varying trains on different routes.

The train which called for a higher degree of skill on the part of both the fireman and driver was the 5.35 in the evening starting from the Scours Lane yard west of Reading. Most of the time when I worked this one I had the assistance of a first-class mate, Mick Bailey. He was only a slightly built young man but had the knack of firing and getting plenty of steam without seeming to exert himself. We could usually expect to have a 'Hall' class on this train. The load was limited to fifty-eight in length, that being the maximum the middle line at Swindon would hold to stand the train in clear.

The first time I worked it I knew what to expect in the way of urgency, every one that could was quite prepared to give advice on how fast to run. Even the guard added his when he gave me the loading.

'You know we're booked very fast on this one, Jack. If you can make it right time we get a good break at Swindon but if we run at all late we shall get put in somewhere for the express Dragon from Paddington to South Wales to pass. We're booked in front of him to Swindon station. He passes us there while you're taking water.'

I listened to all he had to say with interest, he was genuinely concerned about good timekeeping.

'How many vacuum fitted did you say we've got?'

'Twenty, that's a fair amount for the load.'

I turned to Mick. 'It looks like you've got some work to do if we're going to keep away from that Red Dragon, don't want him breathing fire down our necks.'

'It's all right with me. I'll bet you can't do it.'

I asked the guard, 'What are the chances?'

'Not very good, they won't let you run unless you're going pretty well.'

'Right, you tell the signalman we're ready and to give us the road. We'll see what we can do.'

The time came to leave; Mick exchanged hand signals with the guard and we were away. The train of fifty-eight moderately loaded wagons didn't present any difficulty. In no time we were running at the maximum permitted speed of 50 mph with all signals clear. At each of the possible points where we could be recessed for the Dragon to pass we watched and waited. Each time the appropriate distant was off I took stock of the time.

'How are you doing, Mick? Can I give it a bit more?'

'I'm all right. Don't know what you're hanging about for.'

Passing Challow, the check point for the divisional boundary we were just about right time.

'We'll do it, Mick, if we're given a chance.'

The gradient rose a little from here on but the momentum we had gained served us well. On we rolled with every hope of making it to Swindon. As we drew nearer the conjecture was whether they would let us run right into the middle line at the station or slip us into the goods loop at the transfer sidings. Approaching Swindon we were surprised to see first Highworth distant off, then the transfer followed by the station distant at caution. This sequence was what we needed to run straight in. At our best running time we were only booked three minutes in front of the Red Dragon which didn't allow for a steady run in, bearing in mind that the stop at the other end had to be precise enough to take water as well as stop the right side of the signal. This was where I could make a mess of all our effort by not judging my braking. It was hardly the best train on which to make my first attempt. We rolled down past the transfer where the supervisor stood at his doorway to wave and to see who was the madman on board, at least that was what he said later. I stopped more or less exactly where I wanted and, quite pleased with myself, got down to fill the tank. To my surprise the Red Dragon was running down the platform headed by one of the new 'Britannia' class Pacifics right on time.

The slightest delay with the freight and a signalman somewhere would be obliged to turn us inside to let the fast by.

After relief we were spare for the supervisor to use as he thought fit. In most cases he would ask, 'How are you for overtime?'

In general on this sort of turn there was no hurry to get home. Mick and I agreed that we might as well earn a little extra as go home to bed at just after midnight.

'We're good for twelve hours,' I would say.

Knowing this the supervisor picked out a train he wanted taken through to Acton at London or somewhere in that area. One night he asked, 'I've got a banana train coming up from Barry. Will you work it through to Acton for me?'

'Yes, that'll do us fine,' I replied.

We knew what this meant, one of the very rare fully fitted

vacuum-braked trains. The train duly arrived with a 'Hall' on the front and forty-five vans of bananas and a goods brake van on the rear. The guard said, 'See you at Acton,' as he left to go back to his van. Mick and I filled up and made ready before we left. At the time the weather was quite fair and we left satisfied of a good run through to Acton, probably non stop. The loco soon settled down to a steady rhythm, I sat on my seat with the regulator set and reverser in a high cut-off position cruising along watching Mick casually firing. Approaching Didcot the weather turned a bit misty.

'I hope this don't come up too thick,' said Mick. 'It might stop us going through.'

'It's not bad yet. Anyway why should it make any difference?'

'You know how everything gets stopped when it gets thick.'

'Nothing to worry about yet, mate, keep shovelling.'

Within a few miles the fog got thicker until when we got into the Thames valley it was very thick indeed. Unknown to us the fog had thickened here for some considerable time. Fog signalmen had been called out, at every distant we saw their hand lamps repeating the aspect shown by the signal. It was their duty to place a detonator on the line at the distant signal when it showed a caution aspect as an added precaution against the driver missing the signal, this was in addition to the ATC. When the signal changed to the clear position he would remove the detonator and show a green light or flag to the driver.

We were running along under clear signals even though the fog was exceptionally thick, there was no need to even think of reducing speed. Our only real concern was whether the road would be clear through Reading to allow us to run through to Acton. As we approached Reading first Tilehurst distant was off then Scours Lane with Reading West junction lower distant on Scours starter in the clear.

'Keep a good lookout for West Main distant, Mick. It should be off now we've had the others.'

I stood in my corner with my head near to the window peering to where I thought the distant would be although it was difficult to see beyond the chimney. I glanced at Mick, hanging over the side doing his best to assist but before he had a chance to say or do anything the home signal for West junction passed over the top of the chimney showing a red light followed instantly by the explosion of the fogman's detonator and then the signalman's emergency detonator. To add to the drama a shunting pilot in the yard was sounding its brake whistle, nothing whatever to do with the situation we were in, just coincidence but I was not to know that. Without hesitation I shut off steam, fully applied the brake regardless of consideration for the train or guard at the same time shouting to my mate, 'Hold on, Mick.'

Passing the West junction box I could just make out the signalman waving a red light to me. That only made matters worse as regards my fears. All sorts of things flashed through my mind in seconds. Was there a derailment in front of us which had occurred after we were signalled? Had a train broken away from its loco and got left in front? Mick darted about the footplate attempting to put an injector on to stop the boiler blowing off steam.

'For God's sake, leave it, Mick,' I said. 'Hold on tight somewhere. You never know where we're going to finish up.'

I was already hanging on to the upright rail at the side of the cab with both hands. The full emergency application on freight vehicles takes some time to be fully effective. It seemed ages before there was any response. The crossover points for the junction clattered as they passed underneath the wheels and the brake was now biting well. The tug of the train surged us both forward although we were hanging on tightly. Almost as quickly as the panic started it was over, the train came to a very quick stop and we were none the worse other than the shock of the experience.

'What do you reckon went wrong?' asked Mick.

'No idea, mate, never had one like that before. It wouldn't have been so bad if we could have seen in front.'

'I'd better go back to the box and find out what we're going to do now,' he said.

'That's right, mate, go back to the box. Be careful where you walk, get over to the side out of the way of any other train. Sign the book and stay in the box if necessary. I'll wait here until someone tells us what to do. If you can, will you go back to see if the guard's all right.'

Mick departed and left me with my thoughts. Where exactly are we I questioned myself? Unable to see anything I resorted to listening for sounds and came to the conclusion as to my whereabouts. I reckoned that from the time I had applied the brake the train had stopped in about its own length at approximately 50 mph. Very good by any standards but nowhere near good enough to allay my fears at the time. Mick was gone ages. The signalman agreed it was wise to check on the guard.

I sat alone, the one that should know what was happening was going to be the last to find out.

When Mick returned with the explanations it was a bit of an anti-climax. He said the signalman was sorry and had said, 'Tell your mate I'm sorry to scare you in this weather but Scours Lane thought he heard a "hot box" on your train and "belled" me "Stop and examine". I had no choice.'

'How's the guard? Did you go back to see him?'

'Yes he's all right, says he didn't realise what was happening. The brake went on and he rose in his seat then dropped down again without any jolting at all. He said he was afraid to come up in case we started away again and left him behind so he sat tight.'

After some delay an examiner checked the train and found the offending vehicle. An hour passed by the time it was removed from the train and we were ready to leave.

The yard inspector came across to us. 'Don't go away yet, driver. The control are sending relief out to you.'

It ended all the excitement, a fine run spoiled and a few hours' overtime lost. The fog was clearing too.

Mick and I worked well together, I always knew that I could rely on him. His ability as a fireman was without question so that when we worked the 1.15 in the morning freight from Reading West junction yard to Westbury I could rely on having a comfortable trip. Mick simply got on with his job without needing the slightest directive.

The job was made more interesting by always having a class 47xx loco, a 2–8–0 typical 'Churchward' design with the cut-away cab. It was quite capable of both heavy freight or fast passenger work as a standby in the heavy holiday season. Although it had a lot to commend it as a loco the cab let it down from the men's point of view. Apart from the poor cab the sides of the roof sloped down to clear the gauge and with the slightly higher footplate there wasn't much room to look out over the side without ducking low. Many men including myself have given their heads a severe blow by not thinking first. The driver's side had the extra disadvantage of the large reversing lever and rack in the way. Yet, despite these drawbacks, the loco was extremely capable of working our train. The load of sixty-eight mixed freight followed out of the yard and up round the rising gradient round to Reading West and fairly trotted away down to Newbury and beyond facing the pull up through Hungerford without flinching and the stiffer rise round Grafton curve to the summit at Savernake. From then on there was very little need for steam; Mick had worked his fire to perfection knowing that he would not need to put any more coal on for the last thirty miles' easy running.

One night as we ran smoothly over the top Mick was busy in his corner putting the shovel against the corner of the cab and padding the curved back with a big wad of cotton waste.

'What are you up to, mate?' I asked.

'I'm making myself comfortable, don't see why I should sit up on that seat while I can snooze down here.'

'You cheeky blighter, you can't do that. Who's going to look after the boiler?'

'You are, it won't need any for a long time. Goodnight.'

I felt quite lonely trundling through the night all alone. My first days of single manning, I suppose.

The run of sixty-five miles was booked two hours and three minutes, just comfortable with the type of train and a vacuum-fitted head.

A little later we occasionally had the 75000 'Standard' class 4–6–0 on the job. What a difference with the left-hand drive and no ATC. The different brake and reverser and all the trimmings in different places in the dark. Even Mick thought it wise to keep awake.

One Sunday morning working a mixed freight down this road with the late Johnny Bristow we were rolling gently down the bank beyond Patney considering our running time.

Johnny said, 'Don't want to get there too soon, mate, we're not booked at Westbury until after the passenger has gone, might as well take it easy.'

'You'd better wind the handbrake on a bit, John, we'll run too fast down here otherwise.'

John put the handbrake on, not a little but quite positively. We cruised gently down the bank looking across to Devizes castle standing on the edge of rising ground.

'Better ease the brake a little, John, we're coming to a stand.'

'You're not in a hurry, are you?' he asked as he released it rather too much.

I sat on the lever rack looking forward.

'Johnny, will you put the brake on again, please.'

'I wish you'd make up your mind,' he said.

'I wish you would and don't be long about it. There's a red flag in front of us.'

Without batting an eyelid he wound the brake on as hard as he could. I applied the vacuum, on the loco only this time, and we sat back waiting to see what was round the bend. Presently bang, bang, bang as we exploded the three warning detonators. The man with the red flag shouted as we passed 'They've got a rail out down the bank.'

Quite confident of stopping I sat back and waited. When we finally stopped we were in sight of the scene of operations and kept informed of happenings.

We had a guard at Reading who seemed afraid to refuse any extra loading. It was said of him that he would couple the yard stop blocks on as well if he could. One night with Mick he did the dirty on us. We took a train from Reading with his instructions to pick up some more at Newbury. The guard was in charge of the loading and we could only trust him to make certain we were not above the specified load for any route or loco.

'You've got thirty-six on now, picking up another thirty at Newbury making just a full load.'

Before we got to Newbury I had said to Mick, 'I hope they're a light lot to pick up, this train's already heavy enough.'

The loco was a spanking new 'Hall' only recently out of Swindon shops but the load was telling on it.

At Newbury I queried with the guard. 'Are you sure we haven't got a full load on now, they're very heavy.'

'No, you'll have a full load when we've picked these up.'

'I reckon we'll be overloaded, don't think we ought to take them.'

'I'm telling you, we won't be overloaded. We're picking them up.'

Without any option we loaded up and set off. The rise out of Newbury confirmed my fears, it took us ages to get under way. We struggled on and on with no hope of putting any off, there were no sidings about. The rise at Hungerford almost brought us to a stop and when we met the last bit of extra steep bank approaching Savernake the loco was absolutely flat out with the regulator wide open and the lever in full fore gear to get the utmost out of it. Mick had managed to keep a full head of steam and as we struggled round Grafton curve I said, 'We only need the wheels to slip now and we won't make it to the top.' I was dropping sand on the rails to try and avert it but to no avail, the loco slipped throwing masses of sparks into the night sky. I shut off to stop the slip and opened up immediately, knowing that such an action would most likely snatch the couplings and cause one to break. I didn't see what else I could do; if I pussyfooted about I was going to come to a stand for certain, if I broke away the guard could then answer for it. We kept going and it seemed we picked up a little speed.

'I wouldn't be surprised if the train's parted, Mick. We'll pull on to Savernake. Get the detonators out ready, if the back end's broken away they'll quite likely run back and come off the road at the "catch points". Be prepared to put them down outside the box.'

With the train going a little easier I was now convinced that this was the case and looked back anxiously to see if I could see the light on the side of the brake van. Just as I was about to stop at the signalbox the side light came into view a long way back. We hadn't broken away so I didn't stop. As soon as the train was over the top I shut off to run down the other side and for my first and only time ran all the way into Westbury with the train pushing me. I know that if there had been a rail out on the bank that night we would have gone across the fields. The guard must have known how guilty he was, he went the opposite way to us after relief to avoid us. His intentions may have been good but he was dangerous to have on the rear.

As a steam driver I can still recall one other serious incident. I worked the 8.15 evening freight from Reading to Worcester as far as Oxford. All the week I prepared my own loco for the train. On Saturday it was prepared for me to allow me to book on later because of a booked later return.

The driver preparing was a man of good standing, conscientious and reliable. When I arrived at the loco and he told me that all was well I willingly accepted his word and when he pointed out how good the brake was I was quite happy. The loco was 7909 *Heveningham Hall*, one of the 'modified Halls'. It was quite new and it looked as if we were in for a pleasant trip. We left the junction yard on time with a full load of sixty-five wagons and without any difficulty rolled along at between 25 and 30 mph. My mate on this occasion was 'Paddy' Walsh. He had a very sturdy build, capable of any amount of work – not that he needed to be on this particular train. I had the added interest of a speedometer on this loco and watched as it varied with the slight undulations. Soon after passing through Cholsey station it was on 28 mph; better shut off soon, I thought, we'll be able to run to Didcot.

Cruising through Moreton cutting I sighted the distant signal for Didcot at caution. Without a fitted vacuum head I said to

Paddy, 'Pull the handbrake on, mate, we've got it on.' He obliged and then at a suitable moment I carried on by applying the vacuum brake a little. Nothing much seemed to be happening so I made a stronger application, still no response. Then I applied the brake fully.

'Wind yours on as hard as you can, mate. This one doesn't seem to be much good.'

The train had got momentum and didn't seem to want to lose it, it rolled on and on getting nearer to the outer home signal for Didcot East box. Looking over to the main line I could see that a fast was signalled across in front of us to precede us to Oxford. At this particular time I could see no way of stopping clear of the junction and turned to Paddy.

'Get the red flags out, mate, and see if you can stop the fast down the main.'

With Paddy's full strength on the handbrake and the vacuum there was nothing left but to reverse the loco. Here I was again, unable to stop a train and this time in a situation likely to cause a collision. Reluctantly I put this lovely new loco into reverse and opened the regulator a little. The combination of my brake whistle, the red flag waved by Paddy and the driver's own observation of what was happening caused the driver of the fast to stop before he arrived at the junction. As it happened we had passed first the outer home signal and then the home by several yards but had fortunately stopped just clear of the crossover. I phoned the signalman to explain, the fast moved off and I set about finding out why I had suffered yet another brake failure. Most drivers don't get one in a lifetime but here I was on my second.

While my mate and I looked round it was starting to get dark and through the new type 'hopper' ashpan a fair amount of light shone through.

'There's something wrong here, mate. Will you go and get a flare lamp?'

With head down under the wheels I investigated and found that a firebar had dropped down and was poking out through the hopper which had trapped it against the brake rodding preventing it from working. As much as we tried we were unable to move it and asked to be allowed to run to Oxford at a reduced speed where we could take it to shed for attention.

Although some of the incidents I was involved in were quite unusual and may have been considered as reckless, I had a healthy regard for all possible eventualities and worked accordingly. I never took any chances by running too fast for my brake power and was always very observant. I like to think that it was my diligence that just kept me on the right side of trouble.

The little bit of practice I was fortunate to have with my old mate Arthur when he let me drive the 61xx 2–6–2Ts on the local stoppers now came in handy. Having retained my route knowledge to Paddington I occasionally got booked on the same train in my own right as a driver when I was spare. Two trips to Paddington for a day's work was quite enough, stopping all stations. Preparing the loco, making sixty stops, running round the train twice at Paddington and once at Reading, taking water several times and standing up for the whole of the day in the close proximity of the fire made for tiring and tedious work, particularly six days at a stretch. After a week on a turn like this one felt quite professional at braking.

The only passenger train of any consequence in my link was the 7.46 a.m. from Henley to Paddington. It was a train where everyone reckoned to be on their toes. The passengers were mainly season-ticket holders with a fair number of first class passengers. They all seemed to think they had the right to complain at the slightest thing without knowing what they were talking about. The day started with preparing a 'Hall' and taking it light to Henley and being there in good time to heat the train in winter.

The run across the branch with ten on was not easy, stopping at stations too short for the train and booked rather hard as well. From Twyford there was a sharp dash up the relief line to cross over at Ruscombe and get to Maidenhead as quickly as possible. This was where the unusual skill was needed. Every passenger had their own seat and stood on the platform in the exact position where they thought their door should stop. As the train ran in they put their hands out to open the doors and if the door handle didn't come to rest in their hand they reported the driver for stopping in the wrong place! None of them had any idea of the difficulty stopping when it was required to run in at high speed to maintain time. Thirty minutes from Maidenhead to Paddington seems a long time today but on that train it represented one of the maddest dashes I can remember. The time getting up to speed and the time taken braking down to stop left little spare in between, at least 75 mph was required to run right time. Late arrival by a few minutes caused more concern and more complaints. In fact the driver was blamed regardless of whether he had adverse signals or not. This was quite noticeable from the condescending passengers who proffered a newspaper to the driver if he was right time but walked straight past if only a few minutes late, even in foggy weather as well. Of course, quite a few of them were Headquarters office boys who thought they knew.

My experiences had taken me through a demanding yet enjoyable footplate career but things were beginning to change. Firemen were leaving the job. Was it because of the often arduous work and the dirt or was it the unsocial hours at which it had to be done? Certainly they were more enlightened and perhaps they could foresee a future without the interest that I had relished. Either way the best of the older men seemed to be the ones leaving and the new recruits contained more than a fair share of indifferent lads. Difficulty was now arising in filling the vacancies, quite the opposite to when I joined when everyone clamoured for the footplate. The prospect of hard work just for the hope of becoming a driver in the distant future was not sufficient inducement. My own good mate Mick had gone and Paddy soon followed him, both saying they were fed up with the job. Girlfriends and wives probably had quite an influence in their decisions. Or was it those diesels looming up on the horizon making them reconsider? It was early days for the diesels. The 'diesel multiple unit' (DMU) sets as yet were in the distance up in the far Midlands and should not have had any influence but running in our area gas turbines were being experimented with. Number 18000 followed by 18100 were creating quite a stir with tales of their supremacy and how much time they could clip off the times on the West of England road.

I had become intrigued and on several occasions tried to get on board to have a look round but each time I met with the same rebuff. Even when one of these new locos was stationary, either the inspector in charge or the driver managed some excuse to prevent me from following my interest. It was true to say that at the time it was a special loco and needed the attention of a team of maintenance men both from BR and the makers. There really wasn't much room in the cab, not even for a quick peep but I still got the impression that it was hallowed ground. No one was taking such locos seriously from the point of view that they were going to supersede steam; footplatemen in general showed very little interest. When these new locos were so often out of service they were scorned upon and immediately compared with steam for reliability. No doubt quite a few diehards were still with us.

As time passed the success of the DMUs became apparent, more were built and soon after Regions had allocations. Reading, having a high concentration of local and suburban passenger work, was among the first to receive sets. Until now the depot had supported the very old diesel rail-cars originally built in the early 1930s, No 1 being in service until quite recently and the later type modified from the same design still working on the Newbury to Lambourn line. Twin sets of this later style were in operation on the West Drayton to Staines branch.

Looking back one can see that the original rail-car was the direct predecessor of the new DMUs now coming into service. The principle of motive power and the system of control were very much alike, only modern ideas made them any different. A very versatile fleet was built up, able to be formed into various combinations of trains. In fact the modern single-power car is very little changed in principle from the first AEC design.

Bringing in diesels to cover the local services created its own problems. Drivers would have to be taught how to handle them and what to do if any failure occurred on the road. On steam locos they had trained themselves with the aid of their Mutual

Improvement Class and gathered experience as they went through firstly their firing and then the hard way as I had myself. To teach men their new charges tutors were trained and in turn they took the men on an agreed course to be later examined by an inspector.

The problems didn't rest there. The old steam sheds were quite unsuitable for servicing the new sets so special depots were constructed to accommodate them. The servicing facilities I remembered from my cleaning days at Worcester when I assisted to fuel Nos 4, 5 and 6 from a 45-gallon drum standing on a trestle in the carriage shed were far removed from the modern requirements.

As more sets became available it was quite common for a driver to invite others to join him in the cab, more relaxed than the men on the gas turbines. I took my chances and compared them with steam. They certainly had the attraction of the comfort they provided and were much cleaner to work on. To me, at this stage, they were a good replacement for the 61xx 2–6–2Ts on the stoppers, no fireman to worry about but the loneliness of single manning.

The gas turbines had faded into obscurity and by 1958 the first of the five North British-built diesel hydraulics had taken their place on trials, the first locomotive in this series being No 600 *Active*. As before, the footplate was barred to all and sundry so once again I was unable to learn anything about them. All I could gather was that they were diesel hydraulic operated, which meant nothing to me. Ever-greater tales were told of their power and speed and of how the crew managed against adversity when something went wrong with the power output. Once again because of the limited number of these locos only the London Depot at Old Oak Common in our division had any dealing with them.

The steam locos were gradually declining but no one realised that their number was up. As far as I know there wasn't any information given to the men as to the future of the railways or whether we would ultimately change to diesel. We were allowed to carry on in the belief that steam was eternal.

NINE

Initial diesel training

IN THE MIDDLE of September 1961 my turn came to be trained on the diesel multiple units. I booked on in the morning with one of my colleagues, Den Upjohn, and went to the new fuelling point to meet the two tutor drivers, Jack Hillier and Bill Birch. Jack had been my driver for several weeks when I first moved to Reading as a fireman. Den and I were now under his wing again.

Jack said, 'You're both coming with me, Bill has got his pair from last week. First of all we start with a cup of tea while we're waiting for a set to be serviced. Then we'll go out and have a look round it for today.'

Out came an enormous tea can. Jack did the honours and made the tea at the same time outlining the programme for the day.

'That seems an easy day's work, plenty of time to relax,' I said.

'You wait until the end of the day, you won't be saying that. It pays to take it in easy stages.'

While Den and I sat, Jack and Bill planned how they would share the set for training. Bill's men were in their second week and required a different approach to us. Already the conversation was above our heads or was it intended to tease us into thinking we were in for a very rough two weeks?

Both the tutors were highly respected by the drivers they had already taught, well known for their patience. They needed it to cope with the varying attitudes of the men and the various abilities. Two weeks seemed a long time in view of the fact that none of the men in their care knew anything at all of diesels or the methods of controlling them. The names of various controls were quite foreign to them, the tutors no doubt had done a good job.

Before the day was over I realised that Jack's words were of wisdom when he said, 'It pays to take it in easy stages.'

Sitting in the mess room at the end of our day's session Den and I talked over the instruction of the day and both came to the conclusion that to remember what we had been told we would have to write it all down.

The next day I told Jack, 'I'm writing down all you say and intend to use it in evidence.'

'That's good, you'll be able to look at it when you're home.'

I had done quite a lot of studying of steam engines at home so why not now?

We settled down to a pattern, quietly getting to know more, Jack repeating over and over again until he felt we could relax and go out on a train with the two more advanced pupils. They were out for driving experience.

For the first day we watched and listened to what Bill was telling them, not being allowed to have a try ourselves. The one thing noticeable to me was the similarity in outlook to the Auto car trailers. What seemed slow movement to Den, not having any experience of Autos, was familiar to me, the experience had done me some good. There was a difference on these, though, they did have a reliable speedometer and the brake was completely in the driver's hands.

The trip out took us to Westbury via the Devizes branch and through Trowbridge – a route completely new to me before I came to Reading. Fortunately I had done some firing over here with Arthur Millis and got to know it a little; just as well because it was recognised as our training ground.

On the way down at Newbury Jack's milk churn as we called his tea can was trotted out and the whole company enjoyed a cup of tea. The route I had become so familiar with in the night time on freight trains seemed so different from this changed vantage-point. The uphills seemed to be less severe, the diesel engines underneath were getting on with it, no fireman to see slogging away showing just how much work was being done. Running down the other side from Savernake, almost free-wheeling with not a sound of effort, made it imperative to watch the speedometer. The whole route is quite pleasant to work on even under adverse conditions but in this environment it was quite a pleasure particularly in the company of good mates of my own age rather than young lads.

On a steam loco the driver had to use his judgement to get the best out of the machine but the diesel almost told him what to do. One of the instruments on the desk was an engine speed tachometer with indicators to tell the driver when to change to the next gear, either up or down. To the few drivers who, like me, were the proud owners of a car this had some similarity but that was where it ended. 'Forget all you know about a motor car,' Jack said. 'This is quite different.'

One completely different aspect was the free-wheeling when the controller was closed. The set ran quietly as if it would go on for ever, the engine didn't retard the train as it did a motor car. Learning how all the engines in a train responded to the controller at the same time through electric circuits and operated air valves was completely new. How to deal with them if a failure should occur was the important thing. The reason for learning on a steam loco and being examined at Swindon had been to ensure that a driver could get himself out of most troubles he was likely to get into. The diesel was no different in this respect, the driver was the only man around if trouble beset him out in the country. To this end he had to be able to help himself to a great extent. It's true that the sets were designed to make this part of the driver's job easier but to the men who weren't mechanically minded this meant a lot of hard studying and to the older men anguish and worry. Many would have opted out if the opportunity had been given. My own feelings at the time were that if we were going to have diesels to take the place of the 61xx 2–6–2Ts on the stoppers then we might as well accept that in all respects they were better to work on with the one exception that the beloved steam was taking a back seat and had no future. No dirt, clean clothes and a comfortable seat in a weather-proof cab had a lot of advantages; not having to rely on a fireman to supply the power and having it on tap also made for an easier day's work. The loneliness of being single manned was something else to get used to; if one had a poor mate it could be a blessing. At this time the situation was getting worse as regards recruits. The more diesel sets which became available not only cut out firemen but did in fact act as a buffer against them leaving. By now they would be able to judge for themselves that as the local passenger trains became dieselised the work they had been looking forward to would not be available to them, committing them to the rest of their firing days on freight trains on the turns and time they were hoping to get away from.

For my part I was quite interested in learning something new. At this time I had no qualms about what was going to happen in the future, steam locos were going to be around for a long time, these new sets were only taking on the local passenger work.

Den and I put our hearts into learning all we could, in fact it transpired that we tried too hard. At the end of the first week we were both completely bemused that it was a treat to leave it alone over the weekend. Jack had said, 'Go home for the weekend and forget all about it, you've done too much.'

That proved to be good advice; when we resumed on the following Monday everything that had become so muddled became much clearer, the rest of the time was plain sailing: driving taking over the important roll, someone to put me right, no trial and error as on the first Auto car trip. Having passed my examination I was booked to work a turn to Newbury and back through to Slough as my maiden voyage. As was the custom then my tutor accompanied me for my first trip. Arriving back at Reading he said, 'That's it, Jack, you're quite capable of carrying on the rest of the turn alone.'

I may have been but the set had different ideas. I spent ten minutes at Maidenhead dealing with a fault on one of the engines. I thought, it always happens to me.

As a result of my new knowledge and working over the

Devizes branch to gain route knowledge the foreman came to me one morning.

'You know the DMUs, don't you?'

'Yes I've learned them, George. Why?'

'Will you work the 8.10 to Westbury for me? I've got nobody else.'

'Sorry, George, I don't sign the road there.'

George Paxford was the shift foreman on duty and he spoke with a rather pronounced lisp. His entreaties seemed more sincere when he said, 'Go on, do us a favour, mate. I haven't got anybody else. The train will have to be cancelled if you don't.'

'Can't you put a 61 on the job with coaches?'

'It's too late to get one ready now.'

'Do you know that I've been on duty for four hours, George. It's not right for me to start a day's work now.'

'You come down to the office and sign the route. I'll look after you some other time.'

I agreed to help knowing that he would keep his promise if needed.

It had passed through my mind that the tutors would possibly be on the train anyhow. As it happened they didn't show up. No pupils that day. The whole day went well which gave me a lot more confidence in the sets and my own ability with them.

Unfortunately doing George a favour didn't exactly do me one. Although the trip on the DMU went well the fact that I had signed route knowledge turned a bit sour on me some time later.

One of our booked night turns was travel as passenger via Swindon and Melksham to Westbury to work a freight back via Newbury to Reading.

When I booked on duty the foreman said, 'There's a big landslip on the Westbury road. You might have to come back via Swindon.'

I replied, 'Tell them if I have to come back that way I'll need a conductor.'

'Carry on down. I'll let them know,' he said.

At Westbury everything was as usual, the train came in and we were told to relieve in the normal way.

'Which way are we going?' I asked.

'Swindon,' the supervisor said.

'You know I need a conductor that way, don't you?'

After some deliberation with the control he came back. 'You sign the road via Devizes, they tell me. We're sending you that way, you've got some traffic for Newbury.'

'I've never been over the road with a goods train in my life,' I said.

'Can't help that, you sign it and that's all that matters to me.'

Fortunately the train had a fitted head of vacuum which I knew would help where I wasn't too sure of the running on the varying gradients. The night was as black as one could imagine, I was working over the route for the first time in the dark with a freight for the first time. The fireman was good which was a blessing. I was all ready to go when the guard came up and said, 'You'll need a banker from Holt Junction, we've got too many on for the branch.'

'That's going to be interesting, never worked over here with one before. Where will he be? On the front or the rear?'

'He'll come on the rear. Pull round on the branch and he'll come on behind.'

I felt my way round to Holt Junction to upset the signalman a little.

'I want a banker, mate,' I called out to him as I passed his box.

'Why the hell can't they tell me? There isn't one here.'

I stopped the train and went back to him.

'It's no good you stopping there, mate. I can't do anything for you.'

'It's no good me going on either if I've got too many on for the bank.'

He rang Westbury to find out what was happening.

'What shall I do now?' I asked.

'Pull round on to the branch and wait. They're sending a banker round.'

It took the banker nearly an hour to get there and in the meantime I went to chat to the guard.

'Wish I knew a bit more about this road,' I said. 'All right in daylight with a unit, different now.'

He assured me that it was only a short sharp pull up the bank. 'After that it's easy going to Patney.'

I could hear the banker coming so made my way back to my loco. Soon he blew up to indicate he was ready. I replied and we were off. For some distance he wasn't needed, the road was quite level with just a few undulations. From Seend halt it fell a little down to a little bridge over a small river. The bridge had a permanent speed restriction of 15 mph imposed, just what I could have done without. On top of all the other firsts on this road I had never handled a freight train with a banker on the rear. Shutting off and braking down the dip to the bridge and picking up the train again was as tricky job as I had ever needed to accomplish before. Back on the rise I opened up and when I knew we were into the bank got well stuck in. We passed over the road bridge with full regulator and lever well down, the iron girders clattering beneath us. Looking back over the tender I could only just make out the banker in the rear, couldn't tell whether he was doing his share or not. Our 'Hall' was making enough noise for two as it slogged hard up the 1 in 53 gradient. Reflections of my recent struggle up Savernake when I was overloaded.

The last hundred yards or so seemed to be a bit steeper before it levelled off into the station. I said to this fireman as I did before 'If we slip now the banker will have to bail us out.'

The loco kept her feet as we used to say and with mighty heaves just scrambled over the top.

From Holt Junction the driver at the rear had carried the single line token, he would be dropping off when we went through Devizes station, from then on we would carry it through. The signalman came out on to the platform to hand my mate the token and with a joking manner put his hand on the cab rail and pretended to push.

'You should have had a banker,' he said.

'We've got one. Reckon he's not much good though.'

We safely made it through the tunnel and over the brow out

the other end and ran freely down to Patney to rejoin the main line again.

The next night when I was asked to perform the same feat I felt more self-assured but I still went back to the banker driver to ask for a little more assistance.

It seemed to me that I was destined to learn my profession the hard way.

Diesel development was now under way in the form of the 800 'Warship' class, having two diesel engines, the class 42 'Warship' locomotives, having two Bristol-Siddeley Maybach engines of 1000 hp each which powered Mekydro hydraulic transmission to their respective bogies. A complete change from the gas turbines but no doubt being tested because of the general overall efficiency of their predecessors.

Steam locos still worked all the principal services. The new diesels supplemented them rather than replacing them, mainly on the West of England route. The majority of drivers trained at the time had their regular firemen and on certain duties expected to have a diesel booked. They would naturally arrive on duty spick and span with cleanliness and comfort in mind and all too often despair at finding the diesel had developed trouble and a steam loco was booked in its place. This was a blow to their ego but they readily got on with the job, delighted to show their own prowess instead of that of the diesel.

The introduction of diesels was on a rather tentative basis. The other Regions tested various diesel electrics while Western Region were allocated the hydraulics. Many designs were soon in use to test and establish an efficient loco with obviously an eye to running costs and availability.

The cost of building a main-line diesel was stated at the time to be four or five times that of a steam loco. At the time diesel was comparatively cheap to run, coal was also becoming more expensive. Against this the steam loco was confined to shed for much too long for servicing, perhaps doing only eight hours' work or less a day. The diesel was expected to be available at least twenty hours out of twenty-four with a very short servicing time, a quick turn-round being a major factor.

To introduce full dieselisation had its own many and varied problems, one of which was that all drivers would need special training. None could be expected to take charge of these new complicated machines with only steam engine knowledge in their repertoire, even the driving techniques were foreign to them. New knowledge and skills were required, a new type of driver needed to be conceived and this took time.

The diesels were delivered at a very slow rate which led to the impression for a considerable time that none of it was very serious. Rather more like toying with new ideas until steam locos were seen to be laid up at various depots. This became more convincing and the sceptics among us grudgingly conceded that their beloved steam seemed to be dying. The reality that diesel shunters had now enjoyed such a long and successful reign showing ability and reliability with once-a-week servicing was now quite evident. Drivers prepared themselves for training, some pleased but many not ashamed to show their dubious feelings.

It was under these mixed feelings that the senior men at the depot were withdrawn for training, the D600 class being confined to the London depot at O O C as far as our division was concerned. Their introduction followed a similar pattern as the previous gas turbines – fitters everywhere. I did manage to get a little peep one day only to be politely turned off without gleaning any information. In fact I saw more of the D600 class in the scrapyard at Barry.

Drivers were quite excited about the performance of the hydraulic principle and with the reliability of having two engines were becoming more relaxed.

Only five of this 600 type were built.

The introduction of the Swindon-built D800 'Warship' class was a sure sign of further development. At this stage it now became obvious that more drivers would need training. To this end extra tutors were appointed but there was still no definite change from steam to diesel completely, nor were any diesel depots built at this time. The only move at this time was the building of fuelling facilities within the confines of the steam shed.

At this particular stage my depot at Reading was not directly affected.

The 'Warship', being more plentiful, had not become such a sacred symbol. Men who were interested could often get on board and have a look round with sometimes a reasonable guided tour by the driver. Some of these early drivers were quite dubious about imparting their knowledge, some forthcoming, others reticent to expose any shortcomings. After all they were the guinea pigs as far as driving these was concerned. It was from them that the rest of us were able to gain not only knowledge but experience. How much better to learn from someone else instead of the hard way.

I was quite excited at being shown round the driving cab for the first time. The vast array of switches and controls made one realise why the initial drivers were aloof and self-important. Names hitherto unheard of were used to display the driver's superior knowledge, garnished with elaborate stories of faults and failures. Many tales were told of the performance and efficiency of the new diesels and the high speeds they could attain, with firemen in particular commenting that their development had come too late to save themselves a lot of hard toil. From my own point of view I was still in the dark about actual performance but always held the view that my firing days were happy and the work well worth while. I was now a driver with the hard work behind me and I suppose it was safe to take this attitude. I was still interested in driving steam and expected to carry on doing so for some time.

Reading men became involved at times when a diesel was in trouble. Occasionally one would arrive at the station with either one engine stopped or the simpler problem of the train-heating boiler failed. The boilers gave more trouble than any other individual item, either in failing or men being insufficiently trained to operate them; it was a problem that didn't go away until electric train heating was developed.

If a diesel needed assistance because an engine had failed the steam loco could be attached to the front or rear; if it was only for train heating it needed to be between the diesel and the train, inside the train loco as it was termed. Invariably this was where it went because the diesel driver didn't want to be looking at the tender in front of him all day.

Two diesel tutors had been appointed by this time anticipating that the 'Warships' would be covering some of the milk trains to and from the West; trains which Reading men worked would be involved and they would need knowledge. The two Reading drivers Les Willmot and Bill Watts took their new role seriously and worked hard on the senior men who were nearing retirement and didn't much care for making the change. Because the only possible work was of a relieving nature there were no diesels stationed at Reading, nor was it possible to have a standby at the station to cover these emergencies. No trained men and no diesels – the steam loco had to go.

While this may seem a simple remedy the ramifications were much deeper. To start with the men working the station pilot had no route knowledge beyond Westbury which immediately posed the question of whether they should go. Some were quite adamant that they shouldn't while others more adventurous saw no wrong as the diesel driver in front would be responsible. In most cases the argument became academic because very few trains called at Westbury and the assistant would find himself being whisked away round the avoiding line at 80 mph into the unknown with a fair amount of trepidation.

It was from here that the situation became difficult. If the steam driver was providing assistance for power because of one engine failure on the diesel he was in a real quandary as to how much power he should use, when to use it and, more important, when not to. With no route knowledge at all it became a bit of a nightmare; at times the steam driver found himself powering when the diesel in front was braking and then found himself still shut off when he should be powering.

To add to his problems he was quite unable to see the road ahead to judge for himself or to even see the signals, not that he knew them anyway. In most cases he kept on plugging away relying on his ATC to indicate signals at caution. To add to his difficulties all his deliberations had to be made at a much higher speed than was his norm. He was now travelling most of the time at speeds of 90 mph and to quote one fireman: 'I don't think the wheels were touching the rails.'

Perhaps the best story related in the cabin depicting this situation was told by a fireman, a cousin of mine, Wally Styles. He and his driver Charlie Strudley were called upon to assist and duly obliged. Neither of them had ever been behind a diesel before, nor had they been beyond Westbury but with true locomen's grit they sallied forth taking it in their stride. Because of their total lack of knowledge past Westbury the diesel fireman kept walking through to the back cab and gave hand signals and signs indicating what they should do. With this method they were making their way with coal dust flying and hanging on for dear life. When the fireman appeared giving a sign with his hand in a rotary movement they were puzzled and looked over the side. Ahead of them they saw a set of water troughs and realised that they were to pick up water.

'Drop the scoop, Wally,' Charlie instructed.

'Right,' said Wally as he quickly wound the handle.

'Watch it, mate, you'll never get it up again at this speed. Start pulling it up now.'

Wally struggled hard without success. 'Give me a hand, Charlie, the water's holding it down.'

The two of them heaved but the pressure of the water defeated them until the tank filled and overflowed through the air vents at the front of the tender.

'Now look at what you've done. I told you to be careful.' A ton or more of small coal washed down from the tender and swept across the footplate. Before either of them could jump for higher ground their feet were hidden in black wet sludge. Charlie stood back and took stock then let out a tirade at poor Wally – a bit unfair, he couldn't help it.

After some considerable time clearing up and trying to maintain the fire with this black muck they took a look at themselves. Their boots and socks were soaked with jet-black water and several inches up their overall legs. A quick decision was made; take them all off and wash them in the bucket. No sooner said than done and there stood two locomen in bare feet with newspaper for matting and their socks and overalls hanging from the whistle chain, their shoes resting on top of the firebox. A typical Fred Carno situation.

While all this was happening the diesel had been eating up the miles and to their surprise halted at a station, they were at Exeter. A set of men came aboard to relieve them, friendly banter was passed as Wally and Charlie put wet socks and overalls back on causing some delay to the train. An unusual tale, one of the oddest I heard but what can one expect with a Wally and a Charlie on board.

In the early part of 1963 the winter was still with us, dealing out a very severe spell of snow and frost. I was on a night turn, the train we called 'The Biscuits', known as such because it carried produce from the well-known local factory of Huntley & Palmer. It was a simple train: stop to put off at Maidenhead and Slough then slowly make our way to Acton yard. The farther we went the worse the weather got. I was blessing the fact that I had a 61xx 2–6–2T with a closed-in cab.

Normally the shunter uncoupled us to go into the short siding for water and to have our meal break while we waited time for our return train. The wind was blowing an arctic blizzard, the snow swept across as we filled the tank, the return to the relative comfort of the closed-in cab was anticipated with thoughts of thawing out with a strong cup of tea. This was not to be, the tea was made and drank in cold comfort. The snow blew in my side and right through the cab and out the other side, at least that which wasn't stopped either by me or my mate. We were desperately hoping for the shunter to come and direct us to our return train to get away from it all when a diesel pulled up alongside. There in the electrically lit cab sat the two men drinking their tea in the comfort of the heated cab, wearing light overalls and looking very comfortable. As if the sight of this was not enough to sadden any man's heart the driver rose from his seat and crossed the cab to our side, the leeward side, dropped the window and calmly asked, 'Want to change over, mate?'

Before his point had sunk in, much less replied to, he had resumed his driving position and drifted off into the night leaving me even more annoyed and making me think again about the sanity of sticking to steam.

Later in the week, still on the night shift, my train was cancelled because of the atrocious weather and I became spare as did others. The cabin was fairly full with men whose trains were cancelled, we sat around waiting foremen's orders, hoping none would come so that we could avoid going out in such wicked weather. It was not to be, I was soon found a job. A foreman descended on me as if to settle an old score, then politely asked, 'Will you conduct a Southern man to Southall with a train of oil tanks?'

Tommy Neate, the foreman, was a dapper little man who knew his men and they in turn understood and respected him. Asking me politely was his usual manner, the job was mine whether I liked it or not.

'You don't like me much, do you, Tom? What have I done to deserve this on such a night?'

'You were at Southall. You'll know all about it,' he replied.

The night was miserable and cold. The snow had stopped falling but not until a layer of more than six inches had settled. I donned my greatcoat and scarf and rummaged for my gloves, reluctantly preparing for my anticipated hardships. I had arrived in my wellington boots and was now all set for the elements.

Tommy stood in the cabin while I got ready and walked up the shed with me.

'By the time you get to Reading West the train should be there.'

'I hope so, Tom. It'll be a cold wait otherwise.'

I set off and trudged through the snow to the appointed place but the train wasn't there. Alone in this white wilderness in the small hours I stood with my back to the cold easterly wind, collar turned up and scarf round my ears. Ten minutes or so elapsed before I heard a rumbling behind me, although muted by the snow it was definitely an oil train, the tanks had their own particular sound. I looked forward to getting by the fire and thawing out. As the rumbling got closer I became more interested and turned round. To my surprise there was a diesel on the front, its engine throbbing, a noise which I had not been aware of in its approach. As I went up the ramp at the end of the platform the side window was lowered. 'Are you conducting me, mate?' the driver asked.

'Yes please,' was the prompt reply as I gladly clambered on board.

'I'm sorry to be inconveniencing you, getting you out on such a night but I've never been beyond here before.'

Little did he realise that I was going to enjoy my first trip on a diesel.

I felt quite out of place with my snow-covered wellies now starting to drip water on the clean floor.

'Sorry about the mess I'm making,' I said.

'That's all right, if it'll make you feel better put this newspaper down to stand on.'

The coat and scarf were soon on a hanger and the warm cab thawed me out quickly; I became a much happier man.

The journey was over in well under an hour and tea brewed while waiting for the return train. The fireman insisted, 'Take my seat, driver, enjoy your tea in comfort.'

The hour or so waiting was taken up mainly with conversation about the merits of diesel traction, not just the benefits of excluding the weather but its value as opposed to steam. The driver pointed out the versatility of this particular type of loco with its driving position at either side of both cabs.

'This is a class 33 diesel electric, this type are confined to the Southern Region,' he added.

'Do you go into Acton yard at all?' I asked.

'Yes, we've got a train in there at night,' he replied.

'It was probably one of these in there the other night when the driver teased me, asked me if I would like to change over when I was suffering on a steam loco.'

'Probably, some men get a warped sense of humour when they get these benefits.'

The effortless work, the comfort and cleanliness all combined to convince me that diesels were the thing of the future. I had been seduced.

In the shed the next night Tommy Neate came to me again. 'How did you enjoy your trip last night?' he asked.

'Very interesting, Tom. I quite enjoyed the experience.'

'How would you like to work on them regular?'

'It looks like they're here to stay, Tom. There's more about than I thought, the Southern have got quite a lot.'

'I knew you were hooked, that's why I gave you the job,' he explained.

What he didn't know was that he had contributed towards shaping my future.

That particular winter spell gave me an experience quite unlike any I had had before. The following week I was on at noon and Tommy was the foreman again. He asked me, 'Will you take the snow plough to Didcot, they want it over the Newbury branch.'

'Is it ready?'

'You'll need to have a look round. It's fitted to a 22xx over in the loop.'

'What happens at Didcot. Am I expected to go over with it?'

'You'd better wait and see what happens when you get there. Don't forget the speed limit is twenty-five miles an hour.'

It was four o'clock when we eventually left the shed and headed down the main line. It was soon evident why there was a speed restriction. The extended weight out in front of the buffer beam made the loco bounce at the rear end, the long wedge-shaped knife was half the length of the boiler. I turned round the triangle at Didcot and waited in the up loop for orders.

After a while the supervisor came to ask, 'Do you know the road over the branch?' He then saw who I was and added 'Of course you do, you've been over there more than I have.'

'I may have done but not for a long time.'

'Well it hasn't changed one little bit since you last went over there. You can't have forgotten it.'

'Haven't you got a conductor?' I asked.

'No, that's why I'm asking you. If you won't go the branch will have to be shut.'

'Is anyone coming with me? Fitters or anyone else?'

'Bill Miles, the foreman fitter, will be over in a minute.'

Bill arrived before the supervisor left and said he was unable to accompany me.

'We've just had news of a derailment in the yard. They tell me the snow's not too bad, you can run through it by yourself without any trouble.'

I asked, 'How much is there and where is it?'

'It's on the top of Churn in the usual place in the little hollow, about a hundred yards of it.'

'All right then I'll have a go, might as well now we're here. No point in not doing it.'

My mate on this occasion was a chap named Trevor Quelsh, who had been with me for several weeks: an interesting character, never ruffled or upset, always expressionless. At the best of times he could only raise the slightest of smiles. For ever quiet, waiting for things to happen.

'You've never been over this road before, have you, Trevor?' I asked, knowing he couldn't have done.

It was seven o'clock in the evening by the time I introduced him to it.

'We'll be climbing for some time. When we get out into the open will be the time to start looking for the snow. If you can manage to keep plenty of steam it will help when the time comes.'

We made our way through the bleak countryside to the top of the downs. The snow had stopped some time ago and the sky was clearing, the moon popped out now and then to cast an eerie light on the scene.

'I'm going to run steady now, mate, and when we see the snow I shall open up and charge at it.'

Drifting steadily down the slope towards Churn I crossed over to my mate's side, the plough in front hid my view too much from my side. There in front the road looked odd, the rails disappeared, the moonlight wasn't shining on them. Suddenly I realised it was the snow covering them. I moved back to my side quickly and opened up.

'Keep your head in, Trevor, it will all come your side,' I said. Just then we hit the snow and with an almighty swoosh an avalanche was swept up. Trevor timed it just right to take a peep over the side and the top half of him disappeared in the snow. When we emerged he was standing holding the side of the cab looking like a snowman. The wind had turned the snow into his side and on to the tender completely covering the coal.

'Are you all right, mate?' I asked as I shut off and stopped.

'Look at me, I'm plastered,' then raising his hand to his head asked, 'Where's my cap gone?'

It had been swept away, never to be seen again.

After skimming up a couple more small drifts we turned at Newbury and returned to make certain of the up line and to leave the loco and plough at Didcot.

The day ended on a sour note. In the shed we pulled over some points to cross over to the turntable. Trevor called me forward but the loco wouldn't budge. I got down to see why and found we had become derailed by dropping down between the rails and the front of the loco was held up by the plough. We left the loco but not where they had wanted it. That episode concluded my working over that particular line. I didn't get another chance before it was lifted.

The class 35 'Hymek' diesel hydraulic loco, introduced in 1961, was now becoming very prominent in addition to the increase in the 'Warship' fleet. There were insufficient tutors to cover both types. Men who were trained on the 'Warship' were expected to go out and learn for themselves what they could of the 'Hymek'. This turned out to be a failure, modern diesels were too complicated to expect men to be proficient by this method.

The management advertised for two more tutors. An opportunity I had not anticipated had arisen.

Since my introduction to the diesel and the growth of interest developed by me I had confided my thoughts to one of my colleagues, a driver named Doug Brain. We discussed at length the possible direction the development would follow. It was now obvious that diesels were to supersede steam but as yet no one had made any statement to the men concerned. We were all left to come to our own conclusions. By now most had come to realise the end was in sight for steam. Many locos were being laid up and those kept in operation allowed to get into a run-down condition. Coal stacks which had been laid down for many years were being picked up to be burned on these failing locos, in most cases it was rotted away to be very little better than soil and burned almost as well. Those that were still working steam were having a rough time and in many cases the drivers had to cope with a young inexperienced fireman.

Doug and I had talked about all these aspects together with our thoughts on the viability of diesels and each admitted that he would prefer to be working with them than face what was left of steam. I had enjoyed probably one of the best footplate careers both as a fireman and driver. Steam was going so why not look to the future?

The future seemed to be best by going for one of the tutoring posts advertised. As a driver my seniority would keep me off them for some time yet but if I was fortunate enough to be appointed tutor that would advance me considerably.

We both felt that we could cope with the job, both of us having been active in our respective Improvement Classes. One drawback was that neither of us knew anything about main line diesels, only the DMUs. Everyone else was in the same position so we considered our chances were as good as any. Our applications were presented and we waited events.

In the meantime I was moved up to the next higher link and had several weeks' route learning to do before taking on my new duties. The new turns would take me to Bristol and Wolverhampton on routes which I had never covered as a driver and had little known as a fireman.

Before this period was up I had been called for an interview together with Doug. There had been no other applicants which left the chances open and we were both appointed. My route learning was soon to be cut off and my lifetime with steam severed.

TEN

Interlude with 'Warships'

WHILE DECISIONS were being made on how to train us I was allowed to carry on with route learning. To me this seemed a bit unnecessary so I spent as much time as I could scrounging round diesels, more to my benefit.

It was finally decided to use a senior tutor and I began training on 24 June 1963 with Les Wilmott. Les was given a free hand to train us as he saw fit, bearing in mind that our most likely need would be on the new 'Hymek' which was coming in at an ever-increasing rate. Our sessions started in the same manner as did the unit training: a careful look-round, having everything explained carefully, item at a time, its reason and purpose, its possible faults and remedies for any likely failure. At the end of the first day my head was fairly buzzing. The only consolation we got from Les was, 'We haven't started yet, wait until we get going.' We did get going, armed with notebooks and pencils we listened to Les as he took us through the intricacies of the engine and its equipment such as the cooling system, with its special temperature-controlling unit and automatic control of the cooling fans, what to do if it failed and how to get out of trouble. The engine-lubricating oil-system needed quite a lot of explaining, about how the loss of pressure would automatically shut the engine down to save possible damage. Furthermore it was used to assist in controlling the engine speed, an item never to be overlooked. These two items were of vital importance to the good running of the engine. Being of such superb design it needed all the automatic protection it could get.

It was a Bristol-Siddeley Maybach 1700 hp engine constructed to the highest specifications and couldn't be allowed to
work away in the background without any protection at all.
Anyone driving a car is well aware of any problem cropping up
or if not the results are far from being as dramatic as that of a
very expensive engine. While the driver concentrates his atten-
tions to driving he does not have the worry of the engine; in
general that is taken care of.

From the engine we were taken through the functions of the
gearbox or, as it is known on a diesel, the transmission.
Although there is little that a driver can do if a fault develops he
needs a good understanding of it because being automatic it had
an important bearing on his handling of the controller; the
automatic responding to both the road speed and the position of
the power controller. Faults can occur and some remedies can
be carried out but in general very little.

One of the most important items of equipment on any diesel
is the compressed air system. There is a simple adage – 'No air,
no go' – which was coined as a result which simply meant that if
compressed air wasn't available for the brakes to stop the loco
then the loco wouldn't move. The compressor and its automatic
governor had to be working at all times to maintain air. Should
air pressure fail working a train the brake is automatically
applied to stop the train while there is still enough to do so. All
these items have to be fully understood by the driver, the tutor
needed a greater depth of knowledge if he was to be successful
in imparting the amount needed by the driver.

At this time all trains were vacuum braked so vacuum
exhausters were needed to create the necessary vacuum. Even
though there was vacuum available on the loco the brakes were
actually applied by compressed air, controlled by the application of the vacuum – just another little complication.

To add to the new methods of controlling, all the driver's
controls were in effect electric switches, none of them mechanical. To this end a cupboard was placed in the cab one end of
which was full of electric relays, circuit breakers for electric
faults, fault resets and many things the driver didn't need to

know. Unfortunately for the meek the doors had glass panels which revealed the contents making the whole machine look more formidable. On the side of the cubicle a set of seven fault lights were arranged, normally blue but if a fault was indicated the affected one would change to red. This array did nothing to allay fears; so many saw them as a potential source of trouble instead of looking on them as a means of assisting them to identify a fault. Electrical circuits were totally new to many, their limitations being changing a fuse at home. Seeing this and having to know something about it worried quite a lot of the earlier trainees.

The driving controls were reasonably easy to follow because of the similarity to the DMUs and by simply watching a man drive for a while that was soon understood.

The driving cab on the 'Hymek' was rather small, the driver sitting quite near to the window and not much room behind to the engineroom bulkhead. In general, the loco was built to be small and compact which in turn cramped the engine compartment with all the auxiliary equipment. The one end was devoted to housing the train-heating boiler, another item for which the driver was responsible for at this time. The boiler was intended to be automatic, it was in most cases but when it shut down on fault someone had to go back inside to reset or more likely to coax it back to life. The driver couldn't so the fireman although untrained had to do it under the driver's instruction, a very unsatisfactory arrangement.

The preparation of a steam loco was like second sight to a driver after he had been a fireman and seen so much of it in his time. We now had to learn all over again quite a different way of preparation, not an oil can in sight but a serious check on many things mechanical to which I was being introduced for the first time.

The preparation sequence taught had a work-study method and, if carried out correctly, went a long way to assuring that the loco was unlikely to develop a fault and at the same time drummed in the geography of the diesel layout, very important when on the odd occasion a fault did crop up.

Les showed infinite patience yet enjoyed every moment of his position as tutor of tutors. After a while his patience was tried and tested to the limit, he worked very hard but still found himself swamped by our incessant search for knowledge. From the start he was well aware of our keen interest by the probing questions put to him before our appointment. Now we searched even more deeply for detail, always wanting to know. This keenness was not one-sided, Les adopted the attitude that if we wanted to know he was there to teach us and even pushed us along in an effort to subdue us a little. This in turn led to our own research and plenty of swotting, a spiral which had mutual benefits. I'm certain that Les would agree our enthusiasm kept him on his toes.

Being new to the situation we relied heavily on our senior tutor and picked the brains of anyone who dared to show an interest in diesels.

It was obvious to us that some sort of standard should be met and to this end we decided to work together, exchanging information and ideas, more often creating problems not only for ourselves but also for those in a position to help, such as the loco inspectors and the training school instructors.

Until this time diesels had crept in without a concerted training programme. Drivers were trained as and when a depot required them, not all depots were involved at first. Because of this very little literature was available to assist in training or to guide drivers when faults occurred. Fault guides were in their infancy, the provision of which was in the hands of the Regional Headquarters inspectors who, like the rest of us, were learning on a hand-me-down basis. It was very difficult to write a comprehensive fault guide on a machine which had not yet proved itself fully and was quite capable of proving the information doubtful. This point was brought home to me rather forcibly when I once had the temerity to criticise a fault guide for which I was carpeted and challenged to do better. Fools rush in, they say.

Les was required to take two drivers on the 'Warship' class and we were expected to tag along while he taught them. This was a very interesting way to learn because at times he sent us away to fend for ourselves and to return to be questioned later in front of the men he was training. It gave me a better insight into training. It also represented my own training on the 'Warship'.

Having gained knowledge of the 'Hymek' the change to the D800 'Warship' class was more of a conversion. The engines and the transmissions were of a similar design by the same manufacturer, the fact that the main components were basically understood by us made life easier but that was where it ended. The first impression when entering the cab was one of amazement, the whole loco was larger and the cab so impressive. To enter, it was necessary to duck low to enter the doorway and then up two steps to the cab floor centre. The height of the floor level was such that the average person stood with his head just clear of the cab roof, the seats for the crew were set low, on a lower level with the driver on the left. The cubicle for the electrical equipment was ranged right across the middle of the front of the cab and carried on its front a mass of switches, or rather circuit breakers to protect circuits rather than use fuses; there were two rows almost right across, twenty-six in all, quite a formidable array.

Set at the side by the driver there were four gauges of a design which made them look more sinister than they were, the needles instead of having a rotary movement as is normal moved vertically across the slightly curved glass front to register engine water temperature, engine speed, transmission temperature and oil temperature. To make these items a little more difficult they were all capable of shutting the engine down altogether or at least cutting off the power from that engine. In addition there was a test button which if pressed would carry out the automatic function, not to be confused with the normal reset button.

The main point about the bank of circuit breakers was missed by most trainees; to start with, their first thoughts were that they meant trouble and that they themselves would never learn what it was all about. In fact quite the reverse was the case, each one was clearly labelled for what its function was and all the driver needed to know was what that was. If at any time one of them tripped out all the driver had to do was to reset it at an appropriate time. Whatever the fault was it would be clearly indicated and furthermore easily reset. It's all very fine to minimise these simple problems but all the men being trained by Les and Bill at that time were mainly near their retirement and didn't particularly want to make the change. The name tags were completely new to them, none of the names having any meaning at all – completely bewildering to most. After the shock of seeing these the driver was then confronted with the desk, full of driving controls which he had never heard of either. The DMUs had no similarity to this complicated array or to the new names for the various controls and switches. A set of four fault lights faced the driver together with several gauges, horn control, sand control and ATC reset, the fore and reverse lever and the power controller sat in the middle with the power handle incorporating the 'deadman's handle' which must never be released. One hand free to manage the rest seemed an impossible task to many learners. To complicate matters on top of the cubicle there was a small recess with a lid, beneath it lurked several small switches, very much like the miniature circuit breakers on the front but with an entirely different function, they were short-circuiting switches to get out of trouble with but most men needed a lot of convincing.

On top of the cubicle there was another stumbling block, a rotary switch for isolating either of the engines or transmissions if they became faulty, which way to turn it for what muddled so many. I often wondered if it was fair to ask older men to take on such a complicated machine as their first diesel after so many years driving steam. Many did take to them very well and were quite happy when they became more practised.

The engines, two of them, were much like the 'Hymek' except that they were smaller, only twelve cylinders. With the exception of the first they developed 1100 hp, each drove through their own individual transmission to a separate bogie, in effect two separate locos in one, both controlled by the same controller.

The Mekydro transmissions were also similar to the 'Hymek' and again smaller but housed under the cab, hence the raised floor in the centre. When an automatic gear change took place the gearbox made an awful rachetting noise under the floorboards giving newcomers the impression at first that it was falling to pieces.

All this and much more had to be learned in only nine days, not only were the men pushed but the tutors were flogged to the limit. I realised now that although the 'Hymek' had sunk in well my task on these with the older men was going to be tough. Thank goodness some younger ones were coming along by the time I got deeply involved.

To add to the difficulties the D800 'Warship' series was continued with thirty-three locomotives from D833 to D865 using different engines and transmissions. These locomotives were built by North British but used a 1000 hp NBL/MAN engine and Voith transmissions. Externally the loco looked much the same, the engine and its equipment was different which required some extra knowledge.

The MAN engine fitted to the D833 to D865 series was crude by comparison with the Maybach of the earlier D800s and before long gained a bad reputation with tutors and drivers alike; it caused more than a fair share of consternation because it was prone to overheating under full power.

The transmission also gave rise to many worries, it was difficult to reverse quite often and drivers were expected to carry out a manual procedure which normally got them plastered in grease.

The fumes from the hot engine permeated through the bulkhead into the cab and made it very uncomfortable.

The cab layout was basically the same except for the changed indicators applicable to the different equipment.

Whether it was the poorer-quality loco being learned after the better one or the fact that at the onset the extra was the last straw I'm not too sure but I do know that they were definitely disliked.

On the road the different aspect of the diesel cab soon became apparent. The driver's position being on the left-hand side was a departure from the Great Western steam principle. Although the borrowed wartime locos had given most drivers an insight into left-hand drive this situation was quite different. The full front window with unrestricted vision ahead presented quite a new aspect. Judgement of speed took on a new dimension. When looking along a steam boiler there was a definite relationship with the boiler on one side and the lineside features on the other which gave an almost automatic assessment of speed. Without a boiler as a guide and looking straight ahead many men were deceived, particularly when braking.

A lot of my training was carried out on the West of England route on service trains. I had never been beyond Westbury before which not only added to my problems but to those of Les the tutor in directing me as a novice on the diesel and a stranger on the road. I was keenly interested in the route and its many variations as opposed to the main line route I knew, soon finding that line speed restrictions became of paramount importance at such high constant speeds. This was quite a new experience, handling a diesel had an entirely new set of considerations. As mentioned the speed was higher but very deceptive, sitting in the front of an enclosed cab and not having the customary noises which accompanied a steam loco, such as the ticking of the vacuum pump, the throw of the connecting rods and the knock of the big ends. In its place there was almost silence, behind closed windows the external noises were lost to the purr of the engine behind and not a sound of the train following. It was as if the cab constituted the whole, a deception difficult to come to terms with.

Although some steam locos were fitted with speedometers they were rarely used to note the speed, more a matter of interest. Here I found a very important difference, I considered it so much so that I made a point of emphasising its value and importance. When a speed restriction was imposed as low as 5 mph such as on bridge repairs this became the most difficult to negotiate. The initial breaking could quite easily be left a little too late and judgement of speed through the front window

being miscalculated I learned the hard way that the speedometer was the only answer. For some reason the automatic
glance at the lineside for comparison of speed was not used, the
eyes transfixed on a distant point which seemed not to get nearer
but was doing so so much faster than was calculated and to my
amazement loomed up with ever-increasing rapidity – quite
the opposite to what was intended. After the first jolts of bad
braking I recall being quite shaken at my personal failure and
was relieved to vacate the chair and to have a further appraisal of
a qualified driver's efforts, rather than learn from my own mistakes. What I did learn however and was able to pass on was that
it was imperative to use the speedometer to judge the deceleration in relation to the distance still to travel and that anyone
could drive a diesel but the best driver is the master of braking –
a comment I ultimately used to bring the fact home to anyone
who thought otherwise.

Even though the time allowed to actually handle a train was
limited it must be understood this was being superimposed on a
wide experience gained from steam driving.

At the end of my training I passed an exam by a Headquarters
inspector and received the princely sum of 2s 6d a day as a tutor.

My first tutoring job was on nights. One of our turns to
Bristol often had a 'Hymek' on the return train but the link
concerned had not yet been trained on them so this became one
of our duties to instruct the driver in handling and to cover any
faults that might occur.

This first trip all seemed to be going well, tugging hard at a
string of sixty-eight freight wagons, trying to get them swinging
along to face the steep incline through Box tunnel when a red
fault light came up. Now here was a situation which always
proved difficult to resolve. The driver was in charge of the train
with full road knowledge whilst I was responsible for the loco
and no road knowledge, at least very little. Who was to make
the decisions? After a short discussion I left the driver to carry
out my instructions while I ventured into the darkness of the
engineroom with some foreboding. The fault indications had
been quite definite and led me directly to the fault. The

automatic transmission had failed to change gear and we had been flogging away in bottom gear until it overheated, the protection device had worked to say enough is enough. The simple remedy in this situation was to reduce speed to work within the range of the bottom gear and all was soon well except for some nail-biting struggling over the top of the incline. Lessons learned this way were always more effective than all the classroom instruction.

It was directly because of this situation that Doug and I had been appointed, to fit in with the new concept of training. A programme had been devised to give a calculated training period to embrace static training in a depot and follow up with train handling on the road. For this purpose the 'Hymek' was thought to be an ideal loco, graduating to the 'Warship' as required. Classroom training was left in abeyance at this time to be dealt with when the opportunity arose, sometimes months later.

The time came when I was booked to take men for their first insight into main-line diesels, most of whom had become accomplished on the DMUs. It was quite common to see up to ten tutors each with two or even three pupils all at the same time congregating at Old Oak Common depot for basic training. Most of the tutors were my own age with the majority of the trainees twenty years our senior. With no previous experience of teaching except for our own Mutual Improvement Class I was well aware of the position I was in. How well would these senior men accept me? It was certain that I would have to prove myself beyond doubt to gain their respect. I spent many hours studying to gain as much knowledge as possible but this was not the total answer because this raised another and more serious question. How much did the driver need to know? This problem had not been resolved at higher levels which in effect left all tutors doing their best in the allotted time and trusting their trainees would pass. A standard was set indirectly by the examining inspectors who also had very little directive but had to satisfy themselves that drivers were capable of handling and remedying any faults that may occur. This in turn gave us some indication of what level to aim at but in doing so another anomaly crept in, possibly to impress or to solicit confidence. There was also the inescapable fact that mainly because of continued teaching we were getting better ourselves and in turn gave rise to drivers having a better level of knowledge as we moved along. It was not uncommon for some men to get a mental block, a sure sign that they were being pushed too far.

Doug and I were of the same opinion regarding this situation. Having pooled our resources for our own training we decided to join forces to set our aims within the pass requirements without overloading the trainees. To this end we set about simplifying everything to help drivers more readily identify faults occurring on the road. After all it was this that gave them most concern.

Probably one of the most awkward situations in training followed from the fact that all men were not equal in their grasp of knowledge or situations arising from faults. Tutoring two men together is often more difficult than classroom instruction inasmuch that in a classroom the onus is on the trainee to absorb the lessons, the instructor not always in a position to monitor each man's performance; whereas a tutor dealing with two men has the responsibility of ensuring that each man understands stage by stage. His duty is to turn out two qualified drivers, any failure on their part becomes a direct indictment of the tutor's ability.

To start a session with two men of equal calibre was always the tutor's wish whether they be bright, or not so bright. Two bright and willing trainees made for an interesting session because when they reached the required level one could relax. Two slower ones made up for that by needing more persistent pushing, repeating over and over again, explaining points, wondering if they would ever succeed. The last thing one must never do is show frustration at not getting through, even though the winning post sometimes seemed to be getting farther away. By far the most difficult situation was being confronted with two men far apart in aptitude. How did one develop these two along without the bright one realising he was being treated like a moron or the other one thinking it was above his head? It was not easy. Perseverance and gentle persuasion was the key.

One day towards the end of my tutoring days a gentleman approached me on the station and introduced himself as Mr Pointer, the new Traction Officer, my boss. After talking round the various interesting aspects of tutoring he asked, 'What do you think are the important requirements for a tutor?'

This was a point which I had often considered; not wishing to be naïve with the obvious answer of having a good diesel knowledge I replied, 'To be an amateur psychologist.' To which he countered, 'Why?'

A lengthy discussion followed in which I pointed out the difficulties which I have mentioned.

'Do you take it as seriously as that?' he asked.

'Yes,' I replied, 'it's no good doing the job unless I look at it seriously.'

Handling the diesels did seem to come very strange to quite a few men when they first took control even under the supervision of the tutor. I felt that in some cases the men were lulled by the cosy atmosphere and the power on tap as it were, it was all so easy. When it came to braking, especially unexpectedly, their response was lacking in urgency. One example I can quote was when I had a trainee in the chair (the driver's seat) for the first time on a fast train. He sat in the cab of a 'Hymek' serenely running along at 80 mph. I had just finished pointing out to him that he was now travelling faster than he had ever done before and made the point that any brake application would need to be a very positive one. Passing Southall he suddenly pointed ahead with both hands saying 'Look, look.' The signalman had cause to replace the signals to danger to stop us and when the red light came up in his face he failed to react as he should.

'Get the brake in,' I called out. Still the response seemed to be sluggish so I leaned over the driver and made the necessary full application while he was shutting off power. The stop was quite dramatic, the red signal passed by the cab at about 40 mph but we stopped in about four coach-lengths after that.

'Sorry about that,' the driver said. 'I was so surprised. If it ever happens again I'll be ready for it.'

After the emergency had been sorted we carried on to Paddington where I asked the guard, 'How was that sudden stop at Southall?'

'Well, I was at the back of the train walking towards the front along the corridor and suddenly broke into a gallop for no reason. I grabbed hold and looked out of the window in time to see you passing the red light, there wasn't anything in front so I thought no more of it.'

All the hydraulics had an EAB valve fitted, short for emergency application valve. Its purpose was to ensure a full application of the train vacuum brake from any emergency cause, such as a communication cord or a 'deadman's' application and to prevent the driver from attempting to recreate the vacuum to release. Not until the train had been brought to a stand was the driver able to release the brake. The driver's own application was never affected by it because the brake valve had an electrical contact which rendered the EAB valve inoperative, at least it should have done. Unfortunately the wretched thing had a mind of its own and quite often dumped the brake completely even though the driver only intended to make a small application with interesting and face-reddening results. Two of the younger drivers I trained proved the point well when we were working a service train with a 'Hymek' and twelve coaches. The one driving was making what I thought to be a reasonable approach to Slough with just about the right amount of brake application. When he decided to apply a little more for his final stop the EAB valve operated and we came to an involuntary stand half-way up the platform.

It wasn't his fault but he fell for some severe ribbing from the other one. The next day it was his turn to drive. From the start he was too sure of himself, saying, 'I'll show you how to stop at Slough this morning.'

To compensate for a possible repeat performance he ran in a little harder prompting some direction from me to apply more brake. Although he did he still left it a little too late and this time we overran a little, no inconvenience to anyone but a sorry young man sat in the chair to listen to his mate severely chiding him in return, to which he replied, 'Did you know this station was on castors? They've shifted it since yesterday, it was a bit further back there for you.'

When anyone got a bit too clever I preferred to let them learn by their own mistakes rather than keep telling them. I found it easier to explain afterwards than to force them to listen to me at the start. The only snag was that it could inconvenience passengers. When we eventually had a training train of our own we were able to engage in all sorts of specific trials to prove our points and also to be able to set up imaginary faults to get the trainees to analyse and remedy, practical demonstrations which were most beneficial to help the trainees to understand more easily.

The 'Hymek' had a maximum speed allowed of 90 mph, which was intended to prevent any possible damage to the transmission. As a safeguard a device called a locomotive overspeed was incorporated to cut off power and make a full brake application. If the driver exceeded this speed by a few miles an hour it would operate automatically. Most men were very wary of the device and the comments from both their colleagues in training and the scathing of the tutor. Some were careless and tried to initiate such a fault such as the time when I was in charge of the training train from Westbury to Reading with two men named Len and Jack. Len was in the chair, the secondman as he was now called, no longer a fireman, was in his seat on the off side. Jack stood in the centre on the right and I on his left almost behind Len. We were running at 90 mph approaching Newbury and when the gradient fell I reminded Len to ease off a little to avoid an overspeed, 'Watch it, Len, if you get a trip you'll have to go back to reset it.'

Jokingly he replied, 'Not going to bother today. I'm going for the ton, they tell me you issue a leather jacket to anyone that can do it.'

Jack stood there unconcerned as we ran through Newbury with me saying, 'Come on, Len, ease off, you know it's not allowed.' Just then a pigeon flew across in front but failed to get out of the way and it struck the window right in front of Jack's face. Although the second man ducked low by instinct Jack stood there completely motionless without a flicker with the shattered remains of the poor bird spread right across the window in front of his face. At the same time the overspeed tripped bringing us to a stand.

Jack woke from his trance. 'Now look what you've done, plastered the window with dead pigeon, got an overspeed and you still haven't got your leather jacket. I hope you're pleased with yourself.'

Those harsh words from a colleague were more meaningful than any I could have used.

The 'Warship', particularly the D833 to D865 version, was a tutor's delight. With two engines one could be stopped as a fault demonstration without any detriment to the service. At the same time they were prone to overheating of both the engine or transmission, more so when under full power for prolonged periods. This gave rise to misgivings by most men trainees and qualified men alike. I had the same opinion as the Traction Officer, work them to their full and if they failed the maintenance should sort it out. I followed this principle and found that very little difficulty was experienced. We had been living with a myth. What was more positive was the fact that when the engines got old and worn they were more likely to set fire to themselves. The exhaust pipes leaked at all the joints and little jets of flame blew out like a row of small blowlamps which in turn caught alight the deposits of grease and oil on the engine block. There was never a dull moment working an old D833, even if nothing ever happened there was the suspense of waiting for it.

An example of the possible consequences was highlighted one day when I was travelling from Paddington behind D849. From the onset it was throwing out volumes of thick yellow smoke which found its way into the train causing annoyance. At Southall only nine miles out the brake was suddenly applied. I looked out to see clouds of smoke pouring from the loco's side louvres and went immediately to assist. I entered the rear cab and took a fire extinguisher only to find it was empty, previously used. I took the second one and only got a pathetic squirt. The fire on the engine was burning well and the engine would not shut down with any of the normal trips and the manual overriding lever was missing. The engine was running amok without control; although I turned the fuel off it raced away until it finally seized up and stopped with the fire still burning. After this the driver and fireman came back, they had been concerned with putting out a fire on the front engine and were surprised to find me trying to deal with this one. When the main extinguishers were used to completely douse the fires the loco was towed to shed and I'm glad to say for the last time, to be scrapped.

An incident which happened with a similar loco was one day when Doug and I were each tutoring one man each and the foreman at Reading asked us if we would take a D833 light to Newton Abbot with only one engine.

'What do you reckon, mate?' asked Doug. 'We may as well and it will give these two a break.'

'Why not, it'll make a nice change.'

We set off with the front engine running and the rear one and its transmission isolated. This was quite normal and therefore we anticipated no problems. After passing Westbury my man was driving and I sat in the secondman's seat directing him. Rising up to Brewham signalbox we all seemed to smell diesel oil at the same time.

'Have a look, Doug, while I keep a lookout.'

Doug opened the engineroom door and revealed a solid mass of diesel vapour. Without hesitation I reached over and shut the engine down. Ideally we should have stopped at Brewham signalbox but we were too near and as there was a long run downhill there was no reason why we should not keep freewheeling. Doug said, 'You look after the driving. I'll go back and see what's happened.'

He came back quite soon.

'The bleed plug has come out of the fuel injector pump and fuel is spraying up over the room and dripping down on to the hot exhaust pipes.'

'It's a good job I shut down then, mate, could easily have caught fire.'

'What are we going to do about it?' he asked.

'How about if you take the one out of the stopped engine at the back and put that one in.'

'Good idea. I'll do that. You'll have to decide where to stop if I can't get it done quickly.'

Doug disappeared into the engineroom with his spanners while I assessed the situation, we were now rolling freely towards Bruton. There was no need to stop here so I decided to carry on thinking the signalman at Castle Cary would be certain to put us into the loop line out of the way. To my surprise we were signalled right through. To the other driver I said, 'Go back inside, Charlie, and ask Doug how long he's going to be.'

He came back. 'Won't be long now, only a few minutes.'

On the strength of that I decided to keep running but was surprised when the loco lost its momentum and slowed down as it rolled up the slight rise beyond the station. Once over it we picked up speed and ran quite well down the other side towards Somerton and through the tunnel to the station where the signalman was hanging out of his box listening for the engine. I felt sure he would ring the next box at Athelney to tell him of our plight but if he did it made no difference, we were signalled right through again. I had given up hope of ever seeing Doug again. 'Will you go back in, Charlie, and see what's happening.'

Just then the door opened and Doug emerged soaked in diesel oil which had dripped from the roof.

By now we were running through Athelney but with no hope of reaching the next box at Cogload Junction.

'Is everything all right, Doug?' I asked.

'Well I've got the plug in but it's been a bit of a job to tighten it up.'

'Can I start the engine do you think?'

'Yes I think so, it should be all right.'

I turned the switch to start and to our great relief it burst into life immediately, a blessing, our speed had fallen to 10 mph with more than a mile to the next box. Except for Doug smelling very strongly of diesel oil everything had turned out well. Doug had done a very good job. As I have said there was never a dull moment on one of this series of the 'Warships'.

By the time that steam had completely disappeared at the end of 1965 all men were trained on one sort of diesel or another but not many on more than one. The training continued with less urgency mainly for the time being to get men trained on the types they were most likely to be called upon to carry out their link duties.

Rostering of men had become a nightmare, not only did the roster clerk need to have a driver with route knowledge but now a new dimension, diesel knowledge. Clearly, there was still a long way to go.

ELEVEN
Higher speed, better track

THE TERMINATION of steam made all the steam sheds redundant, in some instances temporary use was made of them until
proper diesel facilities were created. Soon they were all demolished together with their landmarks in the way of coal
stages, water columns, emergency coal stacks and the various
wagons that had forever served the sheds. Outside on the road
the familiar water troughs were no longer in use and would soon
disappear. New sheds with redesigned layouts were erected on
or near the old sites together with fuelling facilities to cope with
the now heavy demand. In place of water tanks there stood
diesel fuel tanks. This was a far cry from the 45-gallon drums
lined up on a trestle, remembered from my early days as a
cleaner assisting to fuel the original rail-cars. The gleaming new
sheds with adequate lighting and ventilation replaced the murk
we had so easily become used to. The centrally heated mess
rooms with cooking facilities took the place of our old grimy
cabins lit by a single bulb or even gas but at the same time took
away the character of steam footplatemen swopping yarns with
a huge fire in the grate and the inevitable 2-gallon kettle on the
hob. They lost the interest in talking about their day's work,
diesels had come along and as yet the men were not too sure of
themselves and the interest was not the same.

With this amount of change and the pall of smoke hanging
over the sheds it must be considered that the railways had probably contributed more than anything else to the Clean Air Act.

Together with new cleanliness the men were spruced up with

issues of the new-style uniforms more suitable to their new environment. I, in common with most, was not very impressed and preferred to keep to overalls as long as possible.

In 1961 the first of the class 52 'Western' locos emerged from Swindon works, D1000 *Western Enterprise*, designed by BR but using two German Maybach 1350 hp engines similar to the D800 'Warship' class and two Voith hydraulic transmissions. The combination worked very well together. The power of the two good engines and transmissions soon endeared themselves to all drivers, its new sand-coloured livery and large badge drew attention from all angles.

The first noticeable difference when entering the cab was that it was from a cross corridor behind the cab which also served as a sound barrier from the engine noises. Once inside the cab there were several prominent changes. A flat desk ranged right across the cab below the front window. The window itself spread the whole distance across the cab with only the centre glazing bar to break the view ahead. Without side doors the side windows took up the whole side of the cab above the desk. This arrangement was excellent for observation but it was soon learned that the sun in the summer turned the cab into a greenhouse. Controls similar to the 'Hymek' were used and arranged sensibly with the fault lights conveniently situated near the driver. An additional set of fault lights were placed on the desk the secondman's side to indicate any specific fault on that particular end. A further set in the other cab took care of that end individually.

The cab was set quite high with more upright seats and the panoramic windows presented another new aspect for the driver.

Every driver was by now trained on hydraulics so the training was kept down to a minimum, three days being considered sufficient to convert from one hydraulic to another. Everyone disagreed but we had to make do, we were hard pushed to complete the basic and get in one-day driving as well. The transmissions presented much the same problems as the 'Warship' type, notably awkward to reverse but in hindsight a button had been fitted on the desk to assist. If this failed or if a transmission needed to be isolated for any reason the driver was expected to carry out this procedure manually.

The worst part of the short training period was taking men into the confined space of the radiator fan compartment to show them and get them to do it themselves. Before any attempt could be made it was necessary to clean off the dirt and grease then lift some floor panels and as a further precaution put newspapers down on the floor before lying flat out to reach down to operate the handles. Before letting a driver lie down he was asked to empty his top pockets of all small articles likely to drop out, if they did they would disappear down into the well never to be seen again. The operation was quite difficult and many cursed at being put through such an exercise. With a little thought in design layout this could probably have been avoided.

The day handling was an eye-opener to most men, not just because it was a new loco to them and the outlook was different. The floorboards had removable panels to lift up if the driver needed to operate any of the isolating cocks situated beneath them.

When running along at 90 mph they tended to lift and when a train passed in the opposite direction travelling fast the compression of air beneath lifted the panels to float in the air like magic carpets with clouds of rusty dust blowing up. If side windows were open this made matters even worse.

The value to most drivers was that the loco in general was very efficient and even if one engine did fail the remaining one would nearly always be capable of getting them out of trouble. I'm afraid that for some time the value of this particular two-engined loco spoiled them from taking to any single-engined one.

The single-engined loco was soon to be with us in the form of the class 47, first introduced on to British Railways in 1962. The other Regions had been working them for some time and they were now acclaimed the standard loco. We received our first which immediately created another rush on training, although by this time we were better organised. It soon became apparent that all men would need training so we, the tutors, were put through our paces first.

The loco presented a new challenge by being diesel electric. Apart from a number of Didcot men who had learned on the Southern Region class 33 which were similar none of our men had any idea of electric traction.

The principle of the engine remained the same except for some changed names used by different manufacturers therefore the main training was concentrated on the electric power and a new set of possible faults and the different array of fault lights. A lot of the equipment was different and items like the cooling system were new. The week allowed for basic training was hardly enough but it was followed with a week on the road for handling which made up well.

All the protection devices had the same meaning but now there were more. The blue fault light which was normally dim would indicate any one of eighteen items at fault if it glowed bright. Quite a lot to learn and remember.

Driving needed to be reconsidered particularly when starting away with a heavy train, although various devices were incorporated to eliminate damage and to assist a regulated start the driver was still expected to treat the loco with respect to avoid overloading a traction motor. Having a traction motor on each of the six axles driving their own individual pair of wheels allowed any one wheel to spin freely with bad rail adhesion. The hydraulic principle of each bogie being coupled by the driving shafts eliminated this to a certain extent. The single axle drive allowed each one to run independently. The one benefit was that a faulty motor could be isolated without interfering with any of the others.

The single Sulzer engine caused consternation as expected but this was completely unfounded because the engine was very rugged and gave little cause for concern.

My first training session was taking two Reading men to complete their training which had been left in abeyance, all I had to do really was to take them out handling.

On the first day I took them to Paddington to pick up the 9.10 a.m. to Birmingham with a driver I knew would welcome them. Some drivers were a little opposed to allowing trainees to handle their train. The trainees were in the middle order of seniority with knowledge of all the hydraulics and a reasonable amount of driving experience. Frank Bennet and Sid Ball were their names, between them they drove as far as Birmingham Snow Hill. We left the train there to have our break and to give the crew some respite from the crowded footplate while they carried on to Wolverhampton.

Arrangements were made for us to rejoin them on their return. The train duly arrived with the same loco 1536, with the same twelve coaches.

The driver asked me, 'Do you mind if my secondman drives as far as Banbury? I like to let him practise while I can keep an eye on him.'

'That's all right,' I replied. 'It'll do my chaps some good to watch others.'

The secondman proudly sat in the chair and waited for the 'Right away' signal.

When it was given he quietly opened the controller to allow the train to ease out of the platform through the restrictions over the crossovers and into the tunnel. Satisfied with the start he opened the controller to about threequarters to get the train moving down the drop in the tunnel and up the steep rise out the other end to Bordesley.

Almost as soon as he opened up there were massive blue flashes reflecting on the tunnel walls and our power was lost, a bright blue fault light shone on the desk.

I was standing behind the driver who sat in the secondman's seat.

'What have you done, mate?' he asked.

'I didn't do anything, it just happened when I opened up a bit more.'

'Shut off and try again,' the driver said.

When the power controller was closed the blue fault light went to its normal 'dim' and all looked well for another attempt.

The young man opened up again.

'That's it, mate, I've got power back again.'

No sooner had he completed his words of relief than the flashes started again with a series of sharp whiplash-like cracks, we were not certain where from, either the traction motors or the generator. Either way power was lost again and we were in the tunnel with little chance of getting out under our own power.

The driver turned to me. 'You'd better see if you can find out what it is. You know more than I do.'

This was one reason why most men welcomed tutors because of a certain amount of insurance it provided.

I turned to the flustered young man driving and said, 'Close the controller and just sit there until I come back. Don't do anything at all.'

I went back into the engineroom as we drifted slowly through the tunnel, to where several more fault lights were situated. One of them told me directly what the fault was, a 'power earth fault'. The way out of it was simple but there was no cure. By turning a switch I was able to be certain of getting power for a while which would solve the immediate problem of sticking in the tunnel.

I returned to the cab and told the driver, 'I've turned the earth fault switch. We'll be able to get out but I don't know how far.'

'All right to open up now,' I said to the man in the chair.

Turning the switch allowed us only to regain power, it didn't cure the fault and when the controller was reopened power was back as expected but so was the awful flashing and crackling. I opened the engineroom door to peep inside and found a continuous lightning display.

'Ease down a bit, give just enough power to get us out of the tunnel,' I told the driver.

All this time my two had been standing there completely bemused and silent. I turned to them and asked, 'What do you two think of this? You've had one week's training, you ought to be able to come up with something.'

As we struggled out of the tunnel Sid offered the first reply. 'Blow that, if that's what to expect on these I don't want to know. They're too dangerous.'

Frank answered for me, 'You're windy. There's nothing wrong with that, it can't hurt you.'

'That be blowed for a yarn. You're not getting me in there.'

There was no possible chance of continuing so with the driver's agreement we stopped at Tyseley to ask for another loco.

While the driver went to the signalbox I asked my two to come with me into the engineroom to the electrical cubical to see if we could isolate the fault to carry on. Frank was bold and agreed but Sid needed cajoling by Frank. While I turned various switches with Sid by my side Frank relayed my instructions to the secondman in the chair. When he opened up an almighty flash shot across the generator prompting Sid to try and beat it to the doorway, passing Frank as he did so.

Frank and I followed to the cab, myself satisfied that the loco was of no further use and Frank saying to Sid, 'You're as useless as the loco. Why did you run like that?'

'It's all right for you, you weren't in there.'

'Don't be silly, you passed me in the engineroom like a scared cat.'

'It's all right for this bloke too.' Meaning me. 'He won't get me in there again when there's a fault.'

A little anti-climax followed. When we were at Snow Hill a 'Castle' class steam loco, 7036 *Taunton Castle*, stood in the bay by the side of us. Some banter passed between the two crews regarding the merits or otherwise of the two locos. When we had eventually taken the failed diesel off, the loco to replace it was none other than 7036. The boot was on the other foot when the diesel crew found they had the pleasure of working forward with the steam loco. Like rats we deserted to ride in the train.

The next innovation was the last of the hydraulics, the class 14, a locomotive designed for yard shunting and short-trip work. I had the doubtful distinction of being first to learn on it, after only two weeks I was also the first to sever relations with it for other work but in that short time I came to the firm conclusion that its introduction was mistimed. Diesel electric traction had by now proved itself and this new loco rather more like a toy wasn't needed. In fact it soon got the nickname of 'Teddy Bear'. Some of its points were good, some were poor, particularly from the train working point of view. They were fun to train on and that's about all.

The diesel electric class 50 built by the English Electric Company and leased to British Railways represented a big advance in technology. All the basic components and requirements were there but the electrical side was computerised as much as possible with easily replaceable control cards for quick maintenance and in some cases quick faults. The cab was comfortable and reasonably well liked, the general performance accepted but the terrible state of the engineroom with its soot and grease appalled everyone. A section inside known as the 'clean air compartment' where clean air was preferred was in fact the dirtiest part of the loco. None of the men was keen on entering any part of it. The brake had a rheostatic brake superimposed on the loco and should have assisted in braking but in fact did more to hinder the driver's application, calling for other considerations on his part. Eventually when the fleet was refurbished they changed character and now carry out their work with a good performance.

Classroom training took on a serious role with instructors from the Chief Mechanical and Electrical Engineers section taking charge. All drivers were given an allotted time for each loco they learned, myself included. I spent many weeks in various classrooms thoroughly enjoying myself learning more about the more intricate details. There were several schools of thought about how far this should go for a driver, some of the opinion that he should have the same knowledge as on a steam loco but this was impossible. Some, led by the Traction Officer of the day, thought the door to the engineroom should be locked to keep the driver out. My own feelings were that if a driver understood his charge to a reasonable level he would develop the same affinity as he had with steam and the same mastery.

When diesels arrived, that is from the period which I have outlined, no one could have anticipated such a protracted training programme. Drivers at the start had the responsibility for the train-heating boilers. Later the whole operation was transferred to the secondman which involved another full training programme, a chore which few of the tutors envied. All the hydraulics had train-heating boilers and so did many of the diesel electric locos. At this time all the secondmen had been steam firemen and welcomed the operation of valves and switches instead of shovelling coal. Unfortunately the easier life had its drawbacks, there was very little work to do and sitting just looking out all day didn't create much interest. Drivers on the other hand still had their job driving, even though it was changed quite considerably they were fully occupied.

Before the end of 1967 the odds and ends of training were tailing off but another new project came along, the introduction of air brakes. Southern Region, used to air brakes on their electric stock, also had the class 33 diesel electric locos fitted for air brake working. Now the class 47s were being converted to operate both the vacuum- and air-braked trains with a brake valve referred to as the dual brake. At the same time new vehicles were arriving fitted with only air-brake operation. The new equipment on the locos needed understanding and the operation of the train brake would have to be practised. New regulations were also required to cover eventualities and to assist in smooth operation.

It seemed that there were no lessons learned from the scrappy start on diesel training and here we were again setting out on a new era without a concerted training programme. I was given the job at my depot of starting off the training after a minimal period myself. The few locos fitted could not be spared for training purposes but several vehicles were placed at my disposal to take the men round to show them the equipment and to operate it with the aid of a portable air compressor as used by road diggers. This was a most unsatisfactory method but it did get us going for a time.

Except for this new lease of life for the tutors there was very little training left to do. The management considered that tutors could now be returned to their normal duties as drivers but as training of some sort was anticipated for the foreseeable future it was decided to appoint five training inspectors on a permanent basis in my London division and equal numbers in the other two divisions. In future the inspectorate would be responsible for all training standards.

Applications were invited for the five posts; of the two dozen or so in the division several were not interested in carrying on as inspector and of those that were, quite a few would be disappointed.

I needed very little deliberation on whether to apply; my first love, steam locos, had gone and I was now deeply committed to my new role on diesels. The last five years were now deeply ingrained in me and I felt a need to carry on. My application was successful and in April 1968 I took up my new position, a decision which I never had cause to regret.

With the emphasis on training I was given a course at the railways' own training establishment at Darlington to fit me for classroom instruction. During this period my theme to follow was the new air brakes, a subject which I became completely absorbed in. A subsequent visit to Westinghouse for more instruction put a more professional touch to the job.

Many wondered why it was necessary to change to air brakes. Several reasons combined to make sense, first of all the rolling stock would soon have to be replaced, so why carry on with the old-fashioned vacuum brake when compressed air is used extensively around the world. Most of all, the British two-pipe system would give an even better train operation.

The other overriding factor was speed. Train speeds had been greatly increased but there was no way of speeding up the operation of the vacuum brake. The application of the brake at atmospheric pressure was slow and somewhat inconsistent although effective as regards force. Releasing the vacuum application always presented problems because it was relatively slow, particularly at the rear of the train. Above all, the high speeds now being run regularly needed a brake that would give a more definite response in cases of emergency, vacuum would be quite inadequate.

By comparison the air brake operating at almost five times the pressure with much smaller brake cylinders had a greater degree of flexibility, both for application and release. The rate of each is easily controlled on every vehicle in a train simultaneously enabling the optimum efficiency to be obtained at all times.

Emergency applications are an immediate response, always comforting at these high speeds.

The new freight liner trains of 1500 tons or more are capable of running at 75 mph with the braking efficiency of express passenger trains. Heavy coal trains also run much faster with equally good braking facilities.

The changes become more apparent when one considers that in my firing days the expresses I worked travelled at an average speed of about 65 mph and now freight liner trains are running at 75 mph.

This new era has seen the demise of steam and the introduction of compressed air brakes; faster speeds need faster signalling systems. It's no use having train-running improvements without resignalling, it's all part of the system.

In this respect there was also a dramatic change. The old semaphore arms have been replaced by modern colour light signals with a more intense light than road traffic light signals and fitted with a bull's-eye lens to amplify the light and concentrate the beam, a light that shows up well in daylight as it does in darkness.

Instead of peering ahead for little oil lamps the driver now has a good sighting from far off. The first of these signals in use in my area could be seen from Maidenhead looking west, a distance of about four miles. The brilliance of the light at night was so intense that several oil-lit signals preceding it were completely overpowered until almost upon them. This extraordinary light prompted the shunter at Maidenhead to suggest that drivers would approve because it would shine through their eyelids. It's a fact, they do. These signals have spread throughout the whole of the main line system with only a very few subsidiary branch lines left with manual boxes and signals.

These three items which have changed – diesels, brakes and signals – have made the most significant changes as far as the driver is concerned. Signals which dominated the skyline particularly at junctions where large gantries stood out and made the railway scene have long since gone. In their place are single signal posts capable of giving various diversions, as many as seven routes from one signal and other subsidiary movements. One such signal has almost every type of signal and indicator fitted: positioned at Reading it is known locally as the 'Christmas Tree'. There is no doubt that for anything other than nostalgic reasons these signals are far more superior. The driver has a far better sighting and a more positive indication except that when he reads his signals he must make a mental note of his route, not like the gantry where a mental picture registers. Another good aspect of colour light signalling is that there is a telephone on every signal post giving direct communication with the signalman. With the loss of the manual signalboxes alongside the line the affinity between driver and signalman also went, no longer the friendly wave in passing or the chance of a cup of tea when calling in for rules.

It is quite surprising how bleak the lineside seems without the signalboxes and the masses of signals they controlled, how the line ahead seems to go streaking away into the distance with none of the old familiar lineside landmarks, even the telegraph poles and the lines that rose and dipped in passing have gone, just two ribbons of rail and a purring engine. The colour lights standing at a fixed height and distance from the lineside have no character at all, in fact they are all the same with the exception of those that carry junction indicators.

More consideration and judgement has to be given to the red lights at night, when a driver has to stop at one the deception is far greater than in daylight. The speedometer is now the only guide to deceleration; the red light seen from so far stays deceptively far away and then comes up quickly without seeming to have got nearer in the meantime. In fog they do have a definite benefit. The old semaphore signals were usually high up and the lights were almost impossible to see but with colour lights nearly on a level with the driver's line of sight and their brilliance a patch of colour is detected before the actual signal on occasions.

In addition to this the Automatic Train Control system used by the Great Western Railway has been greatly improved for all Regions and with an inductor placed at a given distance before every signal the driver is doubly indicated, a tremendous aid. The new system, renamed the Audible Warning System, became necessary not only to provide the safety of the GWR type but also to cope with the higher speeds. The physical contact shoe could not be relied upon at such high speeds, calling for a non-contact type. The magnetic inductor became the BR universal system.

Vehicles also took on a new aspect, the old-type wagons that trundled along restricting the speed of trains were no longer of any use. They were in need of replacement and ultimately fleets of purpose-built wagons were taking their place, all with air brakes and roller bearings on their axles, easy running and easy stopping. By reducing the rolling resistance a loco was able to haul a larger payload at a faster speed with the ability to stop. The bulk load trains used the new types including freightliners, 100-ton tank wagons, 'merry-go-round' coal trains and the special car-carrying double-deckers and other various special wagons.

Hand in hand with resignalling came the need for better track. The previous jointed track that had served so well and become known for its rhythmic clicking as the wheels passed over the joints deteriorated too quickly at the joints. The continuous pounding of wheels gradually created depressions and though several innovations were experimented with there was never a real solution.

Almost all the maintenance was carried out manually which was costly in labour and time and on busy tracks the men stood aside as much as they worked. The answer came in eliminating the joints by installing long welded rails. They were taken to the site in lengths of several hundred feet and then welded into much longer lengths in situ with appropriate expansion joints.

The effect of the continuous welded rail was to give a much smoother and also much quieter ride. Gone too was the occasional lurch over a crossover, all unnecessary ones having been removed with the new track layout, those remaining were redesigned for higher speeds. It's commonplace now for basic crossovers to be laid for 40 mph and at some specified junctions even 60 or 75 mph. These new junctions and the new signalling to control them went a long way to getting the best out of the new traction and vehicles.

The maintenance of this type of track called for new machinery. New machines were designed for laying it and in place of men with picks and shovels a new breed of machine took over which is capable of lifting the track and packing it, aligning curves, straightening and also graduating canting on curves, computers calculating all the requirements as it works its way along. A huge benefit is that it can be used continuously when traffic is light and gets much more ground covered at a session.

Trains had been speeded up before the new track was laid but now an even higher speed would be available.

Stations were closed at an ever-increasing rate; only those in the commuter areas remained leaving great gaps of twenty-five miles or more between the major towns, another loss of lineside features. That ribbon of rail with diesels hurtling along bears no resemblance to the railway I once knew and loved.

TWELVE
Full circle

ALL THIS NEW EQUIPMENT was calling for more speed. It came in the form of the High Speed Train (HST).

Many will say this is nothing new, just a faster and more up-to-date version of the now scrapped Blue Pullman. This is possibly so, a compromise between the quality and style of the Pullman service and the more austere needs of modern high speed travel.

It is also argued by some that the high speed is unnecessary but even those will agree that it at least brings cities closer together. A simple example taken from my own journeys from Reading to London: the thirty-six miles took about forty-two minutes in steam days; it now takes only twenty-one. This is emphasised when it takes longer to get a bus home from the station.

The prototype HST progressed through its initial tests before it came to the Western for high speed trials. Our London division was the only one to have a stretch of line made ready for speeds above 100 mph and that was only forty miles long.

Problems had existed regarding manning of the new train and until this was resolved it was agreed that it could run only at speeds exceeding 100 mph providing a traction inspector was accompanying the train.

A few drivers had received training before the train arrived. Several inspectors were also given instruction for the part they were to play and for future training needs.

With very few small exceptions the whole of the prototype

train was of new design from the cab and the electrical power output to the brakes and full electronic controls down to the coaches and maintenance requirements. Everything the driver looked at or touched was changed, even his position in the cab.

Getting acclimatised to his new domain was the driver's first need. The cab was a little claustrophobic because it had no side windows, at least none the driver could see from his seat. The drop-down windows in the side doors were behind his back, the rest of the side was blank. At the time there was a good reason for eliminating side windows. It was generally believed that lineside objects passing by at speed would catch the driver's eye and give a flickering effect which has been known to be distracting. The small forward-looking window also gave rise to feeling shut in. The 'Warships' and 'Westerns' had given such a good all-round visibility but this one restricted the driver to looking straight ahead; to see along the ground the driver would need to stand up if he could or when moving towards another train he lost sight of it too soon. The size of the window was for safety purposes, being calculated at that particular size and thickness to withstand a heavy object hitting it at high speed.

The driver's seat was placed directly in the centre of the cab with his knees in a recess in the desk. On either side of the recess controls for power and brake were very convenient to hand, each had design features where consideration was given to the amount of force the driver needed to operate them freely and they were also made to move on a vertical plane rather than horizontally. The power controller electrically regulated the engine speed at a number of set levels and the brake controller also operated a set of electric contacts to electrically detect the brake level at any of the positions which the driver chose and to maintain the brake at that level throughout the train simultaneously. A brake operating from an electric switch was quite a new experience; just place the controller to a selected position and rely on it working. The response and the very good effect was appreciated.

The main gauges such as the brake pressure level and the speedometer were directly in front of the driver to allow him to read them at a glance with the other less important items ranged round in convenient places.

One of the stumbling blocks regarding manning of the trains was whether a secondman should be used. With the hopes of none the cab was not to be equipped with an extra seat so for the purpose of running the tests and training a second seat was fitted to the bulkhead behind the driver and slightly to his right to accommodate the secondman; the inspector had to stand.

A much more compact Paxman engine was used to drive an alternator, a smaller unit altogether than the main generators in use.

The tests we ran were always carried out in the early morning before the main traffic of the day was about. Our allotted high-speed section was from the 43-mile post to the 63-mile post. We left Reading soon after 4 a.m. and very quickly got up to 100 mph then cruised along giving the driver plenty of chance to settle down and at the same time telling him what would be expected of him during the fast run.

One of the main aspects of the tests was to establish the most suitable level of brake power for the speed. To do this we were to run at 125 mph and at a given point shut off power and fully apply the brake simultaneously, then assess the distance travelled by calculating from the quarter-mile posts.

On all these occasions the cab was rather full with a second man, probably two drivers in training besides myself and the driver. In the train there were several design engineers from Derby and some of our own maintenance men. The inspector received his instructions on which tests to make and relayed them to the driver as required. Because men were now quite used to running at 100 mph they soon settled down with the new arrangement in front of them and the usual relaxed atmosphere existed until at the start of the high speed section when the inspector said 'Open the controller fully now and maintain 125.' With the power of the two engines being a little higher than the ultimate production models the train accelerated very fast and before long all the normal talk in the cab died down and a deathly silence took over. I think it stemmed from the fear of the unknown. Such as when a driver would say 'Shall we be able to stop if we get one on?' meaning a signal at red. The answer was always simple 'You'll prove that for yourself when you make your emergency application.'

At a prearranged spot where it was easy to determine an appropriate mile post right under the bridge at Cholsey the order was given to shut off and apply the brake. The silence changed to sighs of relief as the brake bit and the deceleration could be felt. With varying brake settings varying stopping distances were achieved from which a compromise was decided upon. The train had to be capable of stopping in the required braking distance while at the same time showing consideration for the passengers, too violent a stop was capable of injuring standing passengers and at least of displacing articles of personal belongings – an inconvenience I suffered when such a test was made while I was travelling in a coach. We all had our tea on the table when the application was made and we all finished up with it in our laps. This proved there's more to braking than just stopping.

It was soon realised that stopping was the main concern of all drivers and as soon as that fear was overcome and the brake techniques mastered the men settled down. The men being trained were all from the London depot at OOC and were well used to running fast trains in both steam days and later with the diesels but now they would be running at just about twice the speed they were used to with 'Castles' in their steam heyday. The rest of the training was more or less routine conversion except for all the changed electrical equipment and a few new names to understand.

The train came under their responsibilities to a certain extent; normally it was the guards' but because the air used for the brakes and the coach air suspension system came from both the power cars it was the driver's duty to take care of it. The control cables between the two power cars were also his responsibility, any problem was his.

In 1976 the production models were delivered and training started in earnest. The new trains had been modified in some respects, from the driver's point of view the cab was the most significant. The front window was quite a bit larger giving a better all-round view and the small side windows were included with pull-down blinds in case of side effects. The driver could take a glance at the lineside now if he wished. The desk was slightly changed with no real alteration to the main features. The driver's seat was moved slightly to the left and the co-driver now had a seat by his side on the right of him. The basic functions of the engine and power remained the same except that the engine output was reduced slightly. In general the prototype had proved itself and only slight modifications were called for.

As more and more sets were brought into service they gradually became the mainstay of the express passenger service. Apart from the obvious advantages of high speed they made a great deal of difference as regards operational considerations. A train that can arrive at a station and be turned round for a quick return service in as little as ten minutes in emergency has a huge advantage over loco-hauled stock where a loco has to be provided for each end of the train at terminals.

The limitations of seating is a drawback on some of the more crowded services with only seven passenger vehicles. I sometimes wonder if a class 50 with twelve coaches isn't a better proposition, particularly on routes where the maximum speed cannot be used.

The question now arises, where do we go from here? What is the ultimate? The need for higher speeds in this country does not seem likely and further development of diesels seems only a minimal possibility; therefore we are left with electric traction.

For many years the overhead 25KV system has proved to be efficient, both with unit trains and loco-hauled services. The HST has two power units locked up when the train is out of service, either at night when not required or for general maintenance. An independent electric loco can be used at all times with very little need for maintenance and is capable of high power and high speed, a much more versatile machine.

I would anticipate that this type of traction will be the

ultimate with units for suburban and local passenger work. Unfortunately the need for so many lineside post and gantries to support the conductor wires makes the track and particularly stations and junctions look very cluttered and untidy. My own first impressions when travelling in the cab under the wire at high speed was of running through a long cage. Are we then trapped with nowhere to go? It is impossible to foresee any further development, particularly on the scale of the changes since steam.

Having arrived at the situation where there was no steam left further considerations were needed regarding the training of new entrants to the job. Men working steam automatically learned their skills as they went through the various stages from engine cleaning to firing on shunters then on to local freight and on to passenger to repeat the procedure as a driver and at the same time learn the technical side in his own time. All this training ground was lost, engine cleaning was eliminated and diesel shunters had taken over all the yard work. Local freight no longer existed and local passengers were now diesel multiple units. A secondman's duties now consisted of looking after the train-heating boiler and assisting the driver. The old principle of putting a young man with a driver is out of the question, the driver needs help, not hindrance.

To prepare secondmen so that they would be of some assistance to drivers they were given training in a classroom. This raised more problems. How long should they be given and how much should they be expected to know? It takes a long time to understand loco working even from a practical position, a classroom couldn't provide the right atmosphere. It could be made interesting for them and at least those that passed the final exam were of some use to the driver and in a position to learn more fully as they progressed. Classroom training has become another of the changes forced upon the job by the change from steam to diesel both for men starting and those aspiring to become drivers.

If looking forward is less interesting why not look back? There's certainly plenty to look at in reality with so many enthusiasts restoring everything in sight, recreating the steam scene at many locations all over the country. Even some of the more fascinating diesels have come in for some of their devoted attention.

My own interests in this respect lie in steam at Didcot, the depot of the Great Western Society, and diesels at Bridgnorth on the Severn Valley Railway. These two have rekindled memories of my early firing days at Worcester and Didcot, such a long way off now.

The Western Locomotive Association was formed before the actual demise of the 'Western' class 52 diesel but before they were completely withdrawn they organised a special train and because it was booked over my old terrain I had the pleasure of accompanying it throughout the trip. The train started from Paddington on 27 April 1975 headed by two locos, 1023 *Western Fusilier* and 1051 *Western Ambassador*. With these two powerful locos the train of thirteen coaches presented no problem but as it was a Sunday engineering work delayed us quite a lot until we arrived at Bristol Temple Meads. The two crews were relieved and the locos ran round the train to run to Gloucester where a break was arranged. Unfortunately because of the delay I was forced to reduce the time to get back in schedule.

The driver I had on the front loco was a man who was appointed driver at Southall the same time as myself, a man named Bill, I forget his surname. We departed from Gloucester right time heading for Birmingham New Street by way of Cheltenham, Bromsgrove and the famous Lickey incline, the scene of one of my very first attempts at main line running. We ran through Cheltenham after checking for a speed restriction and opened up to get a good run. It wasn't long before we were aware that something was wrong, the speed wasn't rising as it should. Bill opened the window and leaned out to see if the other loco was working. 'Can't see a sign of any exhaust from his outlets, Jack,' he said. I went into the cross corridor and looked back myself, it was obvious that the loco wasn't being powered. The driver saw me hanging out and gave signs that his loco was in distress.

Bill and I had a consultation about the loading for the bank, wondering if the weight of the train and the dead loco would be too much for our power. 'I've got the load tables in my bag, Bill, I'll check to see if we're within the loading,' I said.

'It's going to take some doing,' said Bill. 'We ought to be doing much more than this,' referring to the speed. We plugged away through Abotts Wood and Spetchley doing 80 mph instead of the expected 90 mph. By now I had confirmed from my tables that we were just three tons under the official loading for the bank, enough to give us confidence. As we neared Bromsgrove at the bottom of the incline we were down to 70 mph with thoughts of a scramble over the top, nearly three miles away. Passing through the station we felt a surge of power and looked back again, the rear loco was giving us all it had. From there on we had no troubles at all, in fact the train went over the top at 50 mph much to the great delight of the hundreds of enthusiasts lining the sides of the track with cameras and recording equipment. How so many people could be so keen on a diesel loco to turn out in such force I couldn't understand, there just wasn't the glamour of steam. It passed through my mind, what speed would we have ascended the summit if both locos had been working all the way. It was a memorable run for me and also my last over that route.

Other runs on individually owned locos also gave me great pleasure. One was on 92203 *Black Prince*, a BR standard 9F 2-10-0, privately owned by David Shepherd, the well-known artist. I was booked to accompany it from Didcot shed to Oxford to pick up a train of thirteen coaches and work via Worcester to Hereford.

Departure from Oxford was right time but before long we were losing time sadly. The fireman failed to get much steam and all of us including David Shepherd riding with us were getting anxious. This was my first steam ride as an inspector and as enthusiastic as ever I had my cine camera with me. At the height of our distress when we were reduced to a speed of about 30 mph I filmed the situation starting with David Shepherd sitting on the fireman's seat with his long hair streaming out behind him, I then panned round to the steam pressure gauge to show it well back on 100 psi instead of 225 then further round on to the back of the fireman. He stood there with his back soaked with sweat and hands on hips looking up at the clock, even from the back it could be seen that he was thinking 'What the hell am I going to do with you.' I stayed with him to watch a few shovelfuls go on the fire and then carried on to the driver. He sat almost unperturbed facing towards the centre of the footplate with a half-smoked cigarette hanging from his mouth, gently rolling with the motion of the loco, not a bit concerned.

My Traction Officer had given me explicit instructions not to assist in any way but I'm afraid I was in charge on the road and disregarded him, I wanted to gave a go anyway. 'Move over, Bob,' I said to the fireman. 'It's time I had a go.'

'I wish you would, I'm almost done in.'

We were approaching Moreton-in-Marsh and running about twenty minutes late, fifteen of them lost in the twenty-five miles or so from Oxford.

I looked at the fire and just shovelled twenty to thirty shovelfuls on and then looked up through the cab ventilator.

'What are you doing, Jack, praying?' asked the owner.

'No, just hoping to see some smoke.'

'There's a little showing.'

With that I gave it the same treatment again and this time clouds of black smoke plumed into the air.

'You're winning,' said David.

It was almost like magic, the steam gauge seemed to move around as we watched, after another round of firing I said to the fireman, 'It's all yours again, Bob. The going's easy from now on.'

I rested on my laurels.

The crowds that turned out for this occasion were phenomenal, every bridge and vantage point was covered with people, nearly all with cameras recording the first steam loco down the line for several years.

A strong reminder of that fact came as we entered Colwall

tunnel; apart from the crowds lining the hill round the portal the fact that no steam locos had passed through the tunnel for so long had left it covered on the inside with the inevitable greasy soot from years of diesel fumes. We were going great guns up the bank running at about 50 mph, the fastest speed I had ever been up there. The terrific blast struck the roof and in effect swept it clean, all of which fell around us. When we emerged from the other end we all looked at each other in amazement, I know that I was the blackest I had ever been in all my railway career. I recall that at Hereford I was unable to get my face clean without using some rather caustic soft soap.

It seems silly but I enjoyed it.

Thanks must be given to the many railway preservation societies for reincarnating the dead as it were. All the wonders of steam would have been lost for ever had it not been for their great enthusiasm. It's easy to understand how myself and my contemporaries were caught up in the fascination of steam and how most of us still are. How men who have never known much of what it was all about can devote so much of their time to the renovation of locos and stock amazes me, their dedication to preservation often leading to neglect of home life and even wives getting caught in the way of life at the weekends. The most some can expect out of their labours is the pride of seeing their finished work and the satisfaction of seeing so many people enjoying what they have done. Most of the men involved in loco preservation at Didcot at least have the opportunity of a footplate ride even if it is only a token trip, a trip of this nature generally realises a lifetime ambition.

One of the more celebrated locos, 6000 *King George V*, has been maintained at the HP Bulmer Ltd Railway Centre at Hereford and for a long time sponsored by British Rail and Swindon Borough.

When Swindon Borough lost its status in 1974 they decided to mark the occasion with a commemorative run with *KGV* as it is affectionately known.

On 25 March that year I had the very great pleasure of being put in charge of the trip. The loco had arrived at Didcot the day previous and made ready with swarms of enthusiasts working on it, all wanting to make it as shiny as new. It looked an absolute picture when I took to it with driver Percy Talbot, one of my old pals from my wartime firing days and his young fireman Bob Cottrell. The train arrived with thirteen coaches hauled by a diesel, a big cheer went up when a real loco backed on to the train. The loco was considered quite capable of running the seventy-three miles to Tyseley without the need for a water stop. From my own experience I knew that it should do at least a hundred miles and had no worries but just the same insisted that we start with the maximum possible amount of water, both in the boiler and tank.

After a long chat with Percy about old times and a few words with Bob I knew that I could let them get on with it. Leaving Didcot North the first comment came from Percy, 'The vacuum's not holding up, looks like I'll have to keep the small ejector open.'

'The pump will probably keep it up when we get running,' I replied.

Bob soon came in with his comment, 'This right-hand injector water feed won't shut off properly, it's wasting a lot of water.'

I assured him, 'That'll be all right, Bob, when you're using it.'

In addition the safety valve seat joint allowed quite a loss of steam if the pressure was maintained at the full amount.

'Keep the pressure down a bit, Bob, that'll save it from being too bad.'

All the little things were brushed aside as we rolled along merrily at our permitted 60 mph, the three of us quite enjoying ourselves.

Percy sat on his seat with his head over the side looking out for signals when he suddenly realised and said, 'What am I sticking my head out here for? You can look out on the fireman's side. I can't see round this big boiler on the curves and this old ATC doesn't work.'

I took up my suggested position and assisted while Bob got on with the firing.

We were stopped at Oxford, someone had reported a defect

on one of the coaches. When we were ready to leave again Percy said, 'You'd better come and have a turn at driving, old mate, you'll probably never get another chance.'

'I intended to ask you,' I said as I took up my driving position.

I proudly sat there and drove this beautiful machine like a boy with a new toy and alas I felt obliged to relinquish it at Banbury to allow the real driver to carry on. To me it was twenty-four miles of living the past and a memory for ever.

As we progressed the right-hand inside piston gland started to blow out steam, the farther we went the worse it got. With all the other little things wasting water we could well have done without any further losses. The run was going fine and we cruised through Leamington Spa and faced the steep rise, the loco taking it in its stride but the water was now becoming quite a worry. Percy and Bob had been handling everything well and conserving all they could but it was getting very low. As we climbed Hatton Bank we considered what our chances really were of making it through to Tyseley.

'We're not going to make it,' said Percy despairingly.

By calculating the miles travelled and those left to go I came to the conclusion that if we didn't get stopped we should just about scrape through.

'We'll get there all right,' I said. 'That's if we don't get caught behind a failed diesel.'

'That's right,' said Percy. 'You would think of something like that.'

'Better take it a bit steady now to be on the right side. Saving water is more important than keeping time.'

After all the nail-biting we arrived at Tyseley with the tank right empty and only half a boiler of water left. We couldn't get into the old Tyseley shed quick enough to get a drink; the day was only just saved.

Unfortunately the loco was due for overhaul and though it looked its best and performed well the little things that wear added together to create more than enough excitement on that memorable day.

My cine camera also worked well to record for me some of the best moments.

When the time came to depart I had a terrible job getting the various enthusiastic workers off, as far as they were concerned they were sticking to it as long as they could. Even Bob the fireman was reluctant but his stint was up and he was required to be relieved. Tony Neale took over for the return. We did manage to get away right time but with the memory of the down trip still fresh I decided that it was wiser to take it steady to start with on the rising gradient and to let the train run on the downhill. With this boiler dodging as we called it we were able to maintain timekeeping and arrive back at Didcot right time with a reasonable amount of water left in the tank.

Of the many preservationists the two which I am most closely connected with are those carrying on with sites on my old patch: the Great Western Society at Didcot and the Severn Valley Railway at Bridgnorth, both of which gave me great pleasure to work at and now help to keep my memories alive.

The SVR always held an attraction for me as a fireman at Worcester, the real old-fashioned line retained most of its old-world charm with the little stations well kept and the line meandering through the valley with the river never far from sight, a pretty and relaxing line to work on. My visits to there in recent years have rekindled memories: the stations are as they were and the enthusiasm of the workers has in fact improved the quality of the track from my days over there.

What surprised me most was the dedication of the men who were passed to drive the locos, they start by proving themselves by doing all the arduous repair work and the various shed duties before getting even considered for driving and then they undergo exams of quite a rigorous nature before taking charge. On the occasions that I have ridden on the footplate I have been quite impressed by their serious dedication and attitude of responsibility, to say nothing of the surprise at their ability to handle a loco and train. One thing I couldn't come to terms with was their liking for getting dirty. 'All part of the pleasure,' one driver said to me.

I leave the steam locos to others and devote what time I have given to the two 'Western' diesels they accommodate and allow to run on their track. These two locos represent for me the twilight of my long railway career.

Didcot is a different proposition for me; not far from my present home and holding as it does memories of my early firing days. The main shed and sidings are preserved as they were in my day with so much more added to interest the visitors, a real live museum. On open days there is something for all, even me. I look back and think this is my depot, in fact I tell them so at times. Their preservation of locos is first class, not only do they steam and run them on the short demonstration lines but present them in such fine condition that they regularly go out on BR metals heading enthusiasts' special trains, often with two locos and in the past with their own 'vintage' passenger train of GWR coaches.

On many occasions I have had the pleasure of riding on these locos as inspector. Each and every trip has given me such a lot of pleasure and with most of them over the routes I worked so many years ago as a fireman.

My pleasure now continues with assisting in the examination of the footplate crews.

In time I foresee that there will be no one left to carry on working locos; BR are fast running out of firemen. It will be a great pity if such a situation did come about because the longer steam locos carry on the more attractive they will become. There are so many young lads who have never seen a working steam loco, they don't know what they have missed.

The cycle has turned full circle and the only reminders of the past glorious age of steam is in the hands of the dedicated preservationists. Let's hope that they will be able to continue to make many people happy as well as themselves. As long as they remain so will the names that endeared each of the former companies to their own interested followers.

To me the letters GWR will always be synonymous with 'Gone With Regret'.

APPENDIX 1

'Star' and 'Castle' class locos worked on by author as cleaner and fireman when stationed at Worcester

		1936/9 Cleaning	1947/9 Firing
4007	Swallowfield Park	x	x
4017	Knight of Liège	x	x
4049	Princess Maud	x	–
4051	Princess Helena	x	x
4086	Builth Castle	x	x
4092	Dunraven Castle	x	x
5017	St Donats Castle	x	x
5042	Winchester Castle	x	–
5049	Earl of Plymouth	x	–
5050	Earl of St Germans	x	–
5063	Earl Baldwin	x	x
5092	Tresco Abbey	x	x
7007	Great Western	–	x

APPENDIX 2

Illustration on following page

2200 HP B.R. TYPE 4 B-B DIESEL HYDRAULIC LOCOMOTIVE
CLASS 42

Engine	(No. Make and Type (No. of Cylinders & Cycle (Max. Cont. Rated Output	– Two, Maybach MD 650 – 12 Cylinders, 4 Stroke – 1135 HP at 1530 RPM
Transmission	Type and other particulars	– 4 Speed Mekydro K104U
Performance	(Max. Tractive Effort ((Cont. Tractive Effort	– 48600 LB at 27.6% Adhesion – 46700 LB at 10.7 MPH
Braking	(Type (For Loco ((For Train (Brake Force (% of Loco ((weight in ((working order	– Air Vacuum – 69.72%
Speed	Max. Permitted Service Speed	– 90 MPH
Curve	(Min. Rad. Curve (without ((gauge ((widening ((At dead ((slow speed	– 4½ chains – 4½ chains
Train Heating Equipment	(Boiler Make and Type (Steaming Capacity	– Spanner Swirlyflow – 1500 LB/HOUR
Tank Capacities	(Engine Fuel) (Boiler Fuel) (Boiler Water	– 800 gallons – 940 gallons

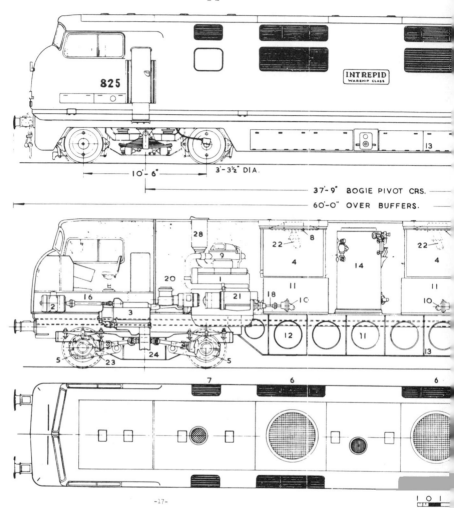

825

INTREPID
WARSHIP CLASS

13

10'- 6"   3'-3½" DIA.

37'-9" BOGIE PIVOT CRS.
60'-0" OVER BUFFERS.

-17-

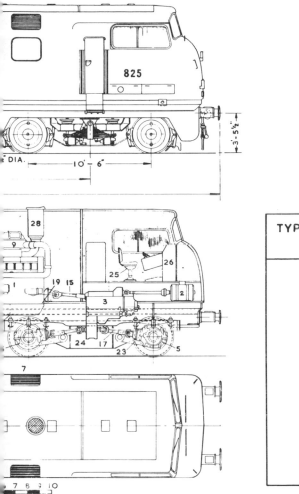

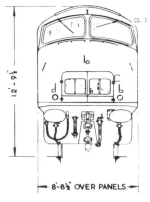

825

12'-9½"

3'-5½"

DIA.

10'-6"

8'-8½" OVER PANELS

28

9

26

25

19 15

3

2

24 17

23

5

7

7 8 9 10

FT.

TYPE 4 DIESEL HYDRAULIC LOCOMOTIVE

1 MAYBACH 1135 BHP ENGINE
2 DYNOSTARTER
3 MEKYDRO TRANSMISSION
4 SERCK RADIATOR
5 MAYBACH FINAL DRIVE
6 RADIATOR AIR INTAKE
7 AIR INLET
8 RADIATOR FAN
9 PRESSURE CHARGER
10 BEHR SERCK FAN PUMP
11 WATER TANK
12 FUEL TANK
13 BATTERIES
14 TRAIN HEATING BOILER
15 PRIMARY CARDAN SHAFT
16 CARDAN SHAFT DYNOSTARTER
17 CARDAN SHAFT FINAL DRIVE
18 DRIVE TO SERCK PUMP
19 VIBRATION DAMPER
20 COMPRESSOR
21 EXHAUSTER
22 FAN MOTOR
23 PIVOTED AXLE ARM
24 WELDED BOGIE FRAME
25 DRIVER'S SEAT
26 CONTROL CABINET
27 ROUTE INDICATOR
28 ENGINE SILENCERS
29 HORNS

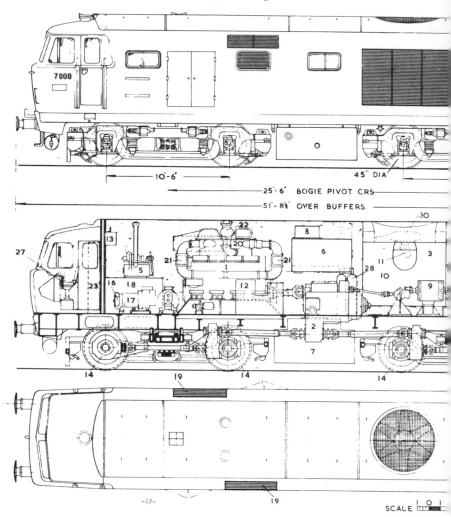

7000

10'-6"

45" DIA

25'-6" BOGIE PIVOT CRS

51'-8½" OVER BUFFERS.

SCALE

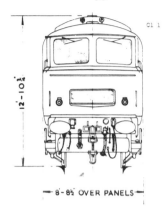

—8'-8½" OVER PANELS—

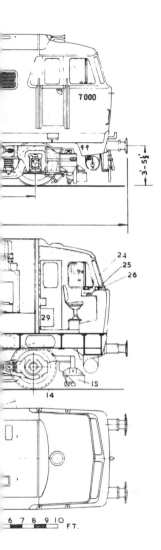

6 7 8 9 10 FT.

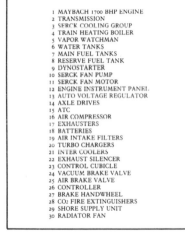

TYPE 3 DIESEL HYDRAULIC LOCOMOTIVE

1 MAYBACH 1700 BHP ENGINE
2 TRANSMISSION
3 SERCK COOLING GROUP
4 TRAIN HEATING BOILER
5 VAPOR WATCHMAN
6 WATER TANKS
7 MAIN FUEL TANKS
8 RESERVE FUEL TANK
9 DYNOSTARTER
10 SERCK FAN PUMP
11 SERCK FAN MOTOR
12 ENGINE INSTRUMENT PANEL
13 AUTO VOLTAGE REGULATOR
14 AXLE DRIVES
15 ATC
16 AIR COMPRESSOR
17 EXHAUSTERS
18 BATTERIES
19 AIR INTAKE FILTERS
20 TURBO CHARGERS
21 INTER COOLERS
22 EXHAUST SILENCER
23 CONTROL CUBICLE
24 VACUUM BRAKE VALVE
25 AIR BRAKE VALVE
26 CONTROLLER
27 BRAKE HANDWHEEL
28 CO2 FIRE EXTINGUISHERS
29 SHORE SUPPLY UNIT
30 RADIATOR FAN

-12-

APPENDIX 3

Illustration on previous page

1700 HP HYMEK TYPE 3 B-B DIESEL HYDRAULIC
LOCOMOTIVE CLASS 35

Engine	(No. Make and Type	- One, Maybach MD 870
	(No. of Cylinders & Cycle	- 16 Cylinders, 4 Stroke
	(Max. Cont. Rated Output	- 1700 HP at 1500 RPM
Transmission	Type and other particulars	- Mekydro K.184u
Performance	(Max. Tractive Effort	- 46600 LB at 27.6% adhesion
	(Cont. Tractive Effort	- 33950 LB at 12.5 MPH
Braking	(Type (For Loco	- Air
	((For Train	- Vacuum
	(Brake Force (% of Loco	- 73.3%
	(Weight in	
	(Working order	
Speed	Max. Permitted Service Speed	- 90 MPH
Curve	Min. Rad. Curve (Without	- 4 chains
	(gauge	
	(widening	
	(At dead slow	- 4 chains
	(speed	
Train Heating Equipment	(Boiler Make and Type	- Spanner and Stone Vapor OK 4616
	(Steaming Capacity	- 1500 and 1750 LB/HOUR
Tank Capacities	(Engine Fuel)	- 800 gallons
	(Boiler Fuel)	
	(Boiler Water	- 800 gallons

APPENDIX 4

Illustration on following page

2750 HP BRUSH TYPE 4 C-C DIESEL ELECTRIC LOCOMOTIVE
CLASS 47

Engine	(Make and Type	- Sulzer 12 LDA 28C
	(No. of Cylinders & Cycle	- 12 Cylinders, 4 Stroke
	(Max. Cont. Rated Output	- 2750 HP at 800 RPM
Main Generator	Make and Type	- Brush TG 172-50 Mk. I
Traction Motors	(Make and Type	- Brush TM 64-68 Mk. IA
	(No.	- Six
	(Type of Suspension	- Nose
	(Type of Gear Drive	- Straight Spur
Performance	(Max. Tractive Effort	- 62,000 LB at 23.8% Adhesion at 7800 amps Main Generator
	(Cont. Tractive Effort	- 30,000 LB at 27 MPH at 1260 amps Main Generator
	(Rail HP at Cont. Rating	- 2160 HP
	(Full Engine Output	- Available between 12.8 and 85 MPH
Braking	(Type (For Loco	- Straight Air and Auto Air
	((For Train	- Auto Air and Air Cont. Vac.
	(Brake Force (% of Loco (weight in (working order	- 85%
Speed	Max. Permitted Service Speed	- 95 MPH
Curve	Min. Rad. Curve (without (gauge (widening at (dead slow (speed	- 4 Chains
Train Heating Equipment	(Boiler Make and Type	- Clayton, Spanner Mk. 111 or Stones
	(Steaming Capacity	- 2500, 1850 or 2750 LB/HOUR
Tank Capacities	(Engine Fuel)	- 810 gallons
	(Boiler Fuel)	
	(Boiler Water	- 1250 gallons

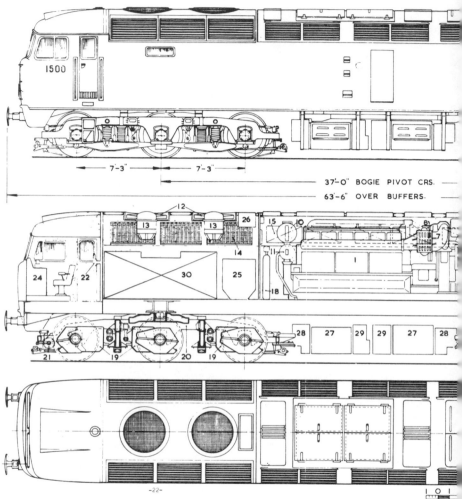

1500

7'-3"   7'-3"

37'-0" BOGIE PIVOT CRS.
63'-6" OVER BUFFERS.

12
13   26   15   10
14
24   22   30   25   11   1
                            18
28   27   29   29   27   28
21   19   20   19

-22-

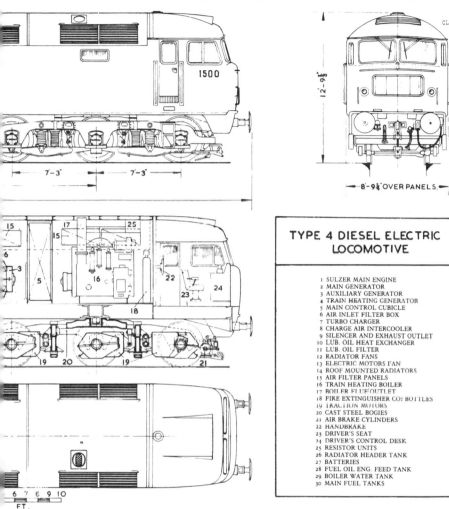

TYPE 4 DIESEL ELECTRIC LOCOMOTIVE

1 SULZER MAIN ENGINE
2 MAIN GENERATOR
3 AUXILIARY GENERATOR
4 TRAIN HEATING GENERATOR
5 MAIN CONTROL CUBICLE
6 AIR INLET FILTER BOX
7 TURBO CHARGER
8 CHARGE AIR INTERCOOLER
9 SILENCER AND EXHAUST OUTLET
10 LUB. OIL HEAT EXCHANGER
11 LUB. OIL FILTER
12 RADIATOR FANS
13 ELECTRIC MOTORS FAN
14 ROOF MOUNTED RADIATORS
15 AIR FILTER PANELS
16 TRAIN HEATING BOILER
17 BOILER FLUE OUTLET
18 FIRE EXTINGUISHER CO2 BOTTLES
19 TRACTION MOTORS
20 CAST STEEL BOGIES
21 AIR BRAKE CYLINDERS
22 HANDBRAKE
23 DRIVER'S SEAT
24 DRIVER'S CONTROL DESK
25 RESISTOR UNITS
26 RADIATOR HEADER TANK
27 BATTERIES
28 FUEL OIL ENG. FEED TANK
29 BOILER WATER TANK
30 MAIN FUEL TANKS

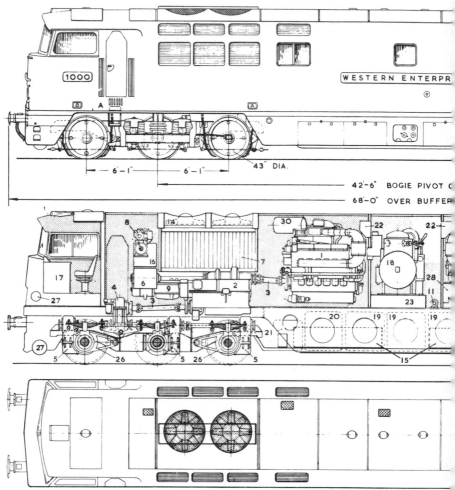

WESTERN ENTERPR

1000

A

43" DIA.

6'-1"   6'-1"

42'-6" BOGIE PIVOT C

68'-0" OVER BUFFER

-24-

1 0 1 2
S

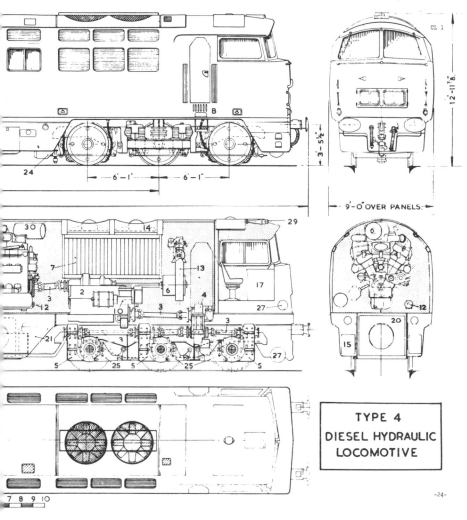

TYPE 4 DIESEL HYDRAULIC LOCOMOTIVE

APPENDIX 5

Illustration on previous page

2700 HP B.R. TYPE 4 C-C DIESEL HYDRAULIC LOCOMOTIVE
CLASS 52

Engine	(No. Make and Type	- Two, Maybach MD 655
	(No. of Cylinders & Cycle	- 12 Cylinders, 4 Stroke
	(Max. Cont. Rated Output	- 1350 HP at 1500 RPM
Transmission	Type and other Particulars	- Voith L6-30rV
Performance	(Max. Tractive Effort	- 66,770 LB at 27.6% Adhesion
	(Cont. Tractive Effort	- 45,200 LB at 14.5 MPH
Braking	(Type (For Loco	- Straight Air and Auto Air
	((For Train	- Auto Air and Air Cont. Vac.
	(Brake Force (% of Loco (weight in (working order	- 75.87%
Speed	Max. Permitted Service Speed	- 80 MPH
Curve	Min. Rad. Curve (without (gauge widening (at dead slow (speed	- 4½ Chains - 4½ Chains
Train Heating Equipment	(Boiler Make and Type	- Spanner Swirlyflo
	(Steaming Capacity	- 1500 LB/HOUR
Tank Capacities	(Engine Fuel)	- 850 gallons
	(Boiler Fuel)	
	(Boiler Water	- 800 gallons

TYPE 4 DIESEL-HYDRAULIC LOCOMOTIVE

1 MAYBACH 1350 BHP ENGINE
2 VOITH HYD. TRANSMISSION
3 CARDAN SHAFTS
4 INTERMEDIATE GEAR BOX
5 FINAL DRIVE GEAR BOX
6 DYNOSTARTER
7 SERCK COOLER GROUP
8 VAPOR WATCHMAN
9 WESTINGHOUSE EXHAUSTER
10 LAYCOCK COMPRESSOR
11 VARLEY FUEL PUMP
12 VARLEY LUB OIL PUMP
13 FIRE EXT. EQUIPMENT
14 SERCK-BEHR FANS
15 BATTERIES
16 DEPOT SUPPLY UNIT
17 CONTROL CABINET AND DESK
18 SPANNER BOILER MK. III
19 WATER TANK
20 FUEL TANK
21 FUEL TANKS, 136 GALLONS
22 FUEL TANKS, 20 GALLONS
23 WATER TANKS, 170 GALLONS
24 A.T.C. SHOE APPARATUS
25 TORQUE ARMS
26 AXLE GUIDE LINKS
27 RESERVOIR
28 ALFLOC TANK
29 WARNING HORNS
30 ENGINE SILENCER

Index